THE
# TOM PETERS SEMINAR
## CRAZY TIMES CALL FOR CRAZY ORGANIZATIONS

**Also by Tom Peters**

*In Search of Excellence*
(with Robert H. Waterman, Jr.)

*A Passion for Excellence*
(with Nancy Austin)

*Thriving on Chaos*

*Liberation Management*

THE

# TOM PETERS SEMINAR

## CRAZY TIMES CALL FOR CRAZY ORGANIZATIONS

**by Tom Peters**

VINTAGE BOOKS
A DIVISION OF RANDOM HOUSE, INC.
NEW YORK

A Vintage Original, First Edition
May 1994

Library of Congress Cataloging-in-Publication Data
Peters, Thomas, J.
     The Tom Peters seminar: crazy times call for crazy organizations.
     /by Tom Peters.
     p.   cm.
     Includes index.
     ISBN 0-679-75493-8
     1. Organizational change    2. Management    I. Title
HD58.8.P483    1994                                            94-4815
658.4'06—dc20                                                  CIP

Page 319 constitutes an extension of this copyright page.

Book design by Ken Silvia Design Group

Manufactured in the United States of America
10   9   8   7   6

*For Evelyn Peters,*
*a talker who raised*
*a talker*

**"Only the paranoid survive."**

— Andy Grove, CEO, Intel

## A NOTE TO THE READER

After my seminars, dozens of participants invariably ask for
paper copies of the 35mm slides I've used as visual aids. This
book is my answer. It's the contents of a typical two-day
Tom Peters seminar, circa early 1994.
Enjoy!

**Tom Peters**
**Palo Alto, California**
**March 1994**

# CONTENTS

# Is it any wonder we're confused?

On October 18, 1993, *USA Today* revealed that the Golden State Warriors offered a $74.4-million, 15-year contract to 20-year-old Chris Webber, who had not played a minute of professional basketball at the time. On the same day, the *Financial Times* headlined the strong threat to the jobs of 400,000 European auto parts workers. Three months later, in January 1994, *Business Week* published a poll reporting that 90 percent of executives foresaw sales going up during the year. Yet, despite this optimism, over half the execs planned to maintain their payrolls as is — or lay off more employees.

The world is wackier than ever.

Go figure. In the span of a few weeks in the summer of 1993, MCI and British Telecom do a huge deal. Time Warner and U.S. West team up, then Time Warner and Silicon Graphics. Then U.S. West and Microsoft and General Instruments join hands. Then Telecommunications Inc. and Time Warner and Microsoft. Like a new solar system forming from galactic dust, a monstrous, multitrillion-dollar computer-software-cable-TV-telecommunications-publishing-entertainment-electronics-information-services megaindustry is born in cyberspace and on my television screen.

Meanwhile, a whole continent, a whole civilization — Asia — breaks loose. China's economy grows 14 percent in 1992, but is expected to "slow" to 10 percent in 1993. However, growth in its first quarter comes in at 15 percent. Sophisticated Singapore's per-capita income passes Britain's. And, speaking of sophistication, advanced electronic design work in Asia now extends far beyond Japan's borders — to Taiwan, Korea, Malaysia, Thailand, China, and India.

When several party delegates to the 1993 Guangdong Communist Party meeting arrive in gold-painted Mercedeses and the Chinese are rioting to acquire stock share applications, is it any wonder that the chairmen of General Motors, IBM, Westinghouse, American Express, and Kodak were all fired within a few months of each other?

Since that day in early 1992 when the stock market value of Microsoft, with $2 billion in revenues at the time, surpassed that of General Motors, with $120 billion in revenues, should it come as a surprise that Boeing, Kodak, Digital Equipment, Compaq, Daimler-Benz, and . . . and . . . ICI, Philips, Hyundai, Volkswagen, and Bosch have announced restructuring "revolutions" — which often decimate the workforce, starting with the whitest of the white collars?

If Hewlett-Packard can run its 9,000-person ink-jet printer business with a "headquarters" staff of four people, and companies in general are flattening and outsourcing at warp speed, is it difficult to believe that Manpower Inc., America's largest provider of temporary workers, now has more than a half-million people on its roles? Or that the temporary worker population in general has risen 250 percent since 1982, while the nation's total workforce increased by only 20 percent? Or that some temp firms are growing like Topsy by supplying transient CEOs and VPs and senior project managers to "networked" companies that view permanence as a mortal business sin?

When we confront an average of 300 programmed electronic microcontrollers each day, and my new Minolta 9xi camera has more "intelligence" than my 1982 Apple II computer, should we be nonplussed by Nintendo, with only 892 workers, racking up $5.5 billion in sales ($6 million per employee) and ranking third in 1992 profits in all of Japan?

And with Nintendo outpacing the world and the Internet gaining a million new members a month, should I wonder that my airplane magazine-reading for a recent trip included *Online Access: The Magazine that Makes Modems Work* and the premier issue of, get this, *Going Bonkers?*

## Into the Beyond(s)

The titles of the nine chapters that follow all begin with the word "beyond" — "Beyond Change," "Beyond Decentralization," "Beyond Empowerment," "Beyond TQM," and so on.

Each "beyond" captures a management model now in vogue.

Though often superficially or only poorly implemented, these models (empowerment, etc.) clearly have utility and value. And yet the intention of my seminars — and of this book — is to push far past today's utility and value to look at tomorrow's.

So you buy the empowerment idea (who doesn't?) and you're struggling to implement it (who isn't?) in your nine-person auto body shop or your 19,000-person telecommunications firm. Fine. Well, fine as far as empowerment goes. But in Chapter 3, I urge you to imagine not just empowering employees but turning them into full-fledged businesspersons. That's right, a company of 100 percent entrepreneurs.

In a sense, each "beyond" constitutes a complete model of organizing; yet each also builds on the "beyonds" that precede it, until a comprehensive notion of organizing and managing emerges in the end.

A comprehensive model? Yes. A comfortable one? Never. In fact, discomfort is the point.

"But hey," you say, "my company still hasn't caught up with the management mandates of the 1980s. This is just too much."

Wanna bet?

## CHAPTER I

BEYOND CHANGE

# TOWARD THE ABANDONMENT OF EVERYTHING

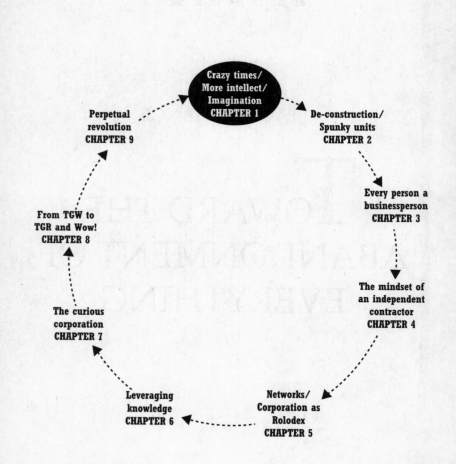

Crazy times/
More intellect/
Imagination
CHAPTER 1

De-construction/
Spunky units
CHAPTER 2

Every person a
businessperson
CHAPTER 3

The mindset of
an independent
contractor
CHAPTER 4

Networks/
Corporation as
Rolodex
CHAPTER 5

Leveraging
knowledge
CHAPTER 6

The curious
corporation
CHAPTER 7

From TGW to
TGR and Wow!
CHAPTER 8

Perpetual
revolution
CHAPTER 9

Change. Change. Change. We must learn to deal with it, thrive

on it. That's today's relentless refrain.

But it's incorrect.

Astoundingly, we must move beyond change and embrace

nothing less than the literal abandonment of the conventions

that brought us to this point.

# Eradicate "change" from your vocabulary.

Substitute "abandonment" or "revolution" instead.

# "There'll be only two kinds of managers— the quick and the dead."

David Vice,
Northern Telecom

Crazy times call for crazy organizations.
Our task in this book is to examine those six words and the stunning mandate for managers, staff professionals, and front-line workers that they imply.

There's little doubt that the times are crazy, and getting crazier — whether you're a banker, software producer, restaurateur, or public official. And if the times are crazy, well, then, what makes more sense than crazy organizations? But if you grant me that premise, then you have to conclude that our principal organizational problem today is the lack of craziness. In short, we're trying to use sane organizations to cope with an insane business world.

I would argue that my thesis is anything but crazy, despite its use of the C-word twice. The six-word sentence is cold, logical, rational: Crazy times → crazy organizations. What has kept me awake at nights since writing *Liberation Management* in 1992 is the growing realization of how stale, dull, and boring most organizations are. And yet even our new theories of management steadfastly ignore the issues of creativity and zest. In fact, more than a few of today's theories actually imply strangling creativity and suppressing zest at a time when they've become the prime creators of economic value.

### The New Metabolism

"The nineties will be a decade in a hurry, a nanosecond culture," said Northern Telecom's David Vice. "There'll be only two kinds of managers — the quick and the dead."

That line invariably gets a laugh in my seminars, but I think what I'm actually hearing is a titter of terror. For white-collar-wearers and blue, for CEOs and receptionists, the bodies are piling up on the street, and, despite a nearly three-year-old recovery, there is no sign that the blood has stopped flowing. On the contrary.

"Recently," wrote Toyoo Gyohten, one-time vice minister of finance in Japan, in *Changing Fortunes,* the book he coauthored with former Federal Reserve chief Paul Volcker, "I was talking to one of Japan's best foreign-exchange dealers, and I asked him to name the factors he considered in buying and selling. He said, 'Many factors, sometimes very short-term, and some medium, and some long-term.' I became very interested when he said he considered the long-term and asked him what he meant by that time frame. He paused a few seconds and replied with genuine seriousness, 'Probably 10 minutes.' That is the way the market is moving these days."

## TRUTH IN NUMBERS

### Tragedy to Movie
Jonestown, 1978—513 days
Waco, 1993—34 days

Most of us aren't in foreign exchange, but I'm not sure it makes much difference what business you're in today. The market's metabolism has raced out of control. "New developments in telecommunications technology seem to come about twice a day," MCI's head of strategy and technology, Dick Liebhaber, told me in late 1992. I don't think he was kidding. "Since 1979, when Sony Corp. invented the Walkman," wrote Steven Brull in the *International Herald Tribune* in March 1992, "the company has developed 227 different models, or about one every three weeks." How would you like to compete with that?

Foreign exchange, telecommunications, consumer electronics, spaghetti sauce (64 new varieties in 1991 alone), and everything else is moving at an accelerated pace. A recent Harper's Index noted that 513 days elapsed between the Jonestown Kool-Aid slaughter, in 1978, and the first television movie covering it; in 1993, the gap between the fiery resolution of the Branch Davidian affair, in Waco, Texas, and the first TV movie was just

34 days (indeed, the movie was under way well before final events took place). That's a 15-fold contraction.

My own innocence about this increasing pace of commerce was bluntly pointed out to me in June 1993, when I purchased a laptop computer. (I was tired of being the only businessperson in the airplane without one, even nervous I would become publicly known as a Luddite.) After a bit of study, I settled on an Apple PowerBook 165c. I came home and proudly showed it to my 27-year-old stepson. "That," he sneered, "is the old one. I think it's been out four or five months." He quickly realized what he'd just said and laughed at himself. But he was right. It *was* an old one — an antique at age 120 days. (It was officially discontinued in December 1993.)

It doesn't matter what kind of business you examine. During a seminar in Philadelphia in late 1992, Hal Rosenbluth, CEO of Rosenbluth International, a travel-services company, said, "Our industry is beyond revolution." Indeed, his company's revenues had grown at a rate that would have seemed incredible not long ago — from $40 million in billings to $1.5 billion in less than 10 years, thanks in part to the introduction of new, proprietary software packages sometimes as often as (shades of Sony) once a month. Voom, varoom! (And yikes!)

Or consider IBM's Austin, Texas, personal computer operation. In the last three years, what was already a thoroughly modern operation has, according to *The Economist*, cut its average manufacturing cycle time from 7.5 to 1.5 days and new product development time from 24 to 8 months, increased its product portfolio from 19 to 85, and simultaneously shrunk the payroll from 1,100 to 423 people.

But an enterprise doesn't have to be high-tech to get caught up in today's acceleration. Few industries are older or more traditional than mineral extraction, yet Australia's Kalgoorlie Consolidated Gold Mines more than doubled production between 1989 and 1992 — at the same time cutting back the number of workers from 1,500 to 720. Ho hum.

Revolution? The word is not too strong. And it's not the same thing as change.

Change? Change! Yes, we've almost all, finally, embraced the notion that "change is the only constant." Well, sorry. Forget change! The word is feeble. Keep saying "revolution." If it doesn't roll easily off your tongue, then I suggest you have a perception problem — and, more to the point, a business or a career problem.

What we do. What we make. How we work. Each is the subject of nothing less than revolution.

## Disembodied Enterprise

Remember the day when all the people needed to do a job worked with you in the same building? When you took it for granted that the best folks for any task were already on your payroll? When you could go months without attending a meeting where outsiders were present? How dated — and silly — all that seems now! Read this description, from Lewis Perelman's *School's Out*, of music recordings being made, circa 1992:

> Most records no longer are mere transcriptions of a group of people in a room playing together. Now recordings are assembled from component parts created all over the world: Tracks are laid down by a lead guitarist in London, a drummer in New Orleans, a keyboard player in Tokyo, a singer in Toronto, and maybe even some riffs by a South African jive chorus and a Czech chamber orchestra. The pieces might be put together anywhere from a Hollywood studio to a barn in the Berkshires.

Perelman, who plumps for "the end of education" (as we know it), then admiringly describes the new, disembodied look of lifetime learning. The National Technological University, he explains, is:

> . . . an electronic graduate engineering school with

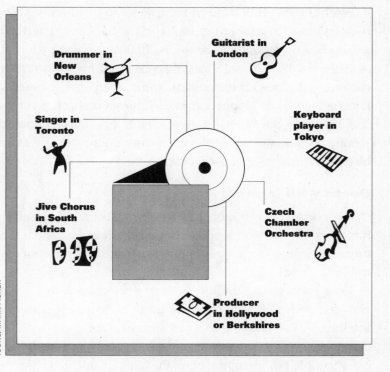

no campus and no full-time faculty, [which] beams its 12,000 hours of courses by satellite from its Fort Collins, Colorado, headquarters to over 5,000 engineers in video classrooms at work sites of scores of subscribing organizations scattered all over the United States. Leading faculty at over forty participating universities nationwide provide NTU's telecourses. Students — generally, engineers with jobs pursuing continuing education and professional development — can attend courses either in real time at the workplace or by taped delay. They communicate with professors by telephone or electronic mail. With new digital signal-compression technology, NTU now can deliver courses anywhere a satellite dish can be put up at one-quarter the cost of a typical college class, according to NTU's president Lionel Baldwin.

We have disembodied enterprises for producing things (recordings), disembodied enterprises for coping with the knowledge revolution per se (individualized lifelong education as delivered by NTU). In fact, dispersed, ad hoc networks are becoming the new, if ephemeral, spine of enterprise based on knowledge — knowledge gathered from whomever, wherever, and instantly packaged to meet customers' fickle demands. Tomorrow's economy will revolve around innovatively assembled brain power, not muscle power.

### Down with Lumps!

"We are trying to sell more and more intellect and less and less materials." These words, spoken by 3M's strategic planner (now retired), George Hegg, will animate much of the discussion to follow.

3M is by birth and tradition a lumpy-object company, a materials company. Yet it is trying to go light on lumps, heavy on intellect. A marketing executive from the company's Austin-based electronics sector told me, "Tom, our salespeople don't carry sample kits anymore. Now the battle is our flowchart versus their flowchart. That is, does our process enable us to custom-engineer a solution [product in yesterday's language] for a customer's specific needs more rapidly than our competitors can?"

LUMPS ➔ BRAINS

Flowcharts and intellect. That's the story, even if a lumpy object (a cable or connector or other device, in the case of 3M at Austin) does eventually change hands. My new Minolta 9xi is a lumpy object, but I suspect I paid about $10 for its plastic casing, another $50 for the fine-ground optical glass, and the rest, about $640, for its intellect: the microprocessors and software that drive the beast and perform acts unimaginable a couple of years ago.

It is a soft world. Nike, a "shoe" company, is consigned to *Fortune*'s service 500 list, not the industrial 500 one. Nike contracts for the production of its spiffy footwear in factories

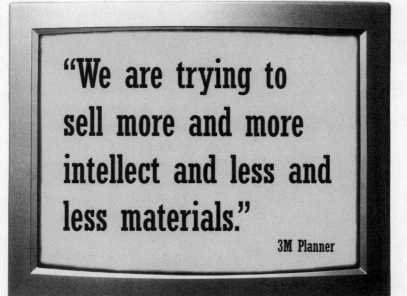

> ## "We are trying to sell more and more intellect and less and less materials."
>
> **3M Planner**

around the globe, but it creates its enormous stock market value via superb design and, above all, marketing skills. Tom Silverman, founder of upstart Tommy Boy Records, says Nike was the first company to understand that it was in the lifestyle business. How else can you explain the "shoemaker" shelling out a $1 million signing bonus, a guarantee of $375,000 a year for 15 years, and Nike stock options to entice Duke basketball coach Mike Krzyewski to chuck his Adidases and "Just do it." Shoes? Lumps? Forget it! Lifestyle. Image. Speed. Value via intellect and pizazz.

### Up with Imagination!

"Microsoft's only factory asset is the human imagination," observed *The New York Times Magazine* writer Fred Moody. In seminars I've used the slide on which those words appear at least a hundred times, yet every time that simple sentence comes into view on the screen I feel the hairs on the back of my neck bristle. "Only," "factory," "asset," "human imagination" — that's a mouthful and a mindful. At any rate, it seems so in an era when most companies, if you look beneath what may be a New Age surface, are still holding onto the management doctrines of the Industrial Revolution.

**"Does anyone know what it means to manage the human imagination?"**

After exposing an audience to the Microsoft quote, I ask a telling question: "Does anyone here know what it means to 'manage the human imagination?'" So far, not a single hand has gone up, including mine. I don't know what it means to manage the human imagination either, but I do know that imagination is the main source of value in the new economy. And I know we had better figure out some answer to my question — quick.

Hegg, of 3M: *more intellect . . . less materials.*

Microsoft: *only asset . . . human imagination.*

The concepts embedded in these two "simple" phrases are turning the world upside down.

### Fractional Value

Look at the new upside-down craziness quantitatively in the form of three fractions. The first is 116/129.

A few years back, Philip Morris purchased Kraft for $12.9 billion, a fair price in view of its subsequent performance. When the accountants finished their work, it turned out that Philip Morris had bought $1.3 billion worth of "stuff" (tangible assets) and $11.6 billion of "other." What's the other, the 116/129?

When I learned accounting, "book value" was what mattered — the meltdown value of the steel in the smokestacks at the Kraft factories and the value of the Velveeta cheese in inventory. But today that story has been turned on its head. **116/129 - - - - -**

You bop in to see your local banker, borrow a cool $13 billion, and after the accountants have turned out the lights and gone home you can figure out where only a billion of your money went. The rest is invested in "other." Call it intangibles, goodwill (the U.S. accountants' term), brand equity, or the ideas in the heads of tens of thousands of Kraft employees around the world.

Welcome to a world where, in the words of one executive I know, "If you can touch it, it's not real." I don't know about you, but that's a tough concept for an old (me) civil engineer (me, again) to get.

It's a tough concept for many managements to grasp, as well. It seems as though the people running most businesses still spend the greater share of their time managing the 13/129 that they can touch — the fixed, tangible assets. They pretty much let "other" (the 116/129) sort itself out. Company managers will devote a half-dozen meetings to a $50,000 capital proposal, then just skim over training issues and go through the whole year without a serious discussion about imagination, which is the basis of all those intangibles.

Here's another fraction to ponder: 97/100.

ABB Asea Brown Boveri is a classic heavy-industry behemoth that competes in such business segments as power plants, power transmission, power distribution, transportation, and pollution control. This $30 billion, Zurich-based outfit is looking to reduce the cycle time of everything it does by 50 percent in the course of the next few years. Success could have an enormous impact on the bottom line.

As part of this so-called T50 program, ABB carefully analyzed the sales-to-delivery cycle (sales, order entry, engineering, specification development, planning, manufacturing, delivery). It turned out that manufacturing accounted for only about 3 percent of cycle time. The rest, the remaining 97 percent, could be labeled "other." As an ABB executive told me, "We manage the

# 97/100

dickens out of the three percent, creating 'manufacturing super-highways'; then we let the rest pretty much take care of itself."

To verify that a similar distortion of concern exists in general, all you need to do is travel down to the local bookstore. You'll find the shelves groaning under tomes on reorganizing the factory. But spot a good book on engineering management or laboratory organization, and you've got a better eye than mine.

Finally, consider 94/100.

One analyst estimates that 6 percent of IBM's ever-dwindling number of employees work in a factory. The remaining 94 percent are engaged in "other" — that is, in intangible, intellectual service activities such as engineering, accounting, personnel, logistics, design, and finance. Moreover, today even the 6 percent working in the factory mostly perform service tasks. Factory "hands" (ah, words!) now spend much of their time working with outsiders in multifunctional teams that streamline processes, improve quality, or customize products. In any case, their strategy ought to be clear, as it is for the other 94 percent: Apply more intellect, apply more imagination.

### Brains R Us (Or Else)

More and more intellect and less and less materials. Only factory asset is the human imagination. Welcome to the world of soft, the world of gray matter. And watch out if you still think brawn defines a worker.

Research by Isabel Sawhill, then at the Urban Institute, throws a scare into seminar participants around the world. Sawhill determined that average U.S. family income grew 20 percent (adjusted for inflation) between 1968 and 1977. In the American tradition, the rising tide lifted all boats equally: High-school dropouts added 20 percent to their paychecks; college grads, 21 percent. Then the Age of Information, Knowledge, and Imagination hit us square in payroll accounting. Over the next decade, from 1978 to 1987, average inflation-adjusted family income jumped 17 percent, but this time the high-school drop-

**- - - - 94/100**

"Travel services? Our industry is 'beyond revolution'."

Hal Rosenbluth, CEO of
Rosenbluth International

out suffered a 4 percent loss, while the college graduate gained a whopping 48 percent. Sufficient reason for revolution? You bet.

The previous economic revolution (the Industrial Revolution) gave us Karl Marx. The information-imagination age hasn't found its Marx. Yet.

## Abandon Everything!

"Every organization has to prepare for the abandonment of everything it does," Peter Drucker wrote in the *Harvard Business Review*. Drucker isn't given to overstatement, yet note the key words in his sentence. Mr. Drucker didn't say, "Most companies ought to be prepared to change significantly in the face of changing times." No, he didn't say "change." He used the words "every," "abandonment," and "everything" — which are dramatically different.

I have said to seminar participants, "Forget your detailed note-taking today. Instead take a single piece of paper and simply write on it, 'every,' 'abandon,' and 'everything.' That's it. Then, when you get back to work, slip the page beneath the glass on your desktop. Refer to it hourly." When I tell them that, I'm in earnest. Coming to grips with no-baloney words — "abandon," not "change" — is a big part of the task we face.

As I've mentioned before and will mention again, the world is turning upside down. This upheaval is of the once-every-two-centuries sort, and that's almost impossible for people who have been alive 25, 35, or even 50 or 60 years to imagine. The technology revolution is getting up to speed just in time to coincide with the arrival of the global village. And there is no place to hide, no placid backwater in which to sit this one out.

During recent trips to Asia, Oceania, Europe, the Middle East,

> **"There is an absolute dearth of new and exciting fashion-forward products."**
>
> David Glass,
> CEO, Wal-Mart

and Latin America, I couldn't help but note that every developed and developing economy is pursuing precisely the same strategy: "Create a value-added, knowledge-based, export-led economy."

**Among the 16,143 new products that hit the shelves in 1991, where is the equivalent of the early microwave oven, the video cassette recorder, or the Walkman...?**

I heard these, or equivalent, words in Argentina, Brazil, Ireland, Singapore, Malaysia, Korea, Australia, New Zealand, and the United Arab Emirates — as well as in the United States, Japan, and Germany. Also in Thailand and Indonesia. And India and China. Everywhere.

A lot of us act as if anyone who doesn't live and work in North America, Western Europe, or Japan is still making sandals. Hardly. Korea's Samsung, barely a player a decade ago, has quickly become the No. 1 producer of commodity semiconductor memory chips, or DRAMs. And in Penang, Malaysia, leading U.S. and Japanese electronics companies no longer limit workers to assembly chores; employees design what they build. Bangalore, India, has become a software design hotbed. (A few wags see it as the world software capital in 30 years.) Singapore, the self-styled "intelligent island," is a global hub for banking, telecommunications, and logistics.

### Shake It Up, Baby!

We're flattening our organizations, shedding our bureaucratic excesses. That's good — and long overdue. But as to entering the Age of Imagination, we're just barely sniffing at the doorway.

In October 1992, I talked with Wal-Mart CEO David Glass. "There's an absolute dearth of new and exciting fashion-forward products," he complained. A dearth?

In 1981, 2,689 new products made their way to the grocery and drugstore shelves in the United States. Just a decade later, in 1991, the number had soared to 16,143. A new product was introduced every half-hour that year. What was Glass complaining about?

Let's look back at what he actually said: ". . . an absolute dearth of new and exciting fashion-forward products." He's right. Among all the new products hitting Wal-Mart's shelves, where is the equivalent of the early microwave oven, the video cassette recorder, or the Walkman — the kind of products, as Glass put it, that sucked people off their couches by the millions and propelled them into his stores?

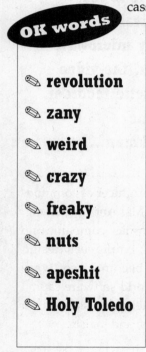

OK words

- ✎ **revolution**
- ✎ **zany**
- ✎ **weird**
- ✎ **crazy**
- ✎ **freaky**
- ✎ **nuts**
- ✎ **apeshit**
- ✎ **Holy Toledo**

New soft and hard products alike are coming at us in increasing numbers from every corner of the global economy, but are they exciting, magical, special? Do they pass the Wow Test (see Chapter 8)? "You can have all these royal weddings and put in place all this [information highway] infrastructure," multimedia expert Gerry O'Connell told *Advertising Age* in late 1993, "but it's going to take real creativity to do something new and exciting." Or as former Apple Computer chairman John Sculley said, "What's the new capability? . . . It's like Rocky IV and Godfather V."

Crazy? No.
So what do we do?
Abandon everything.

## Lessons Learned

- ☑ Crazy times . . . crazy organizations
- ☑ New corporate metabolism (voom, varoom)
- ☑ Disembodied enterprise
- ☑ Learning on the fly, forever
- ☑ More intellect . . . less materials
- ☑ Only asset . . . human imagination
- ☑ Funny fractions (116/129, 97/100, 94/100)
- ☑ "Every organization," "abandon," "everything"
- ☑ Wow! (And the common absence thereof)

### Reprise: A Very Big Deal Indeed

We're trying to cope with the biggest economic change in two centuries. That truth is self-evident. But what does it mean to you? It means that to be scared out of your senses is sensible. To be comfortable is suicidal.

"The obsession with boosting productivity," Roger Swardson wrote in the *San Francisco Chronicle* in the fall of 1993, "has created widely disparate layers of working Americans. One is prosperous, whipping around chanting slogans and wondering what the hell the problem is beyond some bad attitudes; another works each day fearful that it will be the last; and another has fallen through the cracks into dislocation and a dreadful wage depression."

These are crazy times. And hard times. The latter phrase reminded me of a book I hadn't read since adolescence. Last summer I went back and read it again, Charles Dickens's 1854 novel, *Hard Times*. Everything changing. People moving from farms to factories, from village squares to fetid city slums. I wanted to see how people coped then. Not well. Marx described it, if not so entertainingly as Dickens. The Bolsheviks did something about

## Will we all be working for - - - - -

it. They weren't so entertaining either.

Change is here again. What are we doing about it?

Former Citicorp chairman Walter Wriston and writer George Gilder preach technology: Technology, they promise, will set us free. Probably it will, but that isn't a new line. Proponents of change such as de Toqueville preached political liberation the last time around. They turned out to be mostly right. But it took six generations, the transformation of ages-old societies, and two world wars to realize industrialization's democratizing promise. If history repeats itself, and voters' recent hard turn toward extremist candidates everywhere suggests it might, while the impact of these new technology tools will be largely settled in the next 25 years, the social adjustment will require another century.

How, for example, do we deal with the widening wage gap separating the haves and the have-nots in our society? What about the have and have-not nations?

Even those with the moxie to survive revolution face mind-boggling transformations. How does the average educated person replace knowledge that grows obsolete every half-dozen years (or less)? What does the end of job security portend? Will we all be working for Manpower Inc. 20 years from now?

Suppose you buy the thrust of my story so far and reserve the right to quibble later over specifics. What do you get for having signed on the dotted line for madness? I think it makes you better able to assess what is coming.

For instance, you've given yourself permission to feel a little nuts. You've acknowledged that there are no certain answers to lots of today's questions. You understand that we don't even know what questions to ask. For a long time to come a tolerance for ambiguity will be success tool number one for line workers, corporate chiefs, independent professionals, and politicians alike.

You've also acknowledged that hiding from change won't do

any good. In a speech on defense conversion, President Clinton marveled that one hard-hit community had survived a base closure without government help, and wondered how much better off it would have been if aid had been given. I'm not so sure that the answer would not have been: worse off. Most government-aid efforts, however well intended, have the practical effect of insulating folks from the inevitable for only a little while longer. When the money runs out, they're no more prepared than before — and they are further behind. To the extent that we try to "protect" ourselves from the inevitable, we impede our collective ability to adapt to this tectonic shift in our economic base.

By accepting my story, you've agreed to the need to reinvent yourself. Corporations and government must be transformed, and so must we. The race will go to the curious, the slightly mad, and those with an unsated passion for learning and daredeviltry.

And you've agreed that, whatever is happening, it is really big. Maybe that perception alone will make each of us better prepared to weather the shock waves coming our way. Again. And again.

### T.T.D. (Things to Do) and Q.T.A. (Questions to Answer)

❶ Look through a sample of 25 catalogs, from pet supplies to personal computers. They're thick, but are they interesting? How many new offerings take your breath away (those are the right words)? Now try the same thing with your own catalog. If you're in staff services, make a list of your "products." Are they scintillating? Dazzling?

❷ Examine the shift from materials to intellect and services. Look at winning "products" in your industry. Are the service and intellectual components growing? How much? (Try to quantify, akin to the Minolta camera example.) Are you and your colleagues discussing this shift and its implications? Do your priorities reflect the importance of these "soft product" attributes?

❸ Are you seriously concerned (preoccupied?) with nurturing "human imagination" (which goes far beyond empowerment — more later)? Is it an issue? If not, toss this book in the nearest recycling bin.

❹ Do you spend most of your time in the office working with the same old mates? Or are you constantly out and about, working hither and thither, via electronic networks, with an ever-changing group of folks from all over? Do you look outside first, rather than inside, when thinking about the resources (people) you need to launch or execute a project? If not, why not? (Are you so arrogant as to imagine that the best and brightest at everything are already working in your building?)

❺ Are you (meaning you, your unit, your company) prepared to "abandon everything"? Take a cold, quantitative, impersonal look around: How many processes and products have been tossed overboard (not "changed") in the last 12 months? If none or only a handful, why?

❻ What does it really mean to be in the midst of a once-every-two-centuries cataclysm? Are you feeling funny? If not, watch out.

❼ Do you and your colleagues routinely use "hot" words: "revolution," "zany," "weird," "freaky," "nuts," "crazy," "apeshit," "Holy Toledo" (as in "Holy Toledo products")? Do a language audit: How hot/cold is your talk, your notes?

❽ Are you prepared to forswear the word "change" for "revolution"? If not, why not? Because I'm an extremist? Or because you aren't?

❾ On a scale of 1 to 10, how "crazy" (a) are you? (b) is your unit? (c) your company? (d) your most innovative competitor? Are you excited about going to work on Monday? Is the workplace a kick? On a scale of 1 to 10, how dull is your (a) unit, (b) company, (c) closest competitor? How dull are you?

Recall the epigraph to this book:
"Only the paranoid survive" — *Andy Grove, Intel.*

## In the new age, paranoia will not be a disease. Instead, it's the first step toward job security and robust corporate earnings. How about the Paranoid Corporation? Not a bad idea, and perhaps a very good one, these days. There is but one key message in this chapter: We're going far beyond our traditional, and even our more recently stretched, conceptions of how much is enough when it comes to effecting change. Uh, make that *abandonment.*

## CHAPTER 2

BEYOND DECENTRALIZATION

# DISORGANIZING TO UNLEASH IMAGINATION

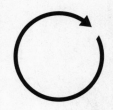

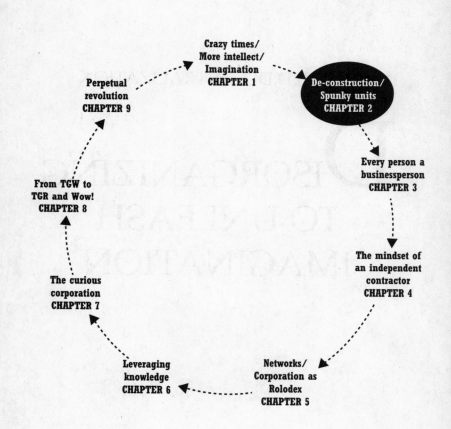

Crazy times/
More intellect/
Imagination
CHAPTER 1

De-construction/
Spunky units
CHAPTER 2

Perpetual
revolution
CHAPTER 9

Every person a
businessperson
CHAPTER 3

From TGW to
TGR and Wow!
CHAPTER 8

The mindset of
an independent
contractor
CHAPTER 4

The curious
corporation
CHAPTER 7

Leveraging
knowledge
CHAPTER 6

Networks/
Corporation as
Rolodex
CHAPTER 5

**More and more** decentralization makes sense when an organization has to deal with an explosion of unknowns. But most corporate decentralization, even circa 1994, utterly fails to unleash the genuine and quirky independence that abides deep within subordinate units. Hence the idea here of moving beyond decentralization and toward **disorganization — or self-DESTRUCTION**, as one corporate chief puts it. It's the logical first step in implementing Chapter 1's "beyond change" message.

**"We removed the entire**

**formal organization.**

**We have a tremendous**

**competitive advantage,**

**because we don't care**

**about formalities."**

Lars Kolind,
President
Oticon

The date was August 8, 1991. The hour was 8:00 a.m. The place was Copenhagen, Denmark. Lars Kolind, the president of Oticon, did something extraordinary. He changed his company into a what he called a "spaghetti organization," a construct without a center.

Oticon, a world leader in hearing-aid manufacture founded in 1904, had been badly sagging. Market share had fallen by half in the past decade. Kolind razed walls, eliminated secretaries, and erased job descriptions and specialties to create a 100 percent project-directed entity in which employees invent the tasks that need to be done, then physically arrange themselves as they see fit to get them done.

To affirm the change, one month later, on September 8, 1991, the company auctioned all its old office furniture to employees. It was a calculated move aimed at certifying the irreversibility of the reorganization. Now people stow their effects in caddies, or personal carts, moving them to appropriate spots in the completely open space as their work with various colleagues requires.

After surprisingly few hiccups, Oticon began to make record profits and regain lost market share. Faced with tougher-than-ever competition from giants such as Philips, it introduced a world-beating new product in half the normal time. When asked if he attributed the miracle (speed and creativity) to his wild and woolly new configuration, Kolind said, "Absolutely. We decided simply to get rid of the former structure. We took away all departments. We took away all managers' titles. And with them went the red tape. There were no secretaries to protect us. We removed the entire formal organization. We have a tremendous competitive advantage, because we don't care about formalities. We only care about performance and results."

Get rid of "the entire formal organization." Strong language indeed. And, apropos of this discussion, what Kolind did at Oticon goes miles beyond decentralization, even as practiced by progressive firms. Kolind has done a lot more than cede some precious authority to the hinterlands. He has put the hinterlands in charge and told them to create, organize, reorganize, and run their own show.

Management consultants Charles Handy and Jim O'Toole call this idea of organization "federal," as opposed to "decentralized." In the latter, the center yields some power to the outlying units. In the former, the outlying units (reluctantly) yield power to the center. If that sounds too far beyond the pale, you and your company are right to be nervous about the future.

## The Value Destroyers

Let's go back for a moment. The year is 1986. A track inspector at the Union Pacific Railroad discovers a problem at a customer-owned rail siding. What does he do? He bucks the news up to his boss, the Yardmaster, who passes it up to the Assistant Trainmaster, who lobs it up to his chief, the Trainmaster, who passes it up to the Division Superintendent of Transportation, who passes it on to the Division Superintendent. The Division Superintendent sends this hot potato to the Regional Transportation Superintendent, who hoists it one more level to the Assistant General Manager, who gives it its final kick up to the General Manager. The siding problem has finally reached the apex of the massive Union Pacific operations hierarchy.

Next it heads across a great chasm to sales and marketing, where it likely lands on the desk of the Assistant Vice President for sales. He sends it down to the Regional Sales Manager, who passes it further down to the District Sales Manager, who informs the sales representative about the problem. And if, actuarially speaking, the customer is still alive, he or she then learns about the rail-siding problem.

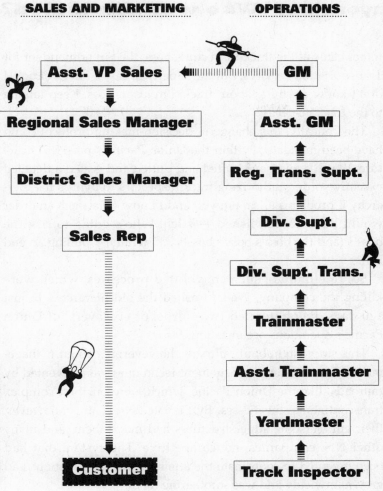

| SALES AND MARKETING | OPERATIONS |
|---|---|

**Asst. VP Sales** ◀━━━━ **GM**

**Regional Sales Manager** ⬇

**Asst. GM** ⬆

**District Sales Manager** ⬇

**Reg. Trans. Supt.** ⬆

**Sales Rep** ⬇

**Div. Supt.** ⬆

**Div. Supt. Trans.** ⬆

**Trainmaster** ⬆

**Asst. Trainmaster** ⬆

**Yardmaster** ⬆

**Customer** ⬆ **Track Inspector**

Honest! This absurd procedure was described to my colleague Marcia Wilkof by one of the frontline track inspectors and confirmed by a boss. The wonder isn't that Union Pacific was in disarray in 1986, but that it was functioning at all.

The railroad appointed a new CEO, Mike Walsh, and in 1987 he undertook a lightning-fast reorganization. Today, if a track inspector discovers a problem at a customer-owned rail siding, he informs the customer directly. If the customer disagrees with the track inspector (a rare occurrence, I'm told), then the customer can call the track inspector's boss, the Superintendent for Transportation Services. But the super will say in effect, "Look, I don't know anything about track. I'm just a boss. Keep talking to the track inspector."

Theoretically, this change in decision-making protocol could have been mandated within the Union Pacific's pre-1987 structure. Walsh could have huffed and puffed and issued a detailed executive order authorizing track inspectors to bypass the hierarchy if problems arise. But you and I know what such an order would have accomplished — zilch. Who's going to risk the boss's (and the boss's boss's boss's . . .) wrath by pulling an end run?

So, to eliminate such convoluted processes, which were killing the company, Walsh trashed the old hierarchy. In just 120 days, he obliterated two-thirds, or six layers, of Union Pacific's operations organization.

This story isn't about railroads, however; it's about management. Many modern management techniques were invented by railroads, like the Union Pacific, which were our first complex transcontinental businesses. By the late 20th century, however, their cumbersome superstructures had made them, and many other U.S. companies, noncompetitive. The system that had been invented to coordinate the affairs of vast corporations had grown unwieldy and was smothering them.

**Question:** Who were the people in those six management layers Mike Walsh eliminated?

**Answer:** The railroad's (and the nation's) best and brightest.

It's true that, in any company, office politics occasionally elevates a nincompoop to a position of authority and responsibility. But, on average, more or less the right person gets promoted to the right job. Those six excised layers at Union Pacific consisted of good, intelligent managers, not dingbats. And, in the unlikely event that similar jobs should ever open up in the future, the railroad presumably would rehire them happily.

But, dear reader, we want to know what value, precisely, did those perfectly competent people add to the gross domestic product of the United States? It's a question I always ask participants at my seminars. Some laugh. Others say, "Damn little." A few say, "Zero."

All are wrong.

The correct, quantitative answer is *negative* value.

I'm not exaggerating. Those extra six layers made it all but impossible for veteran frontline track inspectors to do their job — sorting out problems with track users — thus impeding, not aiding, the conduct of the company's business.

The unpleasant truth that we don't want to hear is that middle management — not the nice people, but their function — doesn't just slow our organizations down. It moves them backward. Middle management clogs our corporate arteries. The effect of middle managers' doing **MIDDLE MANAGEMENT → NEGATIVE VALUE** their specified jobs and following the policy manual is to deduct value. Great gobs of it.

### Letting Go

If garden-variety decentralization were the answer to the track inspector's problems and what ails companies in general today, IBM would be the model to emulate. IBM has reorganized, reorganized, and reorganized again, mostly to no avail. It has also divested itself of some dogs, pieces of the company that senior management decided didn't have a future. One of them, Lexmark, made the fabled IBM Selectric typewriter and now mostly makes printers. Lexmark was sold to its managers in early 1991. In the short space of the next 16 months, the following took place:

■ Managerial ranks were chopped by 60 percent.

■ Line-manager autonomy was increased dramatically.

■ Autonomous strategic business units were created.

■ Procedures were significantly simplified, especially those involving financial approvals.

■ The central staff was decimated and the hierarchy flattened.

■ Radical deintegration took place, with lots of activities outsourced.

■ Manufacturing was totally reorganized.

Net result: The formerly sagging business booked $100 million in pretax profits on $2 billion in sales in the first year away from Mom.

This tale sticks in my craw. Why in the hell couldn't these "obvious" changes have been made while Lexmark was still in the IBM fold? It bugs me, because I can't come up with a good answer. IBM "decentralized." Then decentralized again. And again. But it couldn't let go. Until the newly liberated Lexmark managers had a stake in the action (along with a healthy debt load), until the company was really theirs, until they weren't under IBM's cultural thumb, they didn't, or couldn't, break loose.

Look again at the actions Lexmark took. Collectively, they are impressive, but are any of them surprising? Hardly. These are standard 1980s and 1990s strategies for coping with fast-paced competition. Still, they required a complete break from Mother IBM to happen. Hmmm.

## The Hour of the Pygmy?

*The Economist* purports to be surprised by all this: "New technology has spread around the world, trade barriers have come down, financial markets have been deregulated, and consumer tastes have converged across borders. All these changes were once expected to give big firms even more scope to flex their muscles. Instead they have granted business opportunities to thousands of small- and medium-sized companies, and shown the bodies of many corporate behemoths to be mostly flab. . . . In 1993 'big' no longer means, as it once did, 'successful'; before long it is likely to mean 'failing.'"

As essayist Lance Morrow put it in *Time* in March 1993, "The rise of the knowledge economy means a change, in less than 20 years, from an overbuilt system of large, slow-moving economic units to an array of small, widely dispersed economic centers, some as small as the individual boss."

The Age of the Pygmies in the United States is a case in point. The job-creation machine slowed down in the late 1980s, but it didn't come to a complete halt. Our biggest corporations shed 2.3 million jobs between 1987 and 1992. Ouch! The offsetting news: Our not-so-big companies created 5.9 million jobs, for

**TRUTH IN NUMBERS**

**1987-1992**

Biggest firms    −2.3 million jobs
Small to mid-size firms    +5.9 million jobs

a net addition of 3.6 million. Moreover, and contrary to conventional wisdom, those middle-size and smaller winners added as many high-wage jobs as the giant corporations shed; also, most of the non-high-wage jobs the less sizable companies generated were average-wage jobs. The low-wage jobs created by mid-size and smaller enterprises were only 16 percent of the total (900,000 out of 5.9 million new jobs).

Yet the notion of bigness-is-a-must dies hard. For example, new technologies call for big bucks to start anything. Right? Wrong. *Inc.* magazine's list of 500 top-growth companies contains a few hamburger flippers, but it's also loaded with express-delivery companies, biotech firms, and sophisticated computer and information-technology newcomers. The startling news: 34 percent of the *Inc.* 500 were launched with less than $10,000; 59 percent with less than $50,000; and 75 percent with less than $100,000.

We may be in an age of great sophistication, but a handful of dollars, mostly garnered by putting a second mortgage on the house and shaking down Aunt Sally, will still allow you to get into almost any business you can name.

Still, there may be new tricks the big old gang can learn in order to stay viable — or even become sprightly. If *The*

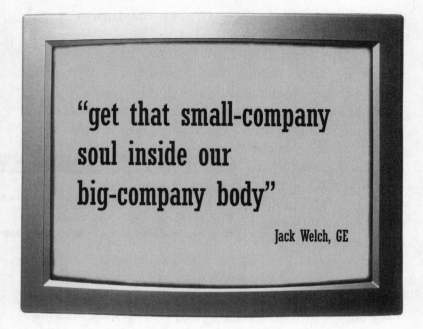

# "get that small-company soul inside our big-company body"

Jack Welch, GE

*Economist* confidently asserts that "the humbling of big firms has only just begun," General Electric CEO Jack Welch nonetheless claims that the best is yet to be.

## Soul Search by Percy, the Mad Organizational Scientist

In his often-quoted 1992 annual report, Welch, a recent convert from liquidation to liberation, said, "What we are trying relentlessly to do is get that small-company soul — and small-company speed — inside our big-company body."

Nobody has pursued that condition more aggressively than ABB Asea Brown Boveri chief Percy Barnevik. The Barnevik strategy: Get rid (almost entirely) of the center; shift responsibility to modest-size, human-scale units.

In 1980, Barnevik moved from head of U.S. operations for Sweden's Sandvik (carbide cutting tools, etc.) to that country's industrial giant Asea. He inherited a central staff of 1,700, which he pruned to 200 in about 100 days. He repeated that feat again and again. Merging Asea with Switzerland's Brown Boveri et

Cie in 1987, he slashed the Brown Boveri's headquarters staff from 4,000 to 200. The Finnish arm of ABB, ABB Stromberg, had a central staff of 880 when Barnevik took over. Today it's 25. (You can check; I'm not making this up.)

About a third of ABB's deposed staffers hit the street; a third went to line units close to the marketplace; and the rest to free-standing units (such as marketing) charged with turning a buck. In the latter case, the central staffers could profitably sell their services to the new, small units or to outside customers — or they could leave.

Barnevik now runs his 210,000-person enterprise with a corporate staff of 150 people: 100 professionals and 50 administrative assistants. The corporate hierarchy, housed in an unimpressive building near Zurich's main railroad station, is bare-bones. Only three layers of management separate Barnevik and his tiny executive team from the 190,000-or-so people on the shop floor who do the real work.

But Barnevik's most impressive accomplishment has been to break the company into 5,000 pieces — each a profit center, each employing on average about 40 people.

The profit center is exceptionally autonomous. Typically, each is led by a chief and four associates (the heads of finance, engineering, operations, and marketing/sales). Almost every center has its own profit-and-loss statement, its own balance sheet, and its own customers.

Barnevik told me that, were it not for the blizzard of paperwork and the legal minutiae, he would incorporate each center. Doing so, he said, would turn the small unit into a real, honest-to-God business — and the unit leaders into genuine entrepreneurs. That's what he's after.

The ABB chief's logic is straightforward. There is a "surplus of everything" in today's crowded markets, he observes, and adds that success will come only to companies that tack fast and add value through quality, service, innovation, and marriage to their customers. Those virtues are achievable, he thinks, only by units that are "spirited, obsessive, and energetic." And, thence, of moderate size. Have you ever heard of a spirited, obsessive, energetic unit of 3,729 people? Or 729, for that matter? I haven't. Neither has Barnevik.

So what is the magic number for a business unit in the intellect-based economy? Barnevik's experience suggests that about 50 makes sense, even in heavy industry. Richard Branson, founder of The Virgin Group (entertainment, real estate, an airline), thinks the same thing. "Once people start not knowing the people in the building and it starts to be impersonal," he told *Success*, "it's time to break up a company. I'd say the limit is about 50 or 60 people. People shouldn't get lost in the corridors of power."

Again and again, in every kind of company, I find enterprising managements that have devised clever ways to split their sizable outfits into surprisingly small units. Maybe the magic number is a little bigger than 50. Maybe it is less than 50. Maybe it's a lot less.

Titeflex, a subsidiary of Britain's TI Group, was bumbling along when, in 1988, Jon Simpson took over and reorganized. He stripped layers of hierarchy and thinned out central staffs. Most drastically, he broke great chunks of the 500-person, high-tech hosemaker into 6- to 10-person business development teams, or BDTs.

Are business development teams self-managing? Yes, but not just self-managing. They are, in effect, small enterprises, like Barnevik's units. The average BDT includes almost all the company old staff functions — accounting, engineering, production scheduling, quality assessment, and human resources. Teams deal directly with customers and vendors, are intimately involved in capital spending, and seek out new business. Each is a genuine profit-and-loss center. A BDT at Titeflex, then, is far more than a self-managing team; it is a "90 percent business," to use a term I've come to like.

This is the age of — I'll say it again — "more and more intellect, less and less materials." This is the age when the "only factory asset is the human imagination." As one executive said to me, "It's clear, for heaven's sake, isn't it? You don't do brainwork in groups of a thousand, or probably even hundreds. You do it in quartets, octets, groups of ten, fifteen, twenty-five."

Or duos.

## Magic Number = 2?

Radical change is coming to health care in the United States. Even without new federal mandates, dramatic reconfigurations of hopelessly archaic hospitals are taking place. Of special

> **" You don't do brainwork in groups of a thousand ...you do it in quartets, octets, groups of ten ... "**
>
> Anonymous Exec

significance is the idea of a "patient-focused enterprise," put forth and tested by Booz, Allen Healthcare vice president Phil Lathrop. Change, he insists, must be radical, not incremental. (Here we go again.)

Why?

In the typical hospital today, with its ludicrous levels of specialization and paperwork, there is — literally — about one clerk per patient. Lathrop jokes that we might as well assign each patient his or her own private clerk.

That isn't all. The typical hospital also employs one relatively senior administrator per three or four patients. So why not break the hospital into three- or four-patient units, Lathrop continues, each with its own CEO?

In fact, only 20 cents on the dollar of hospital expense goes directly to patient care. Thirty percent of frontline employees' time is spent writing things down. And despite the specialization (as many as 600 job classifications, including multiple varieties of floor cleaners, in a huge hospital), most activity is routine.

To begin the hospital revolution, Lathrop wrote in

*Restructuring Health Care: The Patient-Focused Paradigm,* "We have to eliminate the parade of narrow task-doers from the patient's room." What exactly he means by that we'll see in a second.

One of Lathrop's favorite models of the new look is the Lakeland Regional Medical Center, in Lakeland, Florida. This large (897-bed) hospital is in the process of creating five mini-hospitals, each having a surgical unit that's self-contained (like those Business Development Teams at Titeflex) with its own minilab, diagnostic radiology rooms, supply stockrooms, and administrative area. But the breakup doesn't stop there. The minihospital consists, in effect, of microhospitals. The key: Lakeland's "care pairs."

Care pairs are two-person teams, a registered nurse and a technician, who have been trained to perform as "multiskilled practitioners." After just a special six-week course, care pairs can provide 80 to 90 percent — yes, 80 to 90 percent — of pre- and post-surgical care for four to seven patients. Take careful note: In hospitals, the industrial model of specialization has reached its ultimate extreme (those 600 job classifications in a large hospital), but it turns out that just two folks, after a modest dose of cross-training, can run their own hospital. That is, the Lakeland duo can provide most of the care required for a half-dozen patients. What services they can't handle themselves they can coordinate for their patients through a computer terminal found in each patient's room, loaded with specially designed software called "Carelink."

Does it work? You decide. Turnaround time for routine tests dropped from 157 minutes to 48 minutes in the first year or so of patient-focused operations. In diagnostic radiology, a 40-step, 140-minute process was reduced to an 8-step, 28-minute

**CARE PAIR = MICRO HOSPITAL**

■ **Provide 80-90% of pre- and post-surgical care for 4-7 patients**

■ **Coordinate the remaining 10-20% via special software**

process. The pilot unit boasted fewer patient falls and the lowest medication-error rate in the hospital. Registered nurse turnover in the pilot was also the lowest in the hospital. Out-of-pocket costs fell. Both physician and patient satisfaction shot up.

The two most telling indicators, however, are more human. First, the average patient now encounters 13 instead of 48 hospital employees during a stay; second, the registered nurse now spends more than half of his or her time — 53 percent instead of 21 percent — with the patient.

## Tired, But No Tears

But don't the care pairs in places like Lakeland (and those in similarly reorganized units everywhere), performing tasks that used to involve dozens of people, end up running around like characters in a Charlie Chaplin movie? To some extent, yes. But, like most of us, the care pairs don't mind hard work when it has a purpose. Lathrop described the experiences of one veteran nurse, now employed in a patient-focused operation:

> She especially notices the differences on an extremely busy and stressful day. Now when things are really hectic, she goes home more physically tired than in the past. She has more things to do. But she does not go home and cry. That is what happened in the old world when the workload became overwhelming. She would just get frustrated — spending much of her day on the phone trying to get other people to do the things her patients needed.
>
> Eight hours of bickering, cajoling, screaming, and even stretching the truth when necessary were not rewarding. Now, even if she has to hurry between tasks, she and her partners can still get everything necessary done, and they have the discretion to defer things that are not critical. Best of all, the patients see and appreciate her efforts.

Are you beginning to detect a trend here?

Today's turbulent marketplace requires instant response to customer needs, the customization of products and services — and imagination from one and all. None of these attributes were attainable in the cumbersome bureaucracies of the sort originally found at the Union Pacific Railroad, ABB Asea Brown Boveri, Titeflex, or Lakeland Regional Medical Center. Nor in a many-times decentralized IBM, nor at GE before Welch.

## The Pursuit of Spunk

So breaking huge organizations into small and genuinely independent units goes miles beyond the ambitions of traditional decentralization. Many a company, even of rather modest size, is decentralized on paper but in attitude essentially remains centralist.

No one understands the distinction better than Ben Lytle. In 1987, he became chief operating officer of The Associated Group of Indianapolis. Following the sensible management fashion of the day, Lytle split the functionally organized enterprise into five strategic business units. But to his surprise he learned that he had only changed life for about five people — the unit bosses.

"I never will forget one exchange in the elevator," Lytle told us. "I was really excited about having gone from a functional organization into these five major units. A claims processor was in the elevator, too, and I asked her, 'How do you like working in the new structure?' And she said, 'Oh, real well.' And I asked, 'Where do you work now?' I was expecting her to say something like, 'I work in the Commercial Division [one of the five SBUs].' But all she said was, 'On 14.' The only change for her was the location of her office. Nothing else."

(Most senior executives understand the story — even if they fail to act on its lesson. Presenting Lytle's commentary to seminar participants on any continent never fails to elicit a belly laugh or two, along with a roomful of knowing nods.)

After that epiphany, Lytle decided to take an innovative next step: Break the now $3-billion financial services company's product-development, marketing, and service-delivery opera-

"Once it starts to be impersonal, it's time to break up a company."

Richard Branson

tions into 50- to 200-person units called Acordia companies. "The incident in the elevator," he explained, "really made me take a look at how to change culture. You have to change what people see, where they live, how they're paid, everything. When we did the rollouts into the Acordia companies, we changed a lot of things about the way people lived. One of the biggest steps was to decentralize totally into physically separate facilities. Our people even had to interview for jobs in an Acordia company, and we went to more at-risk pay, based on bottom-line results."

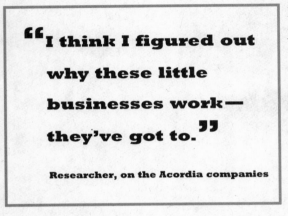

**"I think I figured out why these little businesses work — they've got to."**

Researcher, on the Acordia companies

The Acordia companies, publicly traded as Acordia Inc., are indeed independent. Each one, in addition to having its own separate building (a huge factor, incidentally), has its own chief executive officer and its own board of directors, which includes several outside members. In short, it's a mom-and-pop enterprise that thrives — or goes bust — by serving or failing to serve its small, ordained niche market.

Lytle's concept is to get that independent, do-or-die Acordia unit to leap through burning hoops to serve a small customer — a customer the giant enterprise, even when it was divided into the five strategic business units, probably wouldn't have bothered with.

Acordia Business Benefits, one of the new outfits, operates in 11 Indiana counties. The 300-person Indian Industries came to the Acordia unit with a complex request for a custom-tailored benefits program. Russ Sherlock, the Acordia CEO, decided in a flash to accept Indian Industries' challenge. He's the first to admit he wouldn't have done so under the old structure. But that was on a different planet. Now the new company must serve local industry or die.

My colleague Andrea Meyer visited Acordia Business Benefits for me and wrote up the interview notes in her customarily professional fashion. At the bottom of the last page was this handwritten note: "I think I figured out why all these little businesses work. They've got to." From that comment was born what I call the "gotta unit" concept.

A gotta unit is one of modest size, which may be living in a larger body (The Associated Group), but which routinely does the impossible, not because its members read books (even mine) on getting close to the customer, but for precisely the reason the mom-and-pop grocery store will do almost anything (and then some) to serve its neighbors in the surrounding seven-block area. Without that effort, it goes out of business. Kaput. In other words, they do it 'cause they gotta.

Implementing the gotta unit concept almost amounts to automating spunk — making it absolutely necessary for the unit to deliver a spirited response to every customer.

### The Symbiosis Imperative (Part I)

Take a deep breath!

**Question:** Why are companies putting themselves through all this radical (not to mention agonizing) change?

**Answer:** Because customers are demanding quick, customized solutions to their problems, and smart companies are reinventing themselves to meet their demands.

Zurich Insurance ($15 billion in assets) was feeling the pressure from "a ruinous price war" in "off the shelf" products, *The Economist* reports. Zurich's response was to reorganize into moderate-size specialist companies — in other words, "switch from selling standard products (such as property . . . and accident insurance) to anyone who will buy them, to fashioning customized insurance packages for specific groups." Small-company soul and speed in a big-company body? Zurich calls it being a "specialist insurer on a global scale."

Huge CSR, an Australian minerals and building-products conglomerate, is also thinking small so that it can insinuate itself deep into its customers' businesses, *Business Review Weekly* (Australia) reports. For example, new, small CSR units will become more involved in the installation and distribution of the company's building products. One road-products unit will offer customers a pavement-laying service, in which it will control and vouch for subcontractors. CSR, said the magazine, has calculated that the straight manufacturing business is a low-margin dead end, and it is turning its attention to higher-yielding small-business activities.

In general, companies are figuring out that service "add-ons" are where the loot is — provided the companies can develop a passionate, locally-oriented service-delivery culture. (No small thing, as we have seen, in traditional enterprises.) It all adds up to moving far beyond *In Search of Excellence*'s then-revolutionary notion of close-to-the-customer and toward something like symbiosis — i.e., wholesale, seamless intertwining with customers and other members of the value-adding chain. It's Barnevik's scheme at ABB and Lytle's at The Associated Group — and the very nature of the Business Development Teams at Titeflex and of the care pairs at Lakeland Regional Medical Center. I'll have more to say about it later.

### My Autocorrelation Obsession

The approaches taken by The Associated Group and CSR are still rare. Most so-called decentralization schemes don't decentralize anything at all. In particular, I've become obsessed with what I call "the autocorrelation effect." Let me explain.

A company announces it has decentralized with oomph, and maybe it even grants substantial spending authority to unit chiefs. But digging just a millimeter or two beneath the veneer of this decentralization reveals that each division head runs things the same way he or she did "in the old days." On paper, the new units are independent, but they're not committed to independence. (Recall Lexmark, before and after.) Therefore, they auto-correlate — i.e., they mostly look to one another and over the shoulder at the corporate Mecca for example and precedent.

Certainly that was the case at IBM, where, despite separating out its various products, the mainframe mentality drove the business almost as much in the personal computer, workstation, and minicomputer operations as it did in the mainframe unit itself. And even at Procter & Gamble, home of traditionally vicious brand-versus-brand competition (espoused support for one brand's new product cannibalizing another's profitable sales), decentralization amounts to little more than debate over the number of angels that can dance on the head of a pin. By contrast, companies like The Associated Group have fought autocorrelation and created genuine autonomy of character within their unit heads. Sadly, there are still far more IBMs than Associated Groups.

There is, however, nothing superficial about the decentralization at Random House — a billion-dollar publisher consisting of more than two dozen feisty small-business units, or imprints. (Random House itself is an astonishingly independent unit

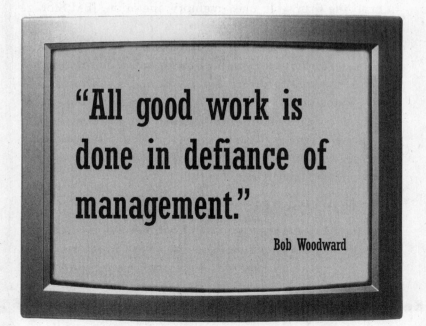

"All good work is done in defiance of management."

Bob Woodward

within S.I. Newhouse's Advance Group.) Sonny Mehta is chief of one of those units, Alfred A. Knopf. But a wisp of a company, just 78 people strong, Knopf is arguably the most prestigious imprint in the United States and among the most prestigious in the world; moreover, Mehta himself may be the most influential individual in book publishing. In conversation, he rarely mentions Mother Random House or its CEO, Alberto Vitale. He's out to do his thing — which is precisely why Vitale can rest easy. With awesome grants of intellectual autonomy and access to big bucks and a superb distribution system, Vitale is able to attract and retain free-spirited, cantankerous folks like Mehta and almost completely avoid the autocorrelation effect. Mehta will (and does) go his own sweet way, and has shaped Knopf as he has seen fit. Period.

I bet deposed IBM chief John Akers wishes he could have said the same about the people heading his subsidiary enterprises. Akers's successor, Lou Gerstner, is sweeping the planet for Mehta-esque folks to run bits of IBM in their own unique ways; for instance, he tapped Ed Zschau, the entrepreneur/politician, to head the firm's big mass-memory operation, IBM Storage Systems.

In this madcap world, the degree to which a chief executive officer can sleep without reaching for Nyquil is directly proportional to the willingness of his subordinates to thumb their noses at him, or, as journalist-turned-manager Bob Woodward told *Esquire*, to remember that "all good work is done in defiance of management." That may be a truth for all seasons, but it is an especially critical truth (more honored in the breach) for these unhinged times. Crazy times . . .

### The Little Shoebox

Some biggies have even started to trade on being small. My Aunt Dorothy sent me a particularly clever Christmas card in 1992. The card company was Shoebox Greetings. Whoops!

**Selling Proposition: "SHOEBOX GREETINGS ....**

Shoebox Greetings is a small, creative, entrepreneurial part of Hallmark. How do I know that? On the back of the card and on the Christmasy red envelope is printed, "Shoebox Greetings (A tiny little division of Hallmark)." Shoebox is publicly making the point that one of the reasons I should like the card, in addition to its clever design, is that it came from an independent, creative, nonbureaucratic, nontraditional offshoot of Hallmark. It's Hallmark. But it's not. The card itself isn't the only clever thing happening here.

Hey, it's so easy to screw it up — subunit independence — I mean, to stomp out spunk.

A while back, and with much fanfare, Xerox reorganized into nine stand-alone businesses. But it retained a single sales force. Executive Vice President Wayland Hicks, the *Financial Times* wrote, "insists this arrangement has not diluted the financial accountability of the nine operations."

Stand-alone businesses? Fat chance. A so-called accountable boss who must funnel his new products (or old ones, for that matter) through somebody else's sales force isn't an independent entrepreneur. Sorry, folks. Keep trying.

At the International Data Group, publisher of *Computerworld* and many other information-industry magazines, founder and CEO Pat McGovern thinks small is beautiful. He's even willing to pay for it. Each publication, for instance, can make its own deals with paper suppliers. Perhaps, he says, he could save a few pennies here and there with centralized paper buying. But, if he did, at the end of the month he could no longer hold his chiefs absolutely accountable.

McGovern doesn't want to hear, "I would have made my numbers except the lamebrains in central purchasing were trying to cut a good deal and delivered our paper supply two days late, which screwed up my pub date, marketing program and profitability." If people running independent operations don't

**.......(a tiny little division of Hallmark)"**

make their numbers, he wants to be able to say to them with a clear conscience, "You made a promise. You didn't come through. You've got a problem." (Not to mention the fact that central purchasing departments' "good deals" are usually bad jokes. By taking the initiative, McGovern's aggressive publishers are likely to end up with a better price on paper stock anyway. That's the nature of "gotta" entrepreneurism.)

## Oh, To Be Naive

How to be spunky? How to avoid the autocorrelation trap? For the individual, the problem is the same as for the corporation.

In an August 1993 television interview, Barry Diller, head of QVC, the home-shopping network, described the joys of a fresh start. He said that you come to a new job in a new industry with "a clean slate." You act "on instinct" and "screw things up" regularly.

All to the good. But pretty soon, he lamented, you "become sophisticated [and] start listening to the market research." You get "captured by the process." In other words, the more you know the less creative you become.

His is a pertinent complaint for everybody in business today — it's innovate, regularly reinvent, or die. Lizards shed their skin to survive. Maybe it's time for a visit to the zoo.

## Just One Strategy

Perhaps these issues of restructuring are ageless. (The principles behind them surely are.) But that's not my point here. These concerns take on special meaning in this jumbled marketplace. "For most companies today," management consultant James Morse wrote in the *Harvard Business Review*, "the only sustainable competitive advantage comes from out-innovating the competition." "Only" and "sustainable" — those are two unambiguous words, wholly warranted.

In *Shadows of Forgotten Ancestors*, Carl Sagan and Ann Druyan wrote, "Active mutators in placid and stable times tend to die off. They are selected against. Reluctant mutators in quickly changing times are also selected against." Today, most of our sizable companies are still reluctant mutators, and these are quickly changing times. They are being selected against.

The last person you would have wanted at the helm of a General Motors or General Electric in 1955 would have been an "active mutator" — a head-case. The times were stable, and stable strategies and stable leaders were called for. (Barry Diller need not apply.) Now the times are unstable, and the reverse is the case. The last thing you want is a passel of ultra-stable folk in charge of subordinate units. (Or at the tippy top, either.) The Random House model of generating 90 percent crazies/90 percent entrepreneurs, à la Sonny Mehta, is an unabashed effort to induce active mutation to fit an active marketplace. Street rap as corporate anthem, anyone?

> **"The only sustainable competitive advantage comes from out-innovating the competition."**
> James Morse

The problem ultimately boils down to cold, statistical considerations. If everybody thinks alike in a so-called decentralized operation, then 14 new-product tries from 14 "autonomous" divisions aren't statistically independent. It's really one try repeated 13 times. Autocorrelation. Low variation.

## Pursuing Variation for All You're Worth

I came across a book called *Understanding Variation: The Key to Managing Chaos.* While the innards consist of a well-rendered treatise on quality improvement through statistical methods to reduce process variation, the exterior — that is, the title — put me off. It's not only wrong, it's diametrically wrong. It's dangerous.

Chaos is with us, that's for sure. But the way to deal with it is to pursue variation, not to manage (stifle) it. The average company, large or small, suffers far more from excess dullness than from excess eccentricity.

Make no mistake, those who will survive will learn to destroy themselves.

## To Self-DESTRUCT Is Glorious

Writing in *Forbes ASAP*, a technology bimonthly, technology mandarin George Gilder says, "In an era of accelerating transition, the rule of success will be self-cannibalization." Likewise, a Wall Street analyst attributed Intel's phenomenal success to its skill at self-destruction. The highest accomplishment for an Intel person or unit is to unseat one of the company's own successful, obscenely profitable products. Intel figures that if it doesn't surpass its own top products quickly, somebody else will. (Remember, "Only the paranoid survive.")

Quad/Graphics, the brilliantly innovative printing company, is as clear as Intel on this point. The theme for a recent set of company strategy sessions (in which all employees participated): "Quad/Graphics must self-DESTRUCT or risk being destroyed." This is the new watchword of a company that already licenses its most advanced technology to arch-competitors for the express purpose of keeping the heat turned up under itself (and making a buck in the process).

Similarly, Nike's perpetually dissatisfied CEO Phil Knight recently proclaimed, "The target now is to invent a new game." That is, these days, when the world is your oyster, grab it! Shuck it! Eat it! And then reach for another. Quickly.

## When 12-Hour Days Are Not Enough

All this coalesced for me during a recent discussion with old friends who run a business north of San Francisco. The trio started about six years ago. Their high-end sporting goods store knocked the socks off the competition — and became the keystone for altering the tenor of a raggedy three-block string of shops.

They welcomed the occasional snoopy visitor trying to figure out what made them tick. Then, about 18 months ago, an energetic challenger opened up a mile away — and leapfrogged my friends' operation. Now the newcomer seems to be taking business away from them at a pretty good clip. (I guessed that the two were in separate markets; I was wrong.)

My pals are still passionate about their work; they chose the business based on love first, commercial prospects second. And over the years they've steadily added new wrinkles. Moreover, they're prepared to keep at it.

But they aren't prepared to abandon their time-tested formula and aim for a quantum leap or order-of-magnitude change.

Given their track record, I'm rather certain they could come up with a sizable chunk of capital, if necessary, for a wholesale repositioning. What's missing is an emotional commitment. What's present is denial.

Oddly (all three are very bright), they don't seem to get it. They've worked like hell to secure what they created (more than any of them dared dream, financially or artistically). They still unflinchingly put in prodigious hours. So why should they, in effect, have to scrap their baby and do something brand new?

I'm not sure I won any gold stars with the unsolicited suggestions I made at the end of what turned out to be a dispiriting dinner. I offered three choices: (1) take six-month (minimum) sabbaticals doing something weird, and see if that whets the appetite for genuine revolution; (2) bring in as an equal a new general partner from somewhere rather far afield, even if it significantly dilutes hard-won equity; or (3) sell the business and avoid future emotional and monetary losses. Each strategy constitutes strong medicine, but will anything weaker do?

All these strategies take guts. Or do they? Look around, and you'll see that business owners and executives who have played pat hands or poked at incremental improvement have been punished in recent times. And the forces administering that punishment are barely loosed. Whether you think of it as bitter medicine or heady challenge, what's the alternative to the sort of radical change I urged on my friends?

I'm not sure how to be any more persuasive about the need for self-destruction, short of packaging a hammer with each copy of this book. My objective in this chapter has been to move the argument far, far beyond conventional decentralization. I am trying to come to grips myself with the idea that businesses or business units with annual revenues of even $2 million (although much smaller companies and even independent contractors should probably take note as well) need to destroy and reinvent themselves.

Frequently. And that necessarily involves failing — and not just failing, but failing with flair. Grab the hammer and start smashing.

## To Lose Is To Win

I'm going to quote three lines from Dwight Lee and Richard McKenzie's *Failure and Progress*. It's one of the most important books I've ever read. (1) "The creation of a market economy . . . is a spontaneous and evolving process that can only emerge from freedom. . . . Freedom is always disruptive." (2) "The case for a market economy has to not only accept but also embrace the failures that are the result of market competition." (3) "The lack of understanding of the essential role of economic failure stands as the biggest political obstacle to achieving free-market prosperity in formerly socialist countries."

These excerpts help make the obvious even clearer: no failure, no progress. Unfortunately, most individuals and companies (countries, too — and not just the socialist ones) don't get it.

"Outsiders think of Silicon Valley as a success story," writes Silicon Valley commentator Mike Malone, "but in truth, it is a graveyard. Failure . . . is Silicon Valley's greatest strength. Every

> **"Silicon Valley is a graveyard ...failure is Silicon Valley's greatest strength."**

> **"Venture capitalists actually like to see a little failure in the résumés of entrepreneurs."**
>
> **Mike Malone**

failed product or enterprise is a lesson stored in the collective memory of the country. We not only don't stigmatize failure, sometimes we even admire it. Venture capitalists actually *like* to see a little failure in the résumés of entrepreneurs." Note the precise nature of Malone's paean to failure. It is, he says bluntly, the greatest strength of this matchless 1,300 square miles of the planet's (not just America's) economy.

Venture capitalist (and Silicon Valley resident) Don Valentine chimes in: "To Washington I say, please don't help us. The world of technology is complex, fast-changing, and unstructured, and it thrives best when individuals are left alone to be different, creative, and disobedient."

What holds for Silicon Valley holds for the average company, tiny or enormous. In 1993, PepsiCo made an utter fool of itself in the Philippines. A procedural goof in a promotional contest led to tens of thousands of claims against the company, amounting to millions of dollars. Several Pepsi trucks and facilities were physically attacked by outraged citizens. When asked what I thought about it, and how it computed with my dictums of maximum freedom, I replied, "Three hearty cheers for PepsiCo."

I am sorry, of course, about the mischief that followed the mistake. But the strength of this feisty $25 billion company (normally "feisty $25 billion" = oxymoron) is precisely that it gives country chiefs, unit managers, brand managers, and damn near

"The world of technology thrives best when individuals are left alone to be different, creative, and disobedient."

Don Valentine

everyone else, very long tethers. And after an error, while it might not promote the perpetrator (though it sometimes has), it also won't create a new set of central controls that stamp out spunk. The predictable price is not just a few failures, but also occasional fiascoes, a wee price to pay compared to the payoff: almost unparalleled craziness and zest from a monster institution.

Or consider what's happened in telecommunications since the breakup of the Bell System in 1984. Now there are eight companies instead of one. None, to be sure, amounts to two folks in a garage. And each one has its own strategic plan. But each is going, recklessly at times, in its own separate direction — trying to ace the others out by poaching on their territories (regularly). Put simply, folks moving energetically in eight different directions are likely to make more interesting mistakes and stumble over more value-producing opportunities than a centrally directed behemoth — like old AT&T (or 1994's version of IBM or GM).

The Nobel laureate in economics F.A. Hayek described competition in the market economy as a "spontaneous discovery process." Competition is costly. It produces waste — i.e., products and services that don't make it. If we knew what was coming, Hayek admitted, we wouldn't need competition. Since we don't and can't know, especially these days, only gloves-off competition — and the concomitant failures, necessarily including big and embarrassing ones — can lead us to discover products and services before the next guy does. So goes the United States, Silicon Valley, High-tech Widgets, Inc., Low-tech Widgets, Inc., Grace and George's Eatery, Inc., and thee and me.

**Three cheers for PepsiCo's screwups**

"Go ahead and fail," says author Tom Robbins. "But fail with wit, fail with grace, fail with style. A mediocre failure is as insufferable as a mediocre success. Embrace failure. Seek it out. Learn to love it." Amen.

## Disorganize or Perish

"People think the president of an outfit has to be the main organizer," Quad/Graphics CEO Harry Quadracci told me. "No, the president is the main *dis*organizer. Everybody 'manages' quite well; whenever anything goes wrong, they take immediate action to make sure nothing will go wrong again. The problem is, nothing new will ever happen, either."

International Data Group's Pat McGovern shares Quadracci's philosophy. For his new magazines, he seeks out publishers with independent track records, who are demonstrably independent in spirit. He acts as their venture capitalist, gives them a new ball to run with, then gets out of their way as they head for the goal line. McGovern summed it up, "If people have total control over their business, they will have the best possible emotional involvement." More eloquent words have rarely been spoken. Nothing would make me happier than to think that 10 percent of the readers of this volume will go away thinking of themselves as "chief *dis*organizers," champions of outrageous public failure, prepared to turn over "total control" to subordinates. Let go! Give it up!

## For Whom Does This Bell Toll?

This chapter, more than any other, seems aimed at top-level corporate managers. It is. And it isn't.

It's for the small company, that's for sure. All the symptoms of the old Union Pacific disease turn up in the average 10-person winery by the end of its second year. The bias toward not reinventing, not embracing failure is often worse in the four-year-old firm suffering from success than in the 44-year-old firm.

As to those stuck in the middle of sizeable outfits, this entire discussion — every word, believe me — is applicable to the supervisor of a 14-person finance or human-resources unit. Disorganizing, creating care pairs, reinvention, mutation, statistically independent tries, embracing failure — all are universal musts today.

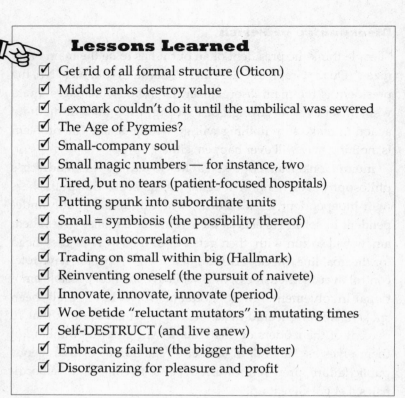

## Lessons Learned

- ☑ Get rid of all formal structure (Oticon)
- ☑ Middle ranks destroy value
- ☑ Lexmark couldn't do it until the umbilical was severed
- ☑ The Age of Pygmies?
- ☑ Small-company soul
- ☑ Small magic numbers — for instance, two
- ☑ Tired, but no tears (patient-focused hospitals)
- ☑ Putting spunk into subordinate units
- ☑ Small = symbiosis (the possibility thereof)
- ☑ Beware autocorrelation
- ☑ Trading on small within big (Hallmark)
- ☑ Reinventing oneself (the pursuit of naivete)
- ☑ Innovate, innovate, innovate (period)
- ☑ Woe betide "reluctant mutators" in mutating times
- ☑ Self-DESTRUCT (and live anew)
- ☑ Embracing failure (the bigger the better)
- ☑ Disorganizing for pleasure and profit

## Reprise 1: The Core Competence Trap

One of the most popular business buzz phrases of the 90s has been "strategic competence" — that is, figuring out what you're good at, stripping out the nonessentials (products, processes, business units), and polishing your main apple like hell. The idea, in other words, is to leverage a few (f-e-w) key skills. It's a good idea for many unfocused companies, which the majority of big corporations are, but to say that the strategic-competence concept can be followed too closely is an understatement. The times are changing, and strategic competence must change right along with them.

Corporation after corporation (IBM and Sears instantly come to mind) is finding that sensible core values can turn into hobbles. Intel climbed to the top of its heap by knowing what it was about — by polishing its core competences. Cannibalization, yes

— but mostly by advanced versions of yesterday's offering. Nonetheless the lesson of IBM looms large. In just a decade, the mainframe went from dominance to near irrelevance. IBM was still the best at mainframes. So what? Intel doesn't want to be caught at the top of a composting heap.

As multimedia "stuff" comes to the fore, somehow blending software, publishing, entertainment, computing, telecommunications, and the like into a super-megaindustry, Intel knows it will have to figure out anew what-we-are and what-we're-about and decide whether its former core competences are still worth polishing. "We all have to go back to school," CEO Andy Grove told *The Economist.* He added that the company must "soften its strategic focus to embrace all sorts of possible new computer and communications technologies."

On the one hand, polish your core competence. On the other hand, soften your strategic focus. Which is it — polish or soften? That's not just the $64,000 question. It's the $64 billion question. And more.

To be good means sharpening your focus, which, by definition, means you'll be easily blindsided by the new. So, be great by being focused . . . and then prepare to commit suicide by softening your focus and learning to tolerate, even welcome, those ominous mutators.

Successful change comes from creating "self-inflicted catastrophes," says Symmetrix CEO George Bennett. "The idea is to build a greenhouse in which to nurture the new order — to test the new organizational forms and the creative use of new technology — to break the rules and invent the future. The greenhouse is then encouraged to cannibalize the customer base and staff of the old organization over time."

Or Carl Sagan and Ann Druyan again: "It's as if, for every million dyed-in-the-wool conservative organisms, there's one radical who's out to change things . . . and for every one of the radicals, only one in a million actually knows what it's talking about — providing a significantly better survival plan than the one currently fashionable. And yet the evolution of life is determined by those revolutionaries." The evolution of life. And the evolution, if any, of our corporations, large and small alike.

### Reprise 2: Any Role for the Center?

We've huffed and we've puffed about blowing down the company and even questioned the validity of the core-competence concept. So, is there any legitimate role whatsoever for the center?

It's a good question. Maybe the mid-size company, joined together in shifting alliances with firms of all sizes, is the best bet for the crazy future. (The Age of Pygmies, etc.) On the other hand, I am willing to acknowledge some role for the center. To wit:

■ Launch key thrusts (3M, a rare feisty giant in PepsiCo's league, has benefited enormously from initiatives, started at headquarters, in time-based competition, quality, environmental awareness, and globalism — but the center is not heavy-handed about it)

■ Inculcate entrepreneurism throughout the organization and far below the division/SBU level; in particular, encourage obstreperous diversity (more Sonny Mehtas)

■ Oversee network and alliance development and management (see Chapter 5)

■ Lead the way in knowledge creation and development throughout the corporate and extracorporate network (see Chapter 6)

■ Keep the corporation curious (see Chapter 7)

■ Set the tone for recruitment and people development (people of imagination, anarchists who may lead you down the bumpy but gold-paved path to an exciting future)

■ Carry the torch for regular reinvention

To suggest these possible roles isn't to yield more than a quarter-inch on the need to decimate the hierarchy. Yes, I could imagine new senior staff slots: vice presidents for, say, customer obsession, venture capital projects (who might subsume the traditional role of the CFO), recruitment of mad geniuses (formerly the HR job), strategic alliances, information technology, knowledge transfer, innovation, and globalism. Yet in my scheme, such new impresarios would fly solo. No staff. No secretary. In my ideal world, no office. The task, instead, is to hoist the center's flag, on the road, for critical issues — and to lead the way in swapping information (and leveraging knowledge) among widely dispersed, highly autonomous operations. This is not, incidentally, far from the role played by ABB's peripatetic, bare-bones central staff.

## T.T.D. (Things to Do) and Q.T.A. (Questions to Answer)

❶ Do you have the guts to admit that most (all?) middle management doesn't add value? That most "specialist" work isn't very special? Can you imagine a company without a headquarters? (Literally.) A giant enterprise with only two layers of management? A completely (or almost) flat structure? Toy with these ideas. See just how radical you and a bunch of your peers can get. Remember Oticon's Kolind: "We simply took away the entire formal structure."

❷ Can you imagine shifting most staff activities (professional services) to self-contained 20-person units? Fifteen? Ten? Eight? Four? Two? (I.e., does the "care pair" notion ring your bell?) Imagine your organization, whatever its size, built entirely around virtually self-sufficient pairs, trios, quartets. Possible? How lean can your residual central staff be? (Hint: Very lean, just for starters.)

❸ Speaking of Kolind, do you have secretaries in your company? If so, why? "The boys" can't type or make coffee? Do you really need secretaries? Says who?

❹ Are your business units (franchises, subsidiaries, whatever) spunky? Do they have their own personalities, their own flavors? Do their chiefs collectively suffer from the autocorrelation effect? Are bosses "90 percent entrepreneurs"? Can they pass the Mehta cantankerousness test? (If yes, redo the test. For example, query outsiders such as suppliers, customers, and Wall Street analysts.)

❺ Are your units small enough, self-contained enough, and focused enough ("gotta size") to achieve "automatic" symbiosis with their customers? Are they ready to do-or-die in their market niche? (Will you let them die if they won't do?) Are you hell-bent to customize any and every product and service, for even modest-size customers?

❻ Recall Barry Diller's observations: Have you and/or your peers been captured by the system? On a scale of one to ten, what is your (you, peers, unit) Naivete Quotient? One equals bad ("We've tried that"). Ten equals good ("Nobody else has done it? Great! Go for it, and we'll pick up the pieces later").

❼ Are you obsessed with constant incremental change (okay as far as it goes — which is not far enough)? Or with reinvention (good)? Or perpetual reinvention (better still)? Can you cope, emotionally and intellectually, with ideas like "self-DESTRUCT"?

❽ How about your business card announcing:

Nancy Doe
Chief *Dis*organizer

Can you visualize that? Send me a copy if you do it.

❾ Does "embrace failure" (big failure, embarrassing from time to time) shock or suit you, your unit, your company? "All success is the result of failure," says economist Jude Wanniski — do you agree? What do *you* think of Pepsi's Philippines fiasco? Had any Philippines fiascos lately? (No? Had any knock-their-socks-off successes?)

In Chapter 1, I proposed the Paranoid Corporation. In this chapter I've argued for the Atomized Corporation, with spirited, often pint-size, subunits with their own personalities and headed by disrespectful chiefs. Each subsection has distanced us more and more from traditional decentralization. And taken us closer and closer to "crazy times call for crazy organizations." **If you think this chapter is about decentralization, reread it or apply for a refund.**

BEYOND EMPOWERMENT

# TURNING EVERY JOB INTO A BUSINESS

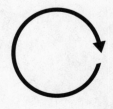

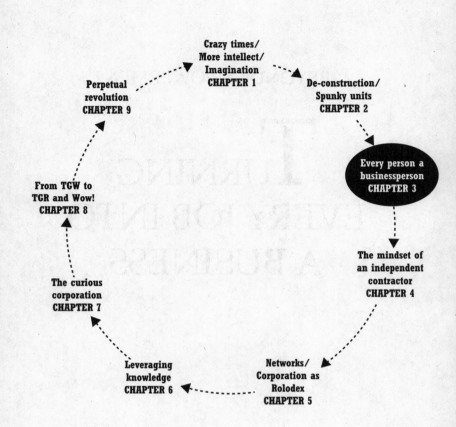

Crazy times/
More intellect/
Imagination
CHAPTER 1

De-construction/
Spunky units
CHAPTER 2

Perpetual
revolution
CHAPTER 9

Every person a
businessperson
CHAPTER 3

From TGW to
TGR and Wow!
CHAPTER 8

The mindset of
an independent
contractor
CHAPTER 4

The curious
corporation
CHAPTER 7

Leveraging
knowledge
CHAPTER 6

Networks/
Corporation as
Rolodex
CHAPTER 5

To atomize the organization (Chapter 2) in order to induce zest, creativity, and almost automatic symbiosis with the customer can be taken another step. Another big step, it turns out: the **entrepreneurizing of every job**. One hundred percent of employees turned into "businesspeople" is, I contend, no pipe dream. It's no cakewalk, either. In any event, just as the atomized company is miles beyond the decentralized company, the organization of businesspeople-entrepreneurs is **miles beyond the empowered organization.**

"Never use the

excuse of following

orders as the

rationale for

following a poor

course of action."

**Roger Meade**

Following a last-minute change of plans, I phoned a hotel early one morning for a reservation. I was disconnected, then put on hold. Finally I reached a living person at the front desk. He flatly declared that he couldn't help me. When I asked why (calmly), he responded (calmly), "I'm not a reservationist."

Such everyday examples explain why I think the most contemptible business terms are "slot filler" and "box server." Yet in early 1994, the average employee in the average firm still fills a slot and serves a box on the organization chart. Most people pass their days following the strictures of some absurdly narrow job description. Boxed in. It's time to break the box.

"We want every employee to be a businessperson," says Ralph Stayer, CEO of Johnsonville Foods. An innocent statement? Far from it. Stayer has done a superb job of breaking his phenomenally successful, $130 million, Wisconsin-based company into small, surprisingly self-sufficient teams and "empowering" frontline people. But he means to dramatically expand the possibilities of empowerment, participation, and self-management when he says each employee should be a "businessperson."

A businessperson is the polar opposite of a slot filler, or, heaven help us, a "reservationist." A businessperson is an entrepreneur (or 90 percent entrepreneur) who has the flair and commitment of mom or pop of Mom & Pop, Inc. A businessperson will go anywhere, find anyone, and break any box to get the job done fast and well.

Stayer insists that 100 percent of any company's employees can become businesspersons. I believe that, and his claim is consistent with the themes of the first two chapters of this book: In a crazy world with a bat's metabolism (Chapter 1) businesses, to compete, have to be not just decentralized but deorganized (Chapter 2). The logical limit of deorganization is the entrepreneur — the business unit of one.

If that's true, two questions arise. How does a company create jobs (microbusinesses?) in which employees can behave like businesspersons? And how do people who have been employees for most of their working lives switch from do-as-you're-told to do-whatever-it-takes? I'll answer question one in this chapter, question two in the next.

## Tom and Joe

At hosemaker Titeflex, which we met in Chapter 2, you'll recall that top dog Jon Simpson handed over the work of the company to Business Development Teams of six-or-so people each. Custom-engineered order lead time plummeted from 10 or so weeks to less than a week. But Simpson added another element, the Rapid Deployment Team.

This team — there is only one — consists of two people, card-carrying Teamsters Tom Strange and Joe Tilli. On their own, these guys can often turn around an order, including custom engineering, in three or four hours. That's right, in a company that was nowhere near death's door, Simpson and friends cut a process that took as long as 2,000 hours (sure, not 2,000 workday hours, but 2-0-0-0 hours to the anxious customers) to three or four hours.

Tom and Joe do it all. They have direct customer contact. They plan and customize the job, doing most of the engineering on their own. (Just as the Lakeland Regional Medical Center's care pairs found they don't need a seven-year professional degree to deliver 90 percent of patient care, Tom and Joe don't need the blessing of an MIT or CalTech degree to perform 90 percent of what is called engineering.) They make the hose, then take it to the loading dock for shipment. They are responsible for client and supplier "relationship management," to use the $29.95-a-minute investment-banking phrase. Their work consists entirely of discrete, value-adding projects.

Most companies could learn some things from Messrs. Strange and Tilli. At the top of the list: The average employee can deliver far more than his or her current job demands — and far more than the terms "employee empowerment," "participative management," and "multiple job skills" imply. How much more?

## JOE AND TOM➞Professional service firm

Well, Tom and Joe are businesspersons. They run a mom-and-pop shop, Strange & Tilli, Inc. Only it happens to be embedded in a company called Titeflex, which itself is embedded in a company called the TI Group. But make no mistake — this is Tom and Joe's little corner of the world, their enterprise. They routinely deal with insiders and outsiders of all kinds, and there is no intervention from management. They take whatever initiative the business requires, which is usually a lot.

What kind of workers are Strange and Tilli? It's a trick question. Consider again the animating theme running through this book: "more intellect, less materials," "only factory asset is the human imagination." Tom and Joe are knowledge workers. They aren't just selling hose. Far from it. They are selling relationship management, customization, and responsiveness. They are, in a word, selling brainware. A lump (hose) is involved, just as it is at 3M in Austin, but the value added (and most of the sticker price) is the knowledge they incorporate into the hose and the service they wrap around it.

In fact, when I got to pondering Tom and Joe, it occurred to me that there's absolutely no difference (none whatsoever) between Titeflex's Rapid Deployment Team and a pair of McKinsey consultants working on their own at a client location. Tom and Joe are proprietors of a two-person professional service firm. They are a couple of frontline Teamsters from Springfield,

Massachusetts, and they are businesspersons, professional service providers, brainworkers. Period.

This is also pretty much the story that's unfolding in the reorganized patient-focused hospitals we discussed (Chapter 2). Consider Phil Lathrop's report about one typical clerical employee's new outlook on her work life:

> Before the restructuring at this hospital, she had been an admitting clerk. She met many patients each day and completed the necessary paperwork for their admission. She was then trained to work on a new patient care center, with duties including admissions, unit-based clerical work, utilization review, and some medical records activities. . . .
>
> In the old world, she did her job well to keep her boss happy. In her new job, she works carefully and well because if she does not, the patients will get hassled by their insurance companies and the hospital business office. . . . She now has control over enough of the patient's paperwork that she herself can assure its accuracy and completeness. Furthermore, she feels an intense personal ownership of the work on the patient's behalf.

An idealization? Not so, says Lathrop's rapidly accumulating evidence. Perhaps even an understatement. Okay, now let's pose the fundamental question again: Can the average (every?) job for the average (every?) employee be turned into a businessperson's position?

Yes.

With a bit of imagination (okay, more than a bit), the average job — actually, every job — can become an entrepreneurial challenge. The cases of Tom, Joe, and the hospital clerk are just the beginning. You'll hear more about others as we develop this

**Q: Can every job be "businessed"?** ▪

idea, and you'll find they all:

- execute mostly self-initiated projects;
- perform ad hoc problem-solving directly for individual internal or external customers;
- work in multifunctional configurations, with self-initiated access to experts inside and outside the company; and
- measure themselves on bottom-line results, based mainly on customer and teammate evaluations rather than a boss's subjective judgment.

### "Businessing"

To "business" a job, "businessing." These words may sound awkward, but they capture the essential idea from the Strange and Tilli case. To be "businessed" is to run one's own show. Such a job within a company must incorporate:

- Cross-training — training in nearly all the skills required to perform the job from start to finish
- Budgeting — responsibility for the formulation, tracking, and amendment of budgets
- Quality-control — quality-measurement, quality-monitoring, and quality-improvement processes
- Autonomy — a place of one's own within a delayered, reengineered organization, as well as the authority to make decisions, including committing substantial resources (money, too) without recourse to higher-ups
- Access to expertise — from instantly available staff specialists (who in effect — no, make that in reality — work at the beck and call of the front line) and outside consultants as required
- One's own real live customers — internal or external, who enhance the businessperson's sense of ownership
- A (limitless) travel budget

 **A: Yes.**

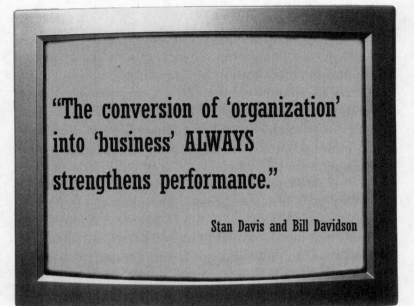

> "The conversion of 'organization' into 'business' ALWAYS strengthens performance."
>
> Stan Davis and Bill Davidson

What's with the last item? Why is it on this otherwise grand list?

Because it contains an important message. Employees don't expect to be able to sign off on an expenditure of millions. (I can't, and I own the majority of shares in my company.) But the businessperson does expect to be able to do what's necessary to move projects forward. You've told your Tom and Joe that their project is important to the company. But when they need to travel, say, with another team member to a distributor on the other side of the country, or to visit a global expert who will be in Osaka only for the next two weeks, you stymie them with a corporate rule that requires four signatures on a travel voucher. You just gang-tackled them. The ball is not in their hands after all. Upshot: Kiss their psychological ownership of the project goodbye.

There's something else (big) a businessperson needs. Information. Shoshana Zuboff coined the word "informate" in her brilliant book *In the Age of the Smart Machine.* To informate is to use technology to invest people with enough knowledge and understanding of the process in which they're working to allow them to exercise, intelligently, the prerogatives normally reserved for management. It's useless to tell people to make decisions on their own (empower them) without giving them the information they need to make the decisions. You can't business a job unless you also informate it.

What kind of information are we talking about? It's simple, really. As a manager or CEO, ask yourself: If I were doing this job, what would I want to know?

Foldcraft, a restaurant-seating manufacturer, did just that. In 1974, Steve Sheppard, one of five senior executives, wasn't privy to the company's annual sales. "If I wanted that information," he recalls, "I had to prove I needed it."

Times have changed. Today Sheppard is CEO, and Foldcraft shares financial information with all employees. Every Wednesday, for example, each department holds a meeting to discuss department and company-wide financial information. And daily sales bookings and product shipments are posted prominently at the company's main entrance.

"If a number [from a specific department] on the income sheet is continually problematic," reports Sheppard, "that department's manager will raise the issue. Because if he or she doesn't, someone else will. If people can finance homes, buy

> **"If I wanted information, I had to prove I needed it."**
>
> **Steve Sheppard**

cars, and send kids to college, they can understand every line on an income sheet."

To inject fun and simplicity into cost-analysis training, financial education director Chuck Mayhew calculates labor, materials, overhead, cost, and sales figures based on a Toll House chocolate-chip cookie recipe. By adjusting pricing, ingredients, and profit margins, employees can fiddle with the model and test various sales and cost-saving techniques. The intent, Sheppard says, is to teach employees to "manage hour-to-hour activities for improved profitability."

Or consider how VeriFone attacks informating. The high-tech company, which has $226 million in annual sales and a 60 percent share of the U.S. market for credit card authorizations, goes even further than Foldcraft. All employees are perpetually accessible to one another via a sophisticated electronic network, and the firm's most intimate data is readily available to everyone. (Many employees have even been registered with the SEC as insiders.) You'll have to wait until Chapter 6, when we discuss corporations as full-fledged, self-designing learning networks, to get the startling details.

If you can honestly say that all the jobs in your company/unit incorporate (most of) the characteristics just ticked off, then you're already light-years beyond "empowerment" and "self-management" as practiced or planned in most organizations. You are on the way to converting the average person into a "90 percent entrepreneur," an honest-to-God businessperson. "The design limit for tomorrow's organization," write Stan Davis and Bill Davidson in *2020 Vision*, is that "each employee becomes a business. . . . The conversion of 'organization' into 'business' ALWAYS strengthens corporate performance." I like those capital letters, ALWAYS.

### Tom and Joe as Metaphor

Tom Strange and Joe Tilli are a metaphor for me — and a rallying cry. They were among the eight people to whom I dedicated *Liberation Management*. Even though the list included Nobel laureate F.A. Hayek and deorganizer-in-chief Percy Barnevik, if I did it again I might go with just Tom and Joe. They epitomize (1) liberation, (2) the transformation of labor into value-added brainwork, (3) unleashing curiosity and imagination across the board, and (4) decentralization taken all the way.

CINDY CHARLES

Why is Virginia Azuelo smiling? Because she can spend up to $2,000 on the spot to fix a guest's problem.

"Can you Tom-and-Joe it?" may be the most important question I ask of seminar participants.

The Ritz-Carlton Hotel chain, one of the few service-sector winners of the Baldrige quality award, has Tom-and-Joe'd it. For one thing, every employee, starting with junior bellhops, can spend up to $2,000 on the spot to fix a guest's problem. No questions asked.

> ## "The only way to make a man trustworthy is to trust him."
>
> **Henry Stimson**

Rosenbluth International, the travel-services firm growing at warp speed, has Tom-and-Joe'd it. Though in a seemingly mundane business, Rosenbluth was ranked one of the 10 best places to work by the authors of *The 100 Best Companies to Work for in America* — mostly for giving exceptional power to employees in characteristically powerless positions.

### It's Simple, Really, If You're Serious

I thought about powerlessness on an icy cold day, when I ventured into the spectacular new Barney's department store at 61st Street and Madison Avenue on Manhattan's Upper East Side. The weather was far worse than predicted, and I needed something to protect my ears. A watch cap, I thought. To my delight, among Barney's finery, I found one. Oh, did I! It was cashmere. But loath as I am to admit it, I would have paid most anything for warmth at that moment. (And besides, there aren't many Army-Navy surplus stores in that neck of the woods.)

I took the cap, which was missing a price tag, to the register. The clerk said he was sure it cost $45, but he couldn't ring it up without a tag. In a couple of moments, he caught the eye of a fellow employee, whom he asked to check the price. She retraced my steps to the hat table, found nothing, and came back a moment or two later, claiming she'd contacted a manager to sort things out.

Another three or four minutes passed. Nothing happened. I left.

It's not the shoddy service (or the cold ears) that got my goat. It's the missed opportunity. I know it's a cliché, but I didn't present a problem to that clerk, I presented a golden opportunity — if Barney's policies, training, recruitment tactics, and frame of mind were what they should have been.

New scenario. Same start to the story, but now that register clerk is Tom Strange redux, that is, Pop of Mom & Pop, Inc. Whether or not he puts bread on the table depends on my satisfaction. Pop says: "Sorry there's no tag. I'm sure it costs $45. Some price for a little cap, huh? But you'll love the cashmere feel; I've worn one myself. Look, I don't want to hold you up, so I'll ring this up as $45, take your address, and if I missed on the high side, we'll send you a refund in tonight's or tomorrow's mail. OK?"

OK? Indeed. Instead of creating an enemy (who tells Barney's stories in seminars — and books), the clerk-alchemist would have created that most valuable of corporate jewels: a lifetime customer (whom he could add to his mailing list).

Ten to one it's not the young man's fault. It's Barney's queasy management — who wouldn't dare trust this clerk with Ritz-Carlton-size power. Yuck.

## Catch-22

There is one whopping Catch-22 to businessing jobs, and I've just hinted at it. "The chief lesson I have learned is that the only way to make a man trustworthy is to trust him," Henry Stimson, U.S. Secretary of War during World War II, declared. To put it another way, you can't trust a person unless you trust the person.

Trust.

*The Virtual Corporation*, by Mike Malone and Bill Davidow, is a superb treatise on the dizzy organizations (which aren't quite organiza-

> "There's no such thing as 'half-trust.' The instructor pilot can't 'half' sit next to you during your first solo."

tions) that are more and more becoming a part of today's economy. After spinning wild, futuristic tales of cyberspace, the authors are drawn back to basics. These flat, ethereal outfits won't work, they emphatically assert, unless we trust the people on the front line.

Britain's first Duke of Wellington (victor over Napoleon at Waterloo) worried about the impact of rail transportation, which was just arriving on the scene. "My Lords," he proclaimed in a speech in the House of Lords, "these iron horses will enable the working classes to move about." Indeed, suspicion of the working class and the reduction of most jobs to insignificance (hyperspecialization) were the bedrock of the Industrial Revolution.

The time has come (it's long overdue, actually) to reverse all that. Technique is important (informating, etc.). But adding trust is the issue of the decade. Keep in mind Tilli, Strange, Lakeland care pairs, bellhops and chambermaids at the Ritz-Carlton, and the people of the Acordia companies. Without trust we cannot expect the human imagination to pursue value-added.

There are two root problems. First, the Duke of Wellington problem — a strong and lingering taste for control, fed by a suspicion that "they" will skylark if not micromanaged. Let me say, if your view of human nature is gloomy, you'll have the devil's own time letting go the reins (which is why we need 95 percent fewer managers — see Chapter 2). Second, there's the "half-trust" problem. As one private pilot put it, "There's no such thing as 'half-trust.' The instructor pilot can't 'half' sit next to you during your first solo." Put another way, people either "own" a task or they don't. Yes. Or no.

All of us bosses would love to "half-delegate." But it doesn't work. What we must do is train till we're blue in the face, let employees graduate through a series of ever more challenging projects, then let go. And the sooner the better. (Hewlett-Packard, EDS, and McKinsey shove employees down the trail to autonomy on day one.) Letting go means letting the person alone to experience those Maalox moments — that is, true, genuine, no-baloney ownership in the gut. If there's no deep-seated, psychological ownership, there no ownership. Period.

CEO Rich Teerlink enumerates the simple but potent official philosophy (write it down) that has turned Harley-Davidson from government mendicant to global star:

- Tell the truth
- Keep your promises
- Be fair
- Respect the individual
- Encourage curiosity

That's it. And one tall order. How does your unit's (10-person accounts-receivable team, division, etc.) philosophy measure up? In theory? In practice?

### Beyond Trust

But maybe even the idea of trust doesn't go far enough. We must encourage the average (every) employee to raise hell. Yes, hell. In Columbus, Ohio, at Marketing Services By Vectra (which produces and distributes more than 13,000 marketing and display items for retail and franchise operations), employees have total access to corporate information — and wittingly use it to bludgeon and embarrass top management. One employee cost-cutting SWAT team, for instance, vetoed plans by their bosses to attend a conference in San Francisco. The $5,000 cannot be spared, they bluntly informed their chiefs.

Nice.

At the information-systems firm Scitor, CEO Roger Meade has made challenging management part of the corporate creed:

Utilize your best judgment at all times. Ask yourself: Is it fair and reasonable? Is it honest? Does it make good business sense in the **All of us would love to half-delegate.** context of our established objectives? If you can answer yes to all of these, then proceed. Remember, you are accountable against this policy for all your actions.

If you find that management's direction is out of touch with the reality of the situation at hand, it is your responsibility to act based upon your best judgment. Never, and I mean never, use the excuse of following orders as the rationale for following a poor course of action. This is compounding stupidity, and it is inexcusable.

Once more: How do you measure up by the Vectra-Scitor standard of mandated sassiness?

## Lessons Learned

- ☑ Every person a businessperson/professional service-provider/90 percent entrepreneur (E-V-E-R-Y)
- ☑ Provide the tools of "businessing" (including big travel budgets and the right — and responsibility — to ring up $45 watch caps without price tags)
- ☑ Inform everyone about everything (Would you need it as CEO? Then "they" need it)
- ☑ Trust (or go bust)
- ☑ Talk back to the boss (as a matter of policy) and monitor his travel expenses

### Jobs and Pride

Any job can be great. "What's wrong with the idea of a *professional* janitor?" asks Bob Argabright, of Chesapeake Packaging, a firm that has gone as far as any in turning employees into businesspeople (which is, by the way, the company's stated objective, using precisely that language). Or consider an oddball article in *The New York Times* on Melvin Reich, Manhattan's premier buttonhole-maker. (Many fashion designers, for example, come to Mr. Reich to have buttonholes made for show garments.) "Buttonholes are what we do," Reich told the *Times*. "We do buttonholes and buttonholes and buttonholes. I am specialized, like the doctors. . . . You think it's nothing. Just a but-

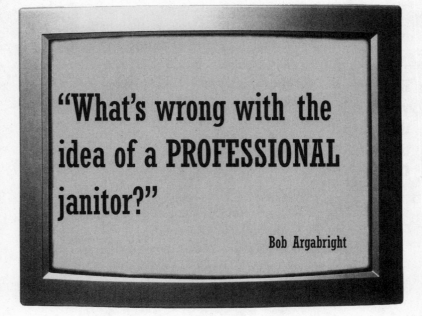

# "What's wrong with the idea of a PROFESSIONAL janitor?"

Bob Argabright

tonhole. But it's something. It's not nothing." And then, asked why he hadn't branched out into zippers: "Zippers are a totally different field. It's a different game. A man can do so much."

I love it. Just like I love to see a first-rate bricklayer at work. The best, plain and simple. I've often stopped, even when embarrassingly behind schedule, to watch such a master artisan. Bricklaying, like buttonhole-making, can be Olympic caliber. And that's the least of it.

I remember catching a TV interview with a food server at an inner-city high-school cafeteria. To say such folks don't get much respect from students and employers is gross understatement. Yet this woman looked the interviewer squarely in the eye and filled the screen when she said, "My job is important. Sometimes this [lunch] is the only hot meal these kids get all day. What I do is important."

That one got to me — the dignity, the pride. Serving food at an inner-city school *is* important. And if we bosses could appreciate the responsibility and pride people take in doing things most of us would be tempted to dismiss as mundane, we'd know how to tap a very profound power.

Employees often do wonders in spite of their half-assed bosses. But if we get it right, if we really try to turn, say, hotel-house-

**How do you stack up against the Ritz-Carlton?**

keeping "chores" into a source of intense pride for the average hotel housekeeper — then wow! Wow for the individual! Wow for me as a boss! Wow for the company! Wow for the customer! Wow for the whole economy! The simple fact is that people — a worker — would rather have a good day than a crummy day. She or he would rather invest in the job than not; rather learn on the job than not. It's insulting to suggest otherwise, to suggest that the average person is a shirker, doesn't want to learn, doesn't want to take charge. "They" defy "us" all the time by turning buttonhole-making — and serving up the midday goop at the inner-city junior high school — into pure art.

### T.T.D. (Things to Do) and Q.T.A. (Questions to Answer)

❶ Within the next two weeks, conduct a phone survey with 25 customers. Ask such questions as, "What's it like to deal with us?" "Does the customer's ball frequently get passed from player to player?" The point: Do you have "reservationists" on your payroll? If so, who's to blame, workers or management? (Hint: workers is the wrong answer.)

❷ Can you imagine e-v-e-r-y job as a Tom Strange/Joe Tilli job? Every employee a value-adding brainworker, a professional service provider? If not, why not? (If you can't, try again!) Today: Take a corner of your organization and a blank piece of paper and Strange/Tilli it. (Excise all un-Strange/un-Tilli jobs. Divvy up drudge tasks, e.g., opening the mail, refilling the fridge, typing, and filing.) How about the idea of *professional* janitor," per Chesapeake Packaging's Argabright?

❸ Recall the former clerk-cipher in the hospital: Does the average employee have identifiable customers? Does she or he own a broad range of "whole tasks" to perform for customers?

❹ Review the list of "businessing" traits. How does your organization stack up (grade rigorously, managers and non-managers alike)? This is an all-or-nothing test. "Pretty good" scores are lousy scores. (And how about those travel budgets?)

❺ Re "businessing": How do you rate on the Ritz-Carlton Scale (where any employee can spend $2,000 to fix a customer's problem)?

❻ Does everyone have complete and timely access to business information (financial, other)? Could *you* do each employee's job adequately with the information available to her or him? Do you train everyone in the business basics, e.g., the Toll House cookie business-simulation model at Foldcraft?

❼ Do "they" trust you? Do you trust "them"? Hint I: One diabolically clever way to find out is to ask via confidential quarterly survey. Hint II: Make evaluations of managers by employees a centerpiece of the performance review process; it should focus those bosses' minds on this apparently mushy topic.

❽ Are employees actively encouraged (via recognition, formal policy statements à la Scitor) to thumb their noses at management as appropriate? Have employees at your company put the kibosh on any of the top dogs' boondoggles?

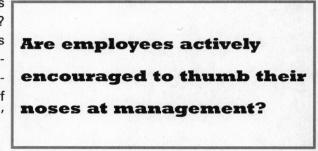

**Are employees actively encouraged to thumb their noses at management?**

❾ McDonald's founder Ray Kroc swore he could see "beauty in a hamburger bun." Can you see beauty in the average frontline job? Can you imagine Michelangelos of housekeeping? (Yes, dammit, I am serious. And if you're not . . .) Draw pictures of the beautifully performed frontline job, worthy of a Broadway production. If you can't, you should worry. A lot.

From the Atomized Corporation (Chapter 2) to the ultimate Businesspersons' Organization (this chapter). Entrepreneurs all. All? Yes, every job a Strange/Tilli job. *Every* is not an approximation. Not for Hal Rosenbluth at Rosenbluth International. And not for you if you're wise. **And if the trust is missing (genuine, unstinting respect), heaven help you, your career, your firm in the changing 90s.**

## CHAPTER 4

BEYOND LOYALTY

# LEARNING TO THINK LIKE AN INDEPENDENT CONTRACTOR

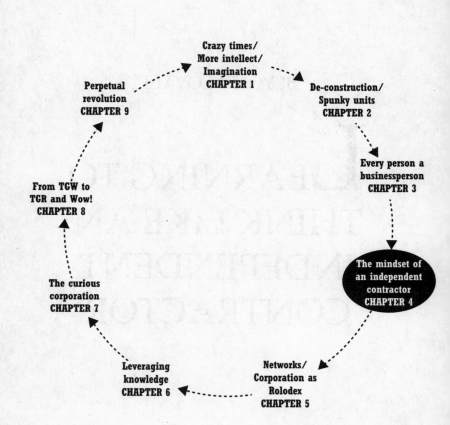

Crazy times/
More intellect/
Imagination
CHAPTER 1

De-construction/
Spunky units
CHAPTER 2

Every person a
businessperson
CHAPTER 3

The mindset of
an independent
contractor
CHAPTER 4

Networks/
Corporation as
Rolodex
CHAPTER 5

Leveraging
knowledge
CHAPTER 6

The curious
corporation
CHAPTER 7

From TGW to
TGR and Wow!
CHAPTER 8

Perpetual
revolution
CHAPTER 9

**Forget loyalty.** Or, at least, loyalty to one's corporation. **Try loyalty to your Rolodex** — your network — instead. In response to crazy times, appropriately paranoid companies (Chapter 1) are atomizing (Chapter 2) and turning every job into a business (Chapter 3). How does the average worker avoid being a pawn in this new board game? By thinking like an independent contractor. Or maybe by becoming one. Ironically, achieving the mindset of an independent practitioner ups the odds considerably of holding on to today's big-company job (should you wish to do so); and not incidentally, your newfound independent streak should be the boss's dream as well as yours.

# "Job security is gone. The driving force of a career must come from the individual."

**Homa Bahrami**

Q. **What do all these people have in common?** Tom Strange and Joe Tilli. Care pairs at Lakeland Regional Medical Center. Russ Sherlock and his Acordia Business Benefits bunch. The average ABB Profit Center employee. An Arthur Andersen consultant.

A. They offer more intellect, less materials; they add value through their imagination; they deliver professional services; whatever they did before, they're now whatever-it-takes businesspeople. How do they do it? More important, how do *you* do it?

### "To Résumé"

Pardon me again for turning another noun (this time résumé) into a verb, but doing so serves a purpose. As the U.S. economy revives, corporate middle managers are still being axed in record numbers. In fact, thinning the middle ranks is increasing while the business performance of the companies doing it is improving. Companies are doing much better with much smaller professional staffs. How come?

Professional staffers, I'm afraid, have been pulling the wool over our eyes. (Not maliciously, or at least not any more maliciously than any card-carrying professional who sincerely believes that only she or her ilk are fit to do a specified job.) Most of what they did turns out not to have been rocket science; in fact, it's well within the reach of frontline employees like Joe Tilli, Tom Strange, et al.

So how do these endangered professional staffers or middle managers deal with the future, now that they've been found naked in the corporate corridors of power? After giving long and hard thought to their plight, I've come up with only one satisfactory answer. But before revealing it, I ask you to consider a particular Arthur Andersen consultant in her third year with the firm, taking stock of her professional assets on December 31, 1993. Here's what she could do:

■ Point to two to three completed projects that have marked her past year

■ Enumerate, quantitatively and qualitatively, benefits she has delivered to each of her clients

■ Provide references from clients who will testify to her existence during the previous 12 months

■ Explain (1) precisely what she learned during the year and (2) precisely how she's more valuable now than a year ago

■ Point to a measurably fatter Rolodex, and name the new acquaintances (mostly far away from her corporate home) she's added to her network (and painstakingly nurtured)

■ Work up a year-end 1993 résumé recognizably different from the one she would have drafted on December 31, 1992.

### Can You Do the Same?

I suggest that if you, as a middle manager or new or seasoned professional staffer, wish to survive, let alone thrive, you'd better be able to résumé. You need to be able to imagine yourself working through a series of fit-for-the-résumé projects, as that Arthur Andersen consultant did, adding value for specific customers, internal and external.

Think résumé. T-h-i-n-k r-é-s-u-m-é.

What does that mean? It means frequently asking yourself six questions:

**1.** What the hell do I do?
**2.** What have I actually done?

**3.** Who among my customers will testify to it?

**4.** What evidence is there that my skills are state of the art?

**5.** Who new do I know, far beyond the company's walls, who will help me deal with an ever-chillier world?

**6.** Will my year-end résumé look different from last year's?

It is a sad fact that the average middle manager or professional staffer can't answer any of these questions effectively. There's an old story about the departure of an 18-year-veteran purchasing staffer from a company. "It's a shame to lose all that experience," one executive said to another. "We didn't lose 18 years' experience," replied the second, "we lost one year's experience repeated 17 times over." The joke is a little too cruel and cynical for me, but only a little. It's like that, as often as not.

> **Who will testify to your existence during the last 12 months?**

Most professional-service-delivery folks on most payrolls don't grow much in the job. Sure, they're good blokes, who help keep the ship afloat from year to year. But, once again, can they do what that garden-variety Arthur Andersen consultant did? Can they draw up a list of satisfied customers (internal and external) who will extol their performance in delivering measurable value-added last year? Can they point to a robust network of outsiders who will (gladly) support them if they shift jobs?

"If you can't say why you made your company a better place," Towers, Perrin consultant Cynthia Kellams observed, "you're out." I'm not sure that's all bad. For quite a long time some of us have acted as if the world owed us a living. We have behaved as if the sinecure on the staff of the big firm, with its $60,000-a-year paycheck and automatic COLA, was a birthright. Myself, I am much more attracted to the independent contractor — the designer, architect, typist, whatever — who lives by the seat of the pants; whose professional existence depends on word-of-mouth endorsement from clients; who regularly adds to her portfolio of marketable skills; who routinely delivers on time, creatively, and for a competitive price (or else).

I suspect that I'm still not being blunt enough. I suggest that every professional staffer or middle manager pass every upcoming or ongoing work activity through the résumé test: Does it meet the résumé standard? Is it résumé-able? If you can't imagine adding what you're working on right now — today — to your year-end, updated résumé, then let it go.

Crude? I don't think so. "Thinking résumé" is a win-win strategy. Sure, it sounds selfish. Actually, it's anything but. The essence of résumé-ing (to continue the barbarism) is having customers who will testify to the value you delivered. You, the professional staffer, will win if you have such customers. And so will your boss and employer.

### From MBO to Résumé-ing (Bosses)

As a matter of fact, I suggest résumé-ing as a strategy for bosses as well as non-bosses. If you're a boss, have all your employees, as a matter of course, update their résumés on a quarterly basis. A prelude to layoffs? An invitation to disloyalty? To the contrary. If their résumés get noticeably better every 90 days (new skills, satisfied customers willing to offer testimonials, completed professional-service-delivery projects), then the employees' current job security will have risen while simultaneously the outfit the boss runs will have delivered demonstrable value to its clients, internal and/or external. Workers will have won. The boss will have won. The company will have won. Not bad.

I further suggest that bosses use résumé-ing as their primary management "control" strategy, replacing the current management-by-objectives scheme and perhaps the traditional employee-evaluation process, too. I imagine the boss sitting down with the employee every three months to review the updated résumé and to help create projects they can imagine will appear on the next résumé update. I can even imagine going public. How about a quarterly résumé-improvement contest?

Again, everybody winds up in the winner's circle. Employees

*Think résumé*

are urged to seek out tools and tasks that up their odds of professional survival, on or off their current employer's payroll; and the employees' successes are automatically the boss's and the firm's.

I see in my mind's eye a well-turned-out individual striding down Madison Avenue. She carries an oversized portfolio containing storyboards for ad campaigns she has contributed to in the last 18 months. The storyboards are her; they're her life and her livelihood. They're what she has to sell on the labor market. If we all thought of ourselves as traveling through life accumulating storyboards that we can brag about (and which have market value), then I suspect that we, our firms, and the whole nation would be a lot better off.

> **You need to imagine yourself working through a series of projects, adding value for specific customers, internal and external.**

### Think Independent

Perhaps the best approach to survival is to assume you're about to be (or just have been) laid off, permanently. That mental image should help make it clear — as it ought to be for all of us these days — that the ball is in only one court: ours. And the shot clock has only a few seconds left.

"People do realize that job security is gone," says University of California at Berkeley professor Homa Bahrami. "But many don't realize what it's been replaced by. The driving force of a career must come from the individual, not the organization." To support her point, Bahrami quotes a saying at the perpetually volatile Apple Computer: "Your sense of job security lies in your employability." Educator and consultant Lewis Perelman likewise imagines every employee as a "free agent," in the big-league-sports sense, "working formally or informally under contract, always with an eye toward their personal value . . . in the marketplace."

A friend of mine who is a TV news producer at ABC under-stands Bahrami's and Perelman's point. The last time I saw him he was in the midst of interviewing prospective agents. He plans to go into business for himself and to sell timely packages (stories ready-made for TV) to the big networks or other players along the burgeoning information highway.

In fact, the representation industry is thriving. For example, Alive Culinary Resources is a new talent agency that plans to devote itself to representing chefs who, while they may be responsible for the unique signature of a superb restaurant, are often treated as chattel by restaurant owners.

Could the age of employee-with-agent be close at hand? Why not?

For bosses themselves, the story stays the same. Writing in *Management Review* about problems along the road to employee empowerment, University of San Francisco management profes-sor Oren Harari discusses a honcho who couldn't let go. Then a family crisis forced him to make plans to leave the company in six months' time. Since he wasn't being replaced, he had to hand over all managerial responsibility to his subordinates. But family circumstances changed, and he didn't have to leave. So, having dismantled his job, he could only stick around if he con-jured up something new to do (which he did). Hence Harari's advice to all bosses: "Pretend you are leaving the company in six months with no replacement, overhaul your organization and train your people to take over your job, and then find a new way to add value. And be prepared to repeat the cycle, over and over again (maybe with different employers) until you retire."

Scary? Yes. But imperative.

## Living with (Cherishing) Ambiguity

It adds up to no less than a brand-new way of living. Career-development expert Bill Charland claims that every position at a company must be created from scratch, a far cry from finding someone to fit a neat job description.

"Given the reality of today's entrepreneurial. . . economy,

**"Pretend you are leaving the company in six months with no replacement."**

Oren Harari

there are few jobs awaiting any of us out there," Charland flatly states. "Instead, most good jobs today are co-created. Jobs are joint ventures [with an employer] in problem solving. They're strategies to solve pressing problems in organizations."

Likewise, Joline Godfrey, author of *Our Wildest Dreams* and champion of women entrepreneurs, says, "In the new economy, learning to make a job is probably going to be more important than learning how to take a job."

Make a job?

Consider MCI, the telecommunications company. "Losers are those who are uncomfortable in unstructured situations," one middle manager there told me. "People around here get responsibility before they're ready. But when are you ready? You're rarely told to do anything. It's hard to find a 'decision-maker.' So it's better to make a decision, on your own, right or wrong. Do something. Make things happen. It's inaction that kills."

I'm an unabashed fan of MCI because of those words —

particularly "hard to find a 'decision-maker.'" MCI works this way: You come aboard without really having a finely drawn job description. It's up to you to invent a job, to figure out how to add value. You do that by creating projects, finding internal "clients," and then you simply move ahead on your own. You learn you can glean advice and gather support from almost anybody. You talk, you listen, you collect information. Once you think you have what you need — well, then, get on with it. You most certainly don't wait for a higher-up to "sign off."

Support for this "Just Do It" mentality, to borrow a phrase, comes from an intriguing study at Bell Labs reported in the *Harvard Business Review*. The researchers analyzed differences between average and top performers. Both types of Bell Labs employees agreed that taking the initiative was the most important thing in getting ahead. Interestingly, both said they regularly took the initiative.

The difference boiled down to two disparate views of what "taking the initiative" meant. The average performer told the researchers that it meant dealing in information — for example, "writing a memo to [a] supervisor about a software bug." The stars, on the other hand, said that taking the initiative meant "fixing [the] bug yourself."

The experience of a director new to CNN confirms the point. He came to the all-news network from one of the Big Three and after a short spell was ready to put his first story on the air. He developed a proposal, then took it to his boss for approval. The boss, he recalled, was flabbergasted, and said, "We don't check adults' homework around here. If it's ready to go, then it's ready to go."

My informant said that the supervisor's reaction gave him quite a jolt. Coming on board as a director meant performing, not talking about it. In the early days of CNN, the now vice chairman of Turner Broadcasting, Burt Reinhardt, put it this way: "'Doing it' means figuring out how to do it yourself. If your way works most of the time, you'll get promoted." Amen, and what a change!

### Véronique and Tommy Lee

Véronique Vienne has spent her career in the fashion industry — as an art director, marketing professional, and freelance writer. When we interviewed her a while back, she had held seven jobs in the last 10 years, and was currently working for Yves Saint Laurent Parfums. She was remarkably straightforward about what she was up to. "My only career strategy is to plan what I can learn, specifically, from each job," Vienne said. "I try to define very clearly two or three things I can accomplish while I'm there." In fact, she added, she chooses jobs more on the basis of what she can learn (and whom she can learn from) than on prospective rank or pay.

I think such a what-can-I-learn-next strategy is pure genius. It's a strategy that frontline employees, in the factory or insurance company's operations department, should follow — not to mention that newly minted Northwestern MBA working in marketing for Kellogg.

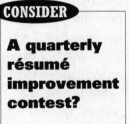

**CONSIDER**

**A quarterly résumé improvement contest?**

While interviewing Vienne, we ran into Sheryl Spanier, an outplacement consultant. She, too, thinks Vienne's approach makes sense: "There's no longer any assurance of a clear, steady career path, no rules you can use to get your meal ticket punched. The key is doing interesting, challenging things professionally, developing a uniqueness and expanding your skills as opposed to fitting yourself into opportunities that present themselves."

Translation: It's far better to move horizontally, even taking a salary cut if necessary, to experience something that spurs your curiosity and adds to your long-term market value. Once again, this logic suggests clearly that you hold the baton. Could we be rediscovering Emersonian self-reliance, which was America's salutary signature for so long? Just ask Tommy Lee Jones.

Actors and actresses are in a tough, competitive business. They understand that their edge over the long haul is brains and inventiveness, not looks. "I've made my living with my imagination all my adult life," *The Fugitive* co-star and Academy Award winner Jones told *Time*. He added, "I hope to continue to grow every day."

### The Age of Homework

The change to job-invention means a shift to self-reliance. And it means that standing still is the kiss of death. Moving forward, or just staying even, calls for getting better, and an audacious commitment to learning. We're in what you might label the Age of Homework.

Thirty-some summers ago, I visited a girlfriend who lived on Cape Cod. It was the first time I'd stayed with a family whose breadwinner was a surgeon. I remember the evenings clearly. Dinner would end about seven, and the old man would disappear into his study to read up on the procedures he'd perform the next day. I was taken aback. Like most of my teenage contemporaries, I dreamed that once you got out of high school, or college, the wretched homework routine was over for good.

Sadly, for many of us, my long-ago dreams have become commonplace nightmares. We attend, sometimes reluctantly, the occasional company-sponsored course (five or 10 days a year, perhaps). And we flip through the pages of a few journals each month. But a commitment to continual learning? Forget it. Not since we got out of school.

In 1994 and beyond, a casual approach to continued learning will not do. Secretaries and receptionists, along with software engineers and lending officers, are already competing directly in the global labor market, and that competitive pressure will only intensify (by order of magnitude) in the years to come.

"My only career strategy is to plan what I can learn from each job."

Véronique Vienne

The way you win, especially if you come from a high-wage nation like ours (and would like to keep those high wages), is to acquire new skills constantly. More bluntly: You need to get (or stay) smarter than the next person, which means that you have to be committed, in some form, to school for life.

> **Education is economics and economics is education.**

As one seminar participant put it, "The family that learns together earns together." That's cute — and also deadly serious. If you're lucky, homework means lots of company-supported training. But, if necessary, homework means you-supported training. In either case, you alone are responsible for setting, and then sticking to, bold and measurable learning/skill-enhancement goals.

No! Back to our earlier discussion of change versus revolution. "Skill-enhancement goals," even bold ones, will not suffice. Your personal program should (must) add up to nothing less than retooling every four to six years. Think of yourself as a machine with a four- to six-year useful life. If you're not investing at least the annual depreciation in reskilling, you're not renewing your capital.

For firms, this continual learning requirement means treating training as a genuine research-and-development investment (regardless of what it's called on the books). For starters: Do you, in your $2 million or $200 million outfit, scrutinize the training budget with the same intensity that you direct toward equipment expenditures and traditional kinds of research? In this brain-based economy, education is economics and economics is education. That's true for the United States, for the State of California, for Intel, for Rosenbluth International, for Véronique Vienne. It's true for me. And for you.

Some people and companies understand the relationship between skill development and strategic necessity very well.

Andersen Consulting, the information-services arm of Arthur Andersen, is obviously in the knowledge business. It spends 6 percent of gross revenue on training, and the average employee is in class 135 hours a year. One hundred thirty-five . . .

Now I happen to think that all of us, from Burger King to Genentech, are in Andersen Consulting's business (professional service delivery). So how does your training expenditure stack up alongside Andersen's? No problem, eh?

### What Do You Want to Be Famous For?

But homework-in-perpetuity and even regular retooling don't go far enough, don't pass the Véronique and Tommy Lee test. There's more to it these days.

Consider David Maister's take on professional service firms. You'd imagine such outfits, where knowledge is the only marketable asset, to be hotbeds of skill building. Not necessarily, says Maister, perhaps the premier observer of these companies. Even when it comes to partners, he finds only 10 percent to 20 percent are what he labels "Dynamos . . . always working to learn something new . . . continually building their practices in new and challenging areas." The rest of the partners, except for a handful of downright incompetents, are "Cruisers," who "work hard, do good work, [and] take care of their clients" — but don't stand out as special talents. The bottom line: The long-term success of any professional service company depends almost wholly on nurturing a higher share of intellectual-miracle-building dynamos than the competition does.

Translating this into an individual mandate for action, Maister insists that far too few of us are concerned (obsessed) with improving our marketable skills. We should, he suggests, be constantly prodding ourselves with such questions as: What's my approach to becoming more valuable in the marketplace this year than last? What new skills do I aim to acquire in the next year? What old skills do I intend to enhance? What is

## Are you satisfied with less than.......

my strategic plan for, say, the next three years?

The bottom-line question is, Maister says, "What, precisely, is it that you want to be famous for?"

That's a helluva thing to ask, isn't it?

## Toward Towering Competence

And along this path we run, merrily upping the ante at every step.

Look, too many of the senior (and not-so-senior) people I encounter in business have lost (or abandoned) their thirst for continued learning and its big brother — towering competence.

Towering competence? I got a graphic lesson years ago on a Friday afternoon outside Rochester, New York. An old friend (then a Xerox executive) and I sat on a rise overlooking the 17th hole of the Oak Hill golf course. We were watching the touring pros play through. One of them stood out. After his approach shot fell, he took a moment, surveyed the course, and made a half-dozen practice swings — presumably pondering the next two days' rounds. Who was this lone ranger? The perennial student of golf, Arnold Palmer.

But the trigger for my concern with towering competence wasn't that afternoon on the links. It was Gita Mehta's 1993 novel, *A River Sutra.* One character, a master musician, reluctantly agrees to take on a new student, his daughter. She tells of the experience:

> My first music lesson extended for several months. In all that time I was not permitted to touch an instrument. . . . Instead my father made me sit next to him in the evenings as the birds were alighting on the trees. "Listen," he said in a voice so hushed it was as if he was praying. "Listen to the birds singing. Do you hear the halfnotes and microtones pouring from their throats? . . . Hear? How that song ended on a

**.....the pursuit of towering competence?**

single note when the bird settled into the tree? The greatest ragas must end like that, leaving just one note's vibrations in the air. . . .

Still, an entire year passed before my father finally allowed me to take the veena across my knees. . . . Morning after morning, month after month he made me play the [scales] over and over again, one hand moving up and down the frets, the other plucking at the veena's strings, until my fingers bled. . . .

I had been under my father's instruction for five years by now. At last my father felt I was capable of commencing the performance of a raga. . . .

Contrast the music student's tale with the ordinary practice of business in 1994. Start with the trainers. Business schools imagine they have a lot to cram into 18 months. Though MBA students may take a few specialized courses their second year, the fact is that these so-called citadels of professional learning turn out dilettantes (would the degree better be called PBA, for Pastiche of Business Administration?) who walk away with an acceptable technical vocabulary but little in-depth knowledge and, worse, because of the abiding focus on finding jobs, little taste for perpetual learning and true mastery.

Nor do they acquire that taste on the job. The excruciating pace of business is the usual excuse. There's no room for listening to the birds sing, for acquiring the sort of mastery Mehta portrays.

Or is there?

Superstar car dealer Carl Sewell will go anywhere and talk with anyone (and has) to learn something new about customer service. Stellar foodmaker Ralph Stayer has spent decades immersed in the study of empowerment. Ditto PepsiCo's Roger Enrico and marketing, GE's Jack Welch and business strategy. Then there's 78-year-old Roger Milliken, who's headed Milliken and Co. for more than half a century. Roger is the Arnold Palmer of the textile business and a passionate student. He's ceaselessly studied manufacturing technology, and it shows in his corporation's manufacturing excellence. In the late 70s, he dove into quality and logged a dozen hours a day of pool time until he had mastered it. Next, customer satisfaction. Studenthood-in-perpetuity is Milliken's signature. Towering competence is his game.

These exceptions, as the saying goes, prove the rule. When I depart from conversations with Sewell and especially Milliken, shaking my still-spinning head, I know I've had an invaluable tutorial (and been thoroughly shaken down for any useful tidbits I might be able to offer). I also know how far these conversations go beyond the norm.

The lesson learned from the Sewells and Millikens of the world might be a tough one to swallow. Whether you're a new B-school graduate, rising marketing exec, or CEO, you need to ask yourself: Am I on the road toward towering competence that can become the basis for startling moves in my industry? If not, precisely what do I plan to do about it? (And when do I plan to start?)

As CEO, look at your top divisional and functional executives as well as the stars below them. Sure, they're "fine performers." But are they those Dynamos that David Maister talks about, are they driving toward towering competence? If not, what do you/ they plan to do about it?

In an age when all value is cerebral, it's high time to take a look at whether or not we're developing an unfair share of gold medalists (who are in hot pursuit of towering competence). Right?

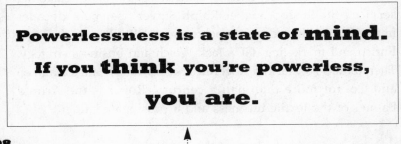

**Powerlessness is a state of mind. If you think you're powerless, you are.**

## How Fat Is Your Rolodex?

Mind your Rolodex. Along with attaining (and maintaining and enhancing) a noteworthy marketable skill, this never-ending job tops the list of must-dos for the wise independent contractor — and for everyone else these days.

A colleague who heads a major business school's executive-education programs laments the timidity of most fast-tracking senior execs who pass through his portals. They ought to "show more loyalty to their Rolodex," he said, somewhat mysteriously. To my "Huh?," he replied that they ought to rely on their extended network for career security, and that in turn should build their nerve "to regularly push the envelope for change in their organizations." To fail to take big risks is the highest risk of all, he added with finality.

Nothing is wrong with seeking or having security. The human animal needs it. It's just that security (or the lack thereof) is not going to come from your company anymore, but instead from your growing (or shrinking) set of external contacts.

How about this for the new higher math: Security is proportional to (1) the thickness of your Rolodex, (2) the rate of Rolodex expansion, (3) the share of Rolodex entries from beyond the corporate walls, and (4) the time devoted to Rolodex maintenance.

## Powerlessness Is a State of Mind

Homework. Towering competence. Must-do elements of the independent mindset. Managing your Rolodex. Another must. Beyond that comes the ultimate intangible, on or off someone's payroll: Your attitude about getting things done.

I've long been offended by the whining middle managers and professional staffers who tell me how tough they've got it. They're bound to their desks by dictatorial bosses who might demand their presence at any moment, they say. They believe in stepping out, but they can't. "Rubbish," is

> **"Assume you have absolute authority."**
> **Richard Perle**

the way Reagan Pentagon staffer Richard Perle feels about such complaints.

"The question always arises as to what authority you have. The answer," Perle said, "is you have to assume you have absolute authority until somebody tells you otherwise, until somebody stops you. Because if you try to derive your authority, your freedom of action, from any other source than yourself, you are not going to have any fun, and you are not going to get much done."

> **It never occurred to Joe Key that he was just a lieutenant commander.**

Perle claimed that he always "operated on the theory that it was within my authority to make decisions and do things and carry them out, right up until the moment that somebody was able to prove otherwise. And it's amazing how much you can get away with, how many people will acquiesce in that, if you seem determined and you seem to know what you are doing."

Perle is right on. I had my epiphany on this score when I thought about Joe Key, also a former Pentagon denizen, and once my boss.

In 1968 I was assigned to the Pentagon and worked for Lieutenant Commander Key. In that building, lieutenant commanders come far cheaper than a dime a dozen. Yet Joe got things done, and without raising a sweat. For years, I wondered about that: What made Joe so successful?

When I read Perle's remarks decades later, the answer suddenly came to me. Silly as it may sound at first blush, it just never occurred to Joe Key that he was a lieutenant commander. Joe, in effect, thought he was an admiral who hadn't bothered to get the thick gold stripe stitched to his sleeve yet.

Joe was fearless. He'd charge into an admiral's office and ask a question. The stunned admiral (who hadn't hung around with lieutenant commanders for years) gave him the answer. Joe took every admiral's aide he could find out to lunch, or at least it seemed that way. Joe knew everybody. He had the place wired.

When he needed something done in a hurry, he called on his network.

Joe was (1) gutsy, (2) a matchless networker 20 years before the term was invented, and (3) sported one of the fattest Rolodexes in the 23,000-person, five-sided building. Powerless? Don't make me laugh. Joe Key, though nominally without clout, was one of the most potent bosses I've encountered. Since those days, my sympathy for people "trapped in the middle," becalmed by "powerlessness," has been zilch.

How do you get the Perle-Key touch if you ain't got it? Good question. A sense of humor and a taste for the absurd can help a nominally powerless person behave like one with clout. Maybe developing those characteristics is even decisive. That is, if you don't take yourself too seriously and are perpetually amused by the peculiar nature of humans singly and in groups, then you're more likely to try most anything, and you won't fret about making a fool of yourself. (After all, the world is such a foolish place. Why not prance in the circus parade with gusto?) In short, powerlessness is a state of mind. If you think you're powerless, you are.

## The Dependent Society Is Dying

Whether it's easy or hard to overcome perceptions of powerlessness is, sadly, beside the point. You've no choice. Powerlessness simply won't do in a commercial world where a nanosecond's power outage can cause commercial chaos.

"Life may be more exciting, but it will also be more frightening," Mary Ann Sieghart writes in *The Times* (London). "The dependent society is dying, the independent society taking its place." Yes, it is a brave, and bold, new world we live in. The social contract has been torn up — or at least the one we and our parents and their parents signed. That social contract had us landing a job at GE or GM at age 18 or 21, staying put for 40 years (raising no sweat during the last 15), then retiring with a gold watch and an adequate pension.

Forget that deal; it's no longer valid. My dad worked for the same outfit, the Baltimore Gas & Electric Company, for 41 years. I thought that was normal. I've worked for four employers since college. I thought that was pretty far out. But now my stepson and his contemporaries (mid-20s) think that switching jobs every couple of years is the way to go. (Many employers, at least in places like Silicon Valley, fret if prospective employees, even youthful ones, can't boast of having several jobs behind them. What's the matter? No zip? No derring-do?)

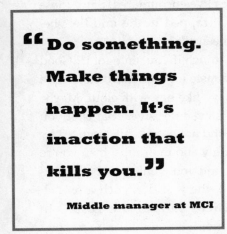

**" Do something. Make things happen. It's inaction that kills you. "**

**Middle manager at MCI**

In his autobiography, *Odyssey,* former Apple boss John Sculley succinctly described what I call "the new loyalty." He said, in effect: Look, Apple can't promise you a job for life. Not even for five or 10 years. Maybe not even for a couple of years. But what Apple can — and does — promise is that, whether you're aboard for three months, six months, six years, or, unlikely as it may be, 16 years, you will be constantly learning, constantly challenged. At the end, you will be demonstrably better positioned in the local or global labor market than you would have been had you not spent the time with us.

I think that's a good deal. It puts the bouncing ball in my court. The playground (Apple) is packed with professional challenges and scintillating peers. So take advantage and learn something, Tom. Become more valuable. Or suffer the consequences. I don't have to depend on smart moves by my employer, whether it's Apple's Mr. Sculley (formerly) or GM's Jack Smith. My true security and superior stipend depend on my own initiative and my own thirst for learning. It's my job (and my life), and I take responsibility for it.

Nostalgia worries me. Too many of us seem to be recalling those big-company jobs as if they were paradise lost. Trust me:

they weren't. I read Ben Hamper's *Rivethead* about life at "the office" (the General Motors production line). It's nothing I'd want. And, frankly, I'm not sure that my dad had such a good deal either. He was an exceptional fella — bright, engaging — but I doubt that the time at work, all 41 years of it, stretched him very much. If he had come under the axman's blow (from his own Percy Barnevik), he would have been no better prepared to confront the labor market 25 years into the job than three years into it. And that is a rotten way to live.

## Toward Brand-New Personalities?

Tack. Jibe. Twist. Turn. The whole (big) idea of routinely moving "horizontally" is critical. The career "ladder" is a dangerous image. It suggests knowable, linear directions. Up = win. Anything else = lose. "Careers" today involve jumping around, up, sideways — and occasionally down. But always grasping for a new learning experience, one that allows you to develop and maintain or enhance skills, your network, and ultimately your labor-market edge.

You've probably figured it out by now: I think this is mostly a good-news story. But it won't be an easy story to live out. The plot is that you'll grow or get left behind — or maybe left out. In bygone days, people worked like hell in their 20s and 30s; then, if they weren't headed for one of the top 10 slots in their outfit by, say, age 45, they could begin to coast. Increasingly, they directed their energy toward off-the-job activities. Nine to five became mostly a pass-the-time drill. No more.

Perhaps you don't have to be as physically energetic at 57 as at 27 — but the requirement for growth does not abate one whit. If anything, the pressure increases as the new twists become increasingly strange and uncomfortable. As the aging athlete can extend a professional career by five to 10 years through guile and headwork and homework, so can we all stretch our career performance. Staying highly engaged with your job until later in life may sound daunting, but it's probably a lot more conducive to long-term mental health — not to mention fiscal health — than the alternative.

In the strange new world, personalities may even have to adjust. Psychologist Kenneth Gergen believes that in a rapidly

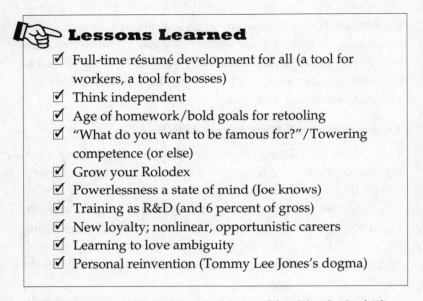

## Lessons Learned

- ☑ Full-time résumé development for all (a tool for workers, a tool for bosses)
- ☑ Think independent
- ☑ Age of homework/bold goals for retooling
- ☑ "What do you want to be famous for?"/Towering competence (or else)
- ☑ Grow your Rolodex
- ☑ Powerlessness a state of mind (Joe knows)
- ☑ Training as R&D (and 6 percent of gross)
- ☑ New loyalty; nonlinear, opportunistic careers
- ☑ Learning to love ambiguity
- ☑ Personal reinvention (Tommy Lee Jones's dogma)

changing society, the traditional mental-health ideal of "firm and fixed identity has become limiting and in many ways incapacitating," political scientist Walter Truett Anderson reported in *Utne Reader*. Gergen believes that people who demonstrate "elasticity" are healthier and more fulfilled. The race, in other words, goes to the labile personalities, the ones who mix the colors of the socks they put on in the morning and revel in change and ambiguity. Hmmm!? Ouch!?

### T.T.D. (Things to Do) and Q.T.A. (Questions to Answer)

❶ As a staff professional or middle manager, how do you fare on the Big Six résumé questions? How does your day — today — rate on the is-it-résumé-able meter? With no ifs, ands, or buts, promptly update your résumé every June 30 and December 31. Forever.

❷ Bosses: Have all employees update their résumés every three or six months (including customer references). Make the résumé creation and review process your chief management tool, replacing any MBO scheme and perhaps your current performance evaluation program. (How about bringing in an out-placement counselor, who understands labor-market value, as an adviser? Really.) Make the process, in part, public. This is win-win; the more customer accolades and the more new skills, the merrier.

❸ Just what have you learned in the last three months, six months, year, 18 months? (Prove it — to yourself, anyway.) Are you taking classes, company-sponsored or not, right now? If not, why not? Do you have a personal skills-development program? As a boss, is every employee engaged in a self-designed learning/homework program with specific goals, reviewed at least twice a year? Is the end product "improvement" or reinvention? (If reinvention, are you sure?) Are you enroute to towering competence?

> **Just what have you learned in the last 3 months, 6 months, year, 18 months? (Prove it.)**

❹ How well does your unit stack up on the MCI test? (Design your own job; don't wait for the decision-makers; act without orders; "inaction will kill you.")

❺ CEOs: Commission a headhunter to assess your division chiefs and other key professionals as to market worth; use this outside review as the centerpiece of your annual appraisal process.

❻ Think network/Rolodex. Do you consider networking "soft stuff" — or do you devote a large share of your time to it? Specifically, is your list of contacts inside and, especially, outside the company growing by the month? Do you have an orderly scheme for keeping in touch? (Some software programs can be a big help.)

❼ Have middle managers and staff professionals discuss powerlessness, their definitions of it, and what they might do about it. Benchmark yourself against peers who do not feel powerless; note the difference, if there is any. (Remember the two definitions of "taking the initiative" at Bell Labs.) Consider Outward Bound or other programs that might help you deal with perceived powerlessness (many are useless, a few invaluable).

❽ As an employee, are you considering a sideways (or downward) career move that will teach you something new and special? Give you a chance to work with someone nifty? Put you into a dysfunctional setting where you confront a challenge head on (and no escaping the consequences of your actions)? Is such an idea repugnant or attractive? Meet with peers, formally or informally, and discuss.

You're as good as your Rolodex, your drive to achieve towering competence, your will to create your own job and abolish your sense of powerlessness, your nerve when it comes to seeking out exciting assignments that call for a downward or sideways shift. That's the story in a futzed-up marketplace, where nothing (person, organization) sits still for more than a few nanoseconds. **The bottom line is equal parts terrifying and liberating.**

## CHAPTER 5

BEYOND DISINTEGRATION

# THE CORPORATION AS ROLODEX

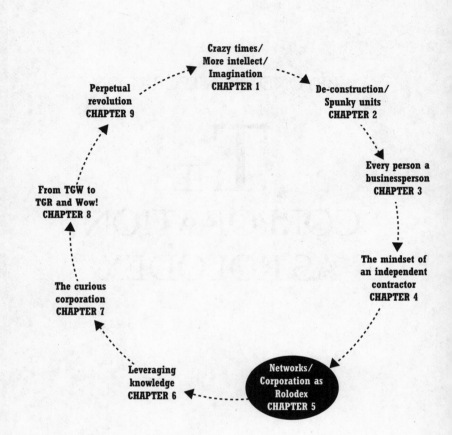

Crazy times/
More intellect/
Imagination
CHAPTER 1

De-construction/
Spunky units
CHAPTER 2

Every person a
businessperson
CHAPTER 3

The mindset of
an independent
contractor
CHAPTER 4

Networks/
Corporation as
Rolodex
CHAPTER 5

Leveraging
knowledge
CHAPTER 6

The curious
corporation
CHAPTER 7

From TGW to
TGR and Wow!
CHAPTER 8

Perpetual
revolution
CHAPTER 9

Atomization and independence and self-definition to deal with fast-paced change. That's been our message so far, for both corporations and individuals. Except, near the end of the last chapter, we introduced the idea of a new dependence; not loyalty to one's company, but to one's network or Rolodex. Now we'll expand on that notion. It's not that two people in a garage can do all tomorrow's work. Instead, **it's the idea of creating an organizational network in a flash by gathering the best talent to exploit an opportunity.**

Call it corporation as Rolodex.

"The lumbering

bureaucracies of

this century will

be replaced by

fluid, independent

groups of problem

solvers..."

**Steve Truett and Tom Barrett**

Consider the "shamrock organization," which sprang from the fertile mind of British business consultant Charles Handy in 1989. A small core of permanent, professional staffers — guardians of the core competence — comprise one leaf of the shamrock. Specialists and independent contractors, to whom a great deal of the organization's work will be outsourced, make up another. Part-timers and temps, who will perform the rest of the work, are the third leaf. Put the leaves together right — and you're in clover.

Handy was prescient.

Recall that Nintendo generated $5.5 billion in 1992 sales and $1.3 billion in pretax profits from just 892 employees. That's more than $6 million in sales per employee. (*Profits*, about $1.5 million per employee, are three times Apple's relatively high *sales* per employee.) Nintendo keeps most of the crucial design and marketing management functions to itself, but lets just about everything else go to partners and licensees.

Welcome to the age of hooked-up, network organizations — whatever that means. What *does* it mean? Answer: It depends.

## The Corporation as Rolodex

In Chapters 2, 3, and 4 we smashed organizations into small, self-sufficient units with distinctive personalities and removed almost all the superstructure above those units; then we imagined that everyone would become a de facto independent businessperson (on the company payroll), and, in effect, create their own jobs. Now we begin the process of putting the demolished companies and independent spirits back together — but not as vertical monoliths, not with jobs that stay the same year after year, not with employees who are around for the duration.

But surely a company can't dominate a market, be it for microchips or potato chips, with two-, five-, 10-, 50-, or even 150-person micro-units. Don't be so sure. Sometimes it can. Sometimes it can't. In either case, there is a need to wire up the specialized resources required to get sizable jobs done (the dictionary definition of organization). It takes such linked-up resources to produce this book, to build a dam, or to create the new Boeing 777.

Oh yes, putting together the right resources to get a job done is as important as ever. It's just that increasingly this hooking up doesn't mean calling on the residents of various functional fiefdoms within a standing organization; no, it means finding and connecting with the best resources anywhere — and in a flash. And then starting all over again, with another one-of-a-kind network, when a new opportunity presents itself. As it will. Soon.

In Chapter 4 we touted Rolodex-power for the individual. She or he would be wise to forget reliance on (and loyalty to) General Motors, Big Blue, or You Name It, Inc.

The new self-reliance (build a towering competence, whether you're a receptionist or computer programmer) also includes a new loyalty — loyalty to one's network peers.

If the bulging and well-tended Rolodex is crucial to individual survival in these tumultuous times, it is also crucial to corporations. They need to do what they do well (towering individual competence, towering corporate core competence), and they need to have bulging and well-tended corporate Rolodexes (alliance candidates and alliance management skills). Could organization-as-Rolodex be the right image for the times?

## Help Wanted, Circa 1994

The corporation as Rolodex? Sound farfetched? Well, it did to me — until I came across this want ad:

> D.L. Boone & Company, one of the first "Virtual Corporations," offers systems, engineering, and management consulting professionals an alternative or supplement to traditional corporate employment or "solo entrepreneurship." Associate Consultants, the members of the company's Professional Services Network, can earn competitive compensation, a 33 percent commission for technical recruiting, a 5 percent finders fee for business development, and an annual profit distribution. Requirements for admission generally include an advanced degree (MBA or MS) in a relevant discipline; a technical BS degree and two years of applicable experience (functional or technical); or a BA/BS and five years applicable experience. Recent college graduates with exceptional academic credentials, and preferably some co-op experience, may also be considered. We are currently gearing up for nearterm proposal development efforts including a joint venture with a Big 6 accounting and consulting firm. E-mail DLBoone to receive information including a summary, corporate overview and the company's accomplishments during September 1993.

Oh, did I mention I "came across" this on America Online, in the Mercury Center (the online version of the *San Jose Mercury News*)? See what I mean?

## De-construct, Reconstruct

In short, today's work — whether in biotechnology or corporate travel services — is unpredictable. The "organization" that executes the work — call it a shamrock, Rolodex, virtual corporation, spider's web, kaleidoscope, rugby scrum, whatever — will look far different than yesterday's model. Essentially, collections of people will gather together — independent contractors, bits and pieces of organizations from hither and thither — to exploit a particular market opening. Then the "organization" will dissolve, never to appear again in precisely the same form.

Take Brenda Brimage, chief executive officer of B&B Communications West, a math textbook developer. "It wouldn't make any sense for me to have employees," Brimage told *Success* magazine in June 1993. "I never know what my projects are going to be." Then there's Rick Smolan, who created the extraordinarily successful *Day in the Life* phenomenon (books, etc.). He grew his company to 18 people, then decided administration was a drag, and in 1987 sold out to Rupert Murdoch. Soon afterwards Smolan founded the aptly named Against All Odds Productions. He and two assistants are the only full-time employees, but the scope of the enterprise is breathtaking — everything from producing best-selling books to developing one of the first successful multimedia products ("From Alice to Ocean"). Smolan gathers whatever partners he needs (ranging from huge sponsors and co-venturers like Apple and Kodak, to independent contractors like the hundreds of professional photographers who shot the *Day in the Life* series); then he lets the network get on with it. Smolan is the Harold Geneen of the 90s, a newfangled conglomerateur, executing numerous projects simultaneously through temporary partnerships. "I consciously decided to farm out everything and work with my friends, many of whom are independent contractors," he told us. Nice. And why not?

Or consider lawyers Robert Esperti and Renno Peterson, who, according to career consultant Bill Charland, had a comfortable estate-planning practice based out of Denver. Except Esperti wanted to live in Wyoming and Peterson in Florida. So they moved to Jackson Hole and Sarasota, respectively, but left the practice intact, thanks to electronic networking tools.

Then they took the next step and formed the electronically-based National Network of Estate Planning Attorneys. Now 350 members strong, it offers education services — publications, videos, electronic bulletin board — and also social support. "We're freeing lawyers from solitary confinement," the duo told Charland. "Now it's possible to share our skills with colleagues on a daily basis, wherever we are."

Or how about Edward McPherson, who has taken these ideas another step forward? He calls InterSolve Group, his oddball consulting company, "just-in-time talent." InterSolve doesn't maintain a stable of MBA trouble-shooters, ready to provide predictable, off-the-shelf solutions. It doesn't even employ a secretary or a receptionist. Instead, it quickly draws together managers, technical experts, marketers — whatever and whenever a client's project requires.

> **"I consciously decided to farm out everything and work with my friends."**
>
> **Rick Smolan**

For one of InterSolve's largest projects, it assembled 26 people in four teams to help First Interstate Bancorp streamline its credit card, loan, and deposit operations. Typically, leader McPherson (one of four InterSolve partners heads each project) knew only one of his team members beforehand. The team worked on the project for about three months, helped the bank realize $14 million in savings, and then disbanded.

"Instead of hiring a conventional consultant, we chose to use InterSolve as an integrator, to pick specialists in certain functional areas," says First Interstate EVP Hayden Watson. "That's how these networks pay off."

## Focusing on the Essentials

And pay off they do. Individuals are gathering on an as-needed basis to provide value-added services to corporations. Corporations are deintegrating, as they learn to focus on the few things they do well, to farm out the rest, and then work together in networks with whatever specialist partners are needed to tackle a particular challenge. Consider an entire industry that's busily reinventing itself, namely banking. Not so many years ago, borrowing, lending, and other services were housed under one roof. No more. "Today, with technologically linked global capital markets and deregulation, most of the services formerly available only in your local bank can be had from any variety of vendors, reachable via networks or 800 numbers, each with its particular specialty," says McKinsey & Co.'s Brook Manville. "The industry is rapidly disaggregating into discrete value-added providers." What is a bank? What is a non-bank? Who knows? (Not any bankers of my acquaintance.)

The story is the same in advertising. Several creative stars left DDB Needham Chicago in the fall of 1993 to form The Leap Partnership. According to the new firm's prospectus, it intends to "unbundle creative services" from the traditional agency structure. "Clients look at the money they're paying their agencies," Leap's George Grier told *Adweek*, "and wonder what, or who, it's paying for. Overhead? Layers of account management? Services they don't use? If you ask clients what they want from their agencies, they say creative advertising that sells the product. We're going to be able to tell clients that their money is going to be spent on people who are generating ideas for their brands all day long."

In 1992, sales per employee at Apple Computer ran $506,000 a year. At IBM the figure was $218,000; at Digital Equipment, $128,000. Although the three companies' product lines differ, they're effectively in the same business, and they ought to look roughly the same. But these statistics tell us they don't. Each company has gone its own way. Digital does just about everything itself. If they don't own an operation and control it, they're uncomfortable — or have been until recently. The same has held true for IBM. Apple, consistent with practice in Silicon Valley, focuses on a few key tasks (design, engineering, advertising and marketing, final assembly) and networks the rest to the best people it can find.

DAN BRYANT

Ed McPherson's "just-in-time talent" saved a client $14 million.

## Outsiders Horn in on the Essentials, Too

But, wait, there's much more to it. It's not just that Apple willy-nilly farms out jobs to the low bidder. Rather, Apple's key skill is the management of networks per se, including the ability to put one together at the drop of a hat. This involves working with both giant partners (such as archrival IBM) and a broad, shifting array of independent contractors. Sometimes I wonder if I have any Silicon Valley friends who haven't worked for Apple on a project, at least for a few months.

Moreover, the company's use of specialized outside resources is not limited to non-core functions. Apple frets ceaselessly about core skills, and because of that routinely brings in outside specialists (firms and individuals) to breathe new life into, say, R&D — an area in which it takes great pride. But not so much pride that it closes itself off to an outsider's fresh take on things.

In fact, the idea of using creative outsiders in essential areas is becoming a groundswell. *Design News* reports that while engineering employment in manufacturing companies has been declining in recent years, it's been soaring at independent engineering-service firms. (The Department of Labor expects engineering employment in such service firms to grow by 57 percent between 1993 and 2005, compared to 12 percent growth at manufacturing firms.) One key reason for the shift: The engineering schools' best and brightest foresee more creative freedom and more rapid growth opportunities at the service firms.

Kingston Technology gets the idea of partners horning in on the essentials. A leading upgrader of computers, the company was, according to *Inc.*, the fastest-growing private company in America in 1992. Kingston bagged $500 million in sales from only 220 employees — which translates into $2.3 million in sales per worker (five times greater than Apple, 18 times greater than Digital). As Kingston grew, *Newsweek* reported, it "stayed small" by creating "a rock-solid network of partners," most of whom rely on a handshake as contract. Here's how Kingston uses its novel form to compress into a few hours a job that typically takes competitors 10 days:

One recent Tuesday, a Los Angeles branch of ComputerLand received a call from Bank of America. It wanted 100 IBM PCs pronto. The problem: they needed lots of extra memory and other upgrades, the better to run Windows, Microsoft's ubiquitous operating system, and link into the bank's computer network. ComputerLand called Kingston, which snapped into action. Within hours it had designed a sophisticated upgrade system — its particular specialty — and relayed the "specs" to a key partner, Express Manufacturing. Express, which specializes in assembling electronic parts, cleared its manufacturing lines, filled Kingston's order and sent the finished systems back that very afternoon. By evening, Kingston had tested all the components and returned them, via FedEx, to ComputerLand. By the weekend, Bank of America's computers were up and running. "You've heard of just-in-time inventory?" asks VP David Sun, referring to Japan's vaunted principle of cost-effective management. "This is just-in-time manufacturing."

No-nonsense Andy Grove, Intel's CEO, told *Business Week* that the idea of a "virtual corporation," which Kingston epitomizes, was just a fad. A couple of weeks later Grove said to *Fortune*, "Anything that can be done in the vertical way can be done more cheaply by collections of specialist companies organized horizontally." Maybe Grove doesn't like the faddish language, but he sure takes a shine to the idea.

## Embracing the Annoying Lingo

Frankly, I like the "virtual org" moniker. It helps us think new. "What will a virtual corporation look like?" Bill Davidow and Mike Malone ask in *The Virtual Corporation*. "To the outside observer, it will appear almost edgeless, with permeable and continuously changing interfaces among company, supplier, and customers. From inside the firm the view will be no less

Sometimes I wonder if
I have any Silicon Valley
friends who haven't worked
for Apple on a project.

Tom Peters

amorphous, with traditional offices, departments, and operating divisions constantly reforming according to need."

What an irritating paragraph! That's precisely why I use it in my seminars. "Edgeless," "permeable," "continuously changing," "amorphous," "constantly re-forming" — these words make the average, conventionally-trained manager squirm. (And make more than a few angry.) Yet we must, regardless of the business we're in, get used to them — and learn to love them.

### The Bedrock Logic

Let's step back and examine the underlying logic. Professor James Brian Quinn of Dartmouth's Amos Tuck School of Business says we'd be wise to imagine companies as collections of "service packages" — logistics, engineering, design, marketing, etc. (Remember one of the magic fractions from Chapter 1: 94 percent of IBMers, for example, work in service activities.) Then the question is: Who should execute these service activities? I put it this way to seminar participants:

■ Isn't it true that 95 percent of what your company does is the performance of services offered by individuals and specialist organizations that you can find in the Yellow Pages?

■ Are you so arrogant as to believe that none of these providers is better than you, more innovative, more quality oriented, more cost efficient?

The fact is, the world is loaded with specialists, totally focused on and expert at "small" tasks. Another fact is that some/many/most of these specialists are likely to be better at their niche activity than generalists are likely to be.

I could generate a 100-page list like the following: Ameriscribe specializes in running mail rooms (customers include National Steel). Serv-Tech does much of Mobil's refinery maintenance (talk about a core task). Total Systems Services does credit card processing for AT&T (AT&T's credit card operation won a Baldrige quality award). Kenco Group runs distribution centers for Whirlpool. And on. And on.

### Hollow or Expand, But Don't Stand Pat

Following Quinn's idea, think of the company as a collection of services: call them Service A, Service B, Service C, Service D. On the one hand, they're all candidates for outsourcing. On the other hand, you can probably offer profitably to external customers some of the services you now perform only for yourself.

In the computer industry, for example, several companies have discovered they've got an edge in manufacturing "services" and are now selling them to competitors (they were previously held sacrosanct). Texas Instruments makes computers for Sun Microsystems; Digital Equipment builds computer boards for Apple; IBM builds computers for Hitachi and PC boards for clonemakers. IBM, in fact, pocketed half a billion dollars in "contract manufacturing" revenue in 1993. In foods the story is the same: Ralston Purina, for example, is the largest manufacturer of private-label cereals for supermarket chains, basically competing with itself.

Or take an internal staff-service activity such as logistics.

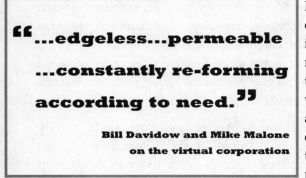

> **"...edgeless...permeable ...constantly re-forming according to need."**
>
> **Bill Davidow and Mike Malone on the virtual corporation**

Kennametal installed a winning just-in-time inventory management system. Customers got wind of it and asked the toolmaker to extend its systems to their companies. Today Kennametal runs, on a turnkey basis, tool rooms. (Hint: Customer toolroom workers, once safe as internal monopolists, now find themselves competing for their lives with a vendor company. Shades of the Age of Homework, eh?)

Or consider Arthur Andersen. The Big Six accounting firms have pretty much divided up the auditing-services business of the world's largest corporations. With such services becoming commoditized, where do you go for growth (and decent margins)? Enter CFM, or Contract Financial Management, among other new Andersen businesses. Just as EDS will take over a corporation's information-services activities (including the employees), Andersen will take over, on a turnkey basis, a corporation's financial-services operation, even providing the chief financial officer.

In much the same vein, Baxter International, with its huge I.V. Systems operation, decided to transport its superior drug-mixing skills to hospitals. In the past, Baxter would pre-mix a few of the most commonly used drugs, and the hospital would do the day-to-day mixing of scores of drugs, with dosages tailored to the needs of hundreds of patients. Enter Patient-specific Intravenous-solution Compounding, a for-profit Baxter service business offering just-in-time, individual-patient drug-mixing to hospitals. In some cases (shades of Kennametal), Baxter has usurped much of the hospital pharmacy's work.

## TI makes computers for Sun, ..............

Baxter also makes and distributes numerous surgical supplies. It has begun packaging its own and other manufacturers' tools in kits for particular procedures — a 200-component appendectomy set, for instance. This, too, puts Baxter directly into its hospital customer's core operational work. And much more is coming. The company increasingly sees itself, regardless of the eventual shape of health-care reform, as working "horizontally" with hospitals to provide turnkey services, deeply embedded in the hospitals' systems, that reduce overall costs. Where Baxter stops and the hospital starts becomes murkier and murkier — purportedly to both parties' benefit.

Such creative extension of services is not the exclusive province of giants. Take the case of Draeger's, a grocery store in Menlo Park, California. What can a single grocery do except sell food (and maybe deliver it)? Lots. A while back I picked up the spiffy 3-month schedule for Draeger's Culinary Center. It begins:

> Draeger's Supermarket is proud to announce a new schedule of classes and product tastings in our Culinary Center. We hope that you will continue to share our excitement about this calendar full of stimulating, educational, and fun events taught by an array of the Bay Area's and the nation's brightest culinary stars.
>
> During this second season of classes, we continue with our in-depth examination of the great regional cooking of Italy. One of our favorite teachers, Carlo Middione, returns to introduce us to the cooking of Emilia Romagna, while Suzette Gresham, one of San Francisco's finest Italian chefs, leads us through Lombardia, Umbria, and the Abruzzi. Chef Patrizio Sacchetto reveals some of the culinary techniques that made his cooking at Blue Fox and Donatello internationally famous. Johanne Killeen, owner and chef of the renowned restaurant Al Forno of

**....IBM for Hitachi, Ralston Purina ......**

Providence, Rhode Island, will present a class on the renaissance of Italian cooking. Local favorite Lou Seibert Pappas will conduct workshops on Biscotti and Pesto.

The calendar includes — burp! — 87 events in the 91 days.

Then there's Lane Group, a British trucking company with $20 million in annual revenues, which has targeted the high end of the hauling market (customers include Body Shop International). First, Lane (shades of Baxter) expanded its essential business idea from "moving goods" to being "a logistics partner" — which has meant thoroughly entwining itself with customers via such techniques as "open book" accounting, where the customer sees all Lane's financials regarding the customer's account (and Lane sees all the customer's logistics numbers, as well).

## BEYOND BISCOTTI

### Draeger's Supermarket

**hosts 87 events in 91 days; creative extension services include tastings, classes, and workshops, conducted by local as well as internationally acclaimed chefs and restaurant owners**

But there's more. Because of illnesses and the like, Lane from time to time would hire drivers from temporary employment agencies. Because a special approach to drivers is part of Lane's core competence, the company is a stickler for driver attitude, dress, fuel-economy habits, etc., and the temps were often disappointing. The answer? Create PL Workforce as a Lane subsidiary (PL is for Peter Lane, the company's original name), which would be an employment agency dealing exclusively in haulage drivers trained to Lane's exacting standards. PL serves Lane's occasional needs and is growing fast by serving Lane's competitors. In fact, it's the only exclusively temp-driver firm in England. Lane discovered a related opportunity in its training department, the engine room of the company's driver standards. It recently founded Training Force, a subsidiary that trains anyone's drivers (again, including rivals') at Lane's

......**is the largest manufacturer of** .......

Bristol headquarters or on the customer's site.

"Services form an envelope around the product," Joseph Fuller, James O'Conor, and Richard Rawlinson write in the *Harvard Business Review.* "Companies make markets by pushing the envelope." That's precisely what Baxter, Kennametal, Arthur Andersen, Draeger's, Lane Group, and others are doing. On the one hand, they're wrapping services around conventional products (Baxter, Draeger's, Andersen). On the other hand, they see that a previously internal-only service has profit potential outside (Kennametal, Lane).

### The Serpentine World

The chain of "value-adds" can become quite complex. Start with (1) a product (lumpy object), such as surgical gloves or a copy machine. Then (2) embed intelligence in the product (self-diagnostics in Otis elevators, Trumpf machine tools, Minolta cameras). Next (3) wrap services around the product (Starkist tuna cans, called "Charlie's Lunch Kit," include 3.25 ounces of chunk tuna plus "2 packets mayonnaise, 1 packet pickle relish, 6 wheat crackers and 1 mixing spoon" — see, this is a game anyone can play). And (4) distribute (Merck paid $6 billion for generic-drug distributor Medco, in part to gain access to information about the 33 million members of its customers' health plans). Next (5) extend distribution services (Baxter's Enhanced Distribution Service offloads customer products, just in time, in the precise order in which they will be stored or used in the hospital). Finally (6) offer turnkey services (a la Kennametal running customers' tool shops).

Imagine it this way:

> Enhanced product = product + embedded intelligence + wraparound services + distribution + extended distribution services + turnkey program management.

............**private-label cereals**

**What a job of parking Marriott did . . . Whoops, make that Professional Parking Services, Inc.**

Add it up and you've totally transformed your product. In fact, you may have transformed the way your customer does business. As in the Baxter case, this calls for extraordinary organizational gymnastics — a wholesale shift from "vertical thinking" (individual product divisions reign supreme) to "horizontal thinking," which makes the product/sales/delivery/service activity seamless and wholly integrated into the customer's systems, rituals, and culture.

When I ponder all this, an odd image comes to mind. I see a pit of slithering snakes: companies tearing themselves apart, hollowing themselves by making decisions to outsource this or that when they find someone better at it. On the other hand, I see them adding services to current products and then darting into the back pockets of other companies (hollowing their customers' enterprises). Visualize a company shipping, say, two-thirds of what it does (those various "service packages") to outsourcers; at the same time, taking most of the rest of what it does (other "service packages," such as IBM's manufacturing prowess and Lane's training excellence) and slipping into customer companies that are looking to do outsourcing. What's left is a complicated, tangled, godawful — and profitable and innovative, if done right — mess. By yesterday's tidy standards.

### Parking Pros Reveal the Clue

Part of what drives this movement toward corporation as Rolodex are computer networks that (at their occasional bests) wildly enhance the ability of disparate and distant actors to be in constant contact with each other. Just as significant is the realization that it is arrogant for individuals or companies to believe that they can do everything better than anyone else. My own epiphany came a couple of years ago when I gave a speech at a Marriott hotel in Orange County, California. The valets did a bang-up job of parking almost 1,000 cars. They were well-dressed, courteous to a fault, and actually ran back and forth from the cars. Some show!

During my speech, I mentioned this and said, "Hats off to Marriott!" There was sustained applause, suggesting others had also enjoyed this spectacle of excellence. After the talk, Paul Paliska came up and introduced himself. Turned out he was the founder of Professional Parking Services, Inc. — valet-parking specialists who subcontract to Marriott.

That really got me thinking. Regardless of the job, from car-parking to biochemical research, there are folks out there who sweat the narrow task as if it were a matter of life and death (which for them it is). I have trouble getting excited about parking, and I expect that Marriott's hotel managers, their platters already balanced with a thousand hot dishes, do, too. But to Paul Paliska and his brother Stephen, parking is a passion, just as the next generation of software is to Microsoft's Bill Gates. And passion makes perfect. (Incidentally, shades of Kennametal, Professional Parking Services will also take over the entire hotel "front" operations. Slither. Slither.)

## Make a Buck or Pack Your Bags

When you get the hang of thinking this way (someone out there probably can . . .), you'll realize that all staff service providers can and probably should be placed on notice — sell to outsiders as well as insiders (profitably), or else. "The division managers pay for the headquarters services from their own budgets," Robert Potter, president of Monsanto Chemical Company, the biggest arm of Monsanto Inc., told *Fortune* magazine. "If they think they're paying too much for support staff, we simply eliminate the [headquarters] job."

But it seems only fair to give the headquarters gang a chance to reach beyond its own borders and become profitable. Take IBM's creation of Workforce Solutions, formerly a sizable (over 2,000 people) part of the IBM human resources staff, mostly responsible for creating and overseeing benefits packages throughout the vast corporation. In May 1992, *Business Week* reported, IBM spun out WFS as a stand-alone company. It's first "customers" were the 13 now substantially independent "Baby Blue" units of IBM. As part of the move to make those units genuinely independent, each is allowed to create unique benefits offerings suitable to its industry. (Before, each unit had provided the same package.)

Knowing it was heading for a free-for-all in the marketplace, WFS quickly pruned its bloated ranks by a third and began to innovate with a vengeance. Then, starting in late 1992, WFS began to take on non-IBM business — and netted $7 million from outsiders in 1993. On the one hand, WFS is encouraged to do as much business as possible outside IBM. On the other hand, the 13 so-called Baby Blues may choose their own benefits providers, from IBM or elsewhere.

### A Wealth of New Species

In this brief review we've seen:

■ "Companies" with a couple of people (B&B Communications West, Against All Odds Productions, InterSolve Group) which build significant market positions while subcontracting almost everything.

■ Networks formed (National Network of Estate Planning Attorneys), which add to the clout (and market value) of scattered, independent contractors.

■ Groups spinning out of big firms, gutting the big firm's core competence and offering precious parts of previously bundled services to clients (the Leap Partnership — unbundled creative advertising services); and prospering service industries that encompass manufacturers' former core competence areas, but attract the best and the brightest to more sprightly settings (the shift to independent engineering-service providers).

■ Companies (Kennametal, Lane Group, IBM) taking internal staff functions (J.I.T. inventory management, training, benefits provision) and creating for-profit arms that at times take over customers' or even competitors' inhouse staff activities (Kennametal runs customers' toolrooms); likewise, formerly captive customers (IBM's business units in the case of WFS) are permitted to shop around for "staff" services.

■ Companies (Baxter I.V., Andersen CFM) taking a product and wrapping a service around it so that they become turnkey service providers to their customers (hospital pharmacies in Baxter I.V.'s case).

■ Companies (IBM, Ralston Purina) offering a formerly sacrosanct core-competence line activity (manufacturing) as a service to outsiders, including archrivals.

■ Companies (Kingston Technology) so completely entwined with core-competence providers (Kingston's manufacturers) that they can provide customized, just-in-time service to customers so far beyond the norm that it, de facto, reinvents an industry.

Which leads to these questions:

■ Can somebody handle any of your "service packages" better than you can? If the answer is "yes" (Professional Parking Services), seriously consider outsourcing.

■ Can you extend your staff services (Kennametal inventory management, Lane Group training, IBM employee benefits) to a customer's or competitor's shop?

■ Can you leverage your core line competence (Ralston Purina) by selling it to outsiders including competitors?

■ Can you routinely refresh your few remaining core-competence areas by using outsiders extensively (Apple)?

■ Can you "wrap-and-integrate" (add service to a product and deliver a larger, integrated package to customers, as Baxter does)?

Pause and reflect: If you buy into the relevance of this list of new organizational arrangements, and even shorter list of questions, then you have: (1) completely redefined what an "organization" is/can be; and (2) cut the legs out from under traditional notions of business strategy. In short, life becomes a permanent floating crap game and the answer to "Is there a there there?" becomes elusive to the point of being laughable (were it not for the trillions of dollars of jitterbugging global wealth at stake).

## Toward Total Interconnection

But when it comes to the destruction of all those old walls, there's even more on the horizon. As change accelerates and network relationships gain in importance, a special new form of wraparound service — keeping everyone in constant touch with everyone else — becomes an ever more valuable part of companies' product/service packages.

"Introducing TotalTrack. It's like getting live broadcasts from the scene of your package" — so read a full-page ad in *USA Today* placed by UPS in early 1993. Until recently, Federal Express was giving UPS fits. Though often more expensive, FedEx's phenomenally sophisticated tracking system enabled clients to know where a package was at a moment's notice. In today's connected, drum-tight commercial world, that's as important as getting the thing there. UPS has spent billions catching up.

In fact, the speedy-parcel-service business has more or less boiled down to a Spielberg-like war between PowerShips and MaxiShips. As of September 1993, the *Wall Street Journal* reported, FedEx had given 26,500 PowerShip tracking terminals and software to big customers. By placing PowerShips at Disney Stores, FedEx has vaulted its share of that client's quick-parcel-delivery business from 60 percent to 95 percent. Johnny-come-lately UPS has so far placed 15,000 MaxiShips with clients, and reports that doing so increases its share of express business, on average, 20 percent. "The more information intensive your service becomes," a UPS exec told the *Journal*, "the more valuable it is to customers." And there's lots more to come. Customers are now clamoring for integrated, one-source, real-time tracking for all shipment and inventory-management services.

Then there's EDS, offering 10,000 General Motors dealers (already hooked up with each other and the parent via the GM/Hughes "dealer satellite network") something called Dealerline. This includes subsystems labeled Partsline, Businessline, Serviceline, and Salesline. Everyone will be chatting up everyone else. There are intra- and interdepartmental nets within the dealership; there are also direct links to the General Motors Acceptance Corporation, outside-credit bureaus, GM parts-distribution centers, parts plants, GM factories, GM zone offices, and other GM dealers. The works, in other words.

Or consider the professional service firm Coopers & Lybrand, which recently introduced TNN, the Tax News Network. This is C&L's way of reaching into its clients' operations. The live communications channel offers regularly updated programs, according to its spiffy, four-color marketing brochure, such as "weekly C&L briefings on key tax developments," "tax highlight/summaries from tax analysts," "federal tax perspective online," "multi-state tax perspective online," "benefits perspective online," "DowVision," "tax notes today," "state tax notes," and "tax notes international." Several of these services are already interactive, though there's lots more to come with the advent of new multimedia technologies.

Such services are, as one observer put it, changing the nature of provider-buyer communication from "monologue to real-time, 24-hours-a-day, global dialogue." The bigger point is that "wrinkles" like these are becoming the most valuable parts of service or product offerings — and the best (only?) way to secure your pitons and gain a sustainable competitive advantage in a fickle marketplace.

## And Then Some

Total integration indeed. But there's even more than more. The last words (for now) go to an early-1994 television ad for MCI, recited by 11-year-old Academy Award winner Anna Paquin:

> There will be a road.
> It will not connect two points.
> It will connect all points.
> Its speed limit will be the speed of light.
> It will not go from here to there.
> There will be no more there.
> We will all only be here.

Hmmm. Or aaarrrggghhh?

## To Describe It Is Not to Do It

Describing the new network forms of organizing is one thing (and no mean feat), but getting there is another. Networking is life itself for many leading-edge firms. For MCI, as for Apple, the ability to create — then manage and then disintegrate — networks of assorted sizes and flavors is arguably core competence No. 1. MCI *is* the various networks it participates in.

The devil, as always, is in the details. I smiled when I read an article about the network software company Novell and came across the title of one of its senior officers. Darrell Miller's calling card reads "Executive Vice President of Strategic Relationships." Telling, eh?

If you're serious about corporation as Rolodex and alliance creation and management, then putting the necessary knitting skills at the top of the strategic agenda is job one. A title like Miller's suggests that Novell takes this stuff very seriously. Novell, Apple, MCI, Federal Express, and a few others are, simply, professional weavers of spider's webs.

One more word on words. David Kelley, chief of the potent industrial design firm IDEO, begs employees not to talk about "outsourcing." And though he doesn't go as far as CNN's Ted Turner, whose obsession for globalism includes fining employees who utter the word "foreign," Kelley does strongly urge the use of "out-

> ### TRUTH IN NUMBERS
>
> **Alison Peterson, networker**
>
> internal activities, 21%
> end-user issues, 5%
> network partners, 74%

partnering." Sure, it's only a word — but, then, words are about the only things that distinguish us humans from our hairy ancestors.

Well, no. One of the tiny companies inside my small company was until recently run by Alison Peterson. I asked her in 1992 to record, for a week, 15-minute chunks of the way she spent her time. She and her company do business via a series of projects invariably involving alliance partners, tiny to huge.

Alliance making and maintenance are the company's strategy. She did it well, and the chief reason popped out unmistakably from the calendar she kept for me. During the week she tracked, Alison spent 8 percent of her time on administration within her own company; another 13 percent working with members of sister companies in our outfit; and about 5 percent went to end-user customers (most of our contact with them comes via distributors). The remainder, 74 percent (seven hours a day), was spent with outside contractors and venture partners. Want to get good at something? Want to put it at the top of your strategic agenda? Your calendar doesn't lie. It clearly says you're serious. Or not.

## That Danged T-Word, Again

When we discussed going far beyond empowerment and turning each employee into a business, we stumbled on the missing link: trust, or the absence thereof. In a firm that commits almost all authority to the front line, it's trust or bust.

Trust is also the oft-ignored glue that holds the newfangled virtual organization together. "The thing that nobody talks about is the profound role of trust," Xerox chief scientist John Seely Brown told *Upside*. "One of the problems with these virtual corporations is that people forget the fact that an alliance lasts for a year or so before it ends. What is left behind is a set of experiences. If those experiences led to a shared understanding and trust between the group that you were just working with and yourself, then you have the basis for future work with them. But the virtual corporation ain't gonna work unless you have a growing web of trust."

Once more, to say it is not to do it. That's for sure. Time spent, language ("outpartnering" for "outsourcing"), and hierarchical importance (EVP of strategic relationships) help. But much more must be done on working with "outsiders" as trusted comrades in arms. For a first-rate discussion of this classic and novel topic, you'll do no better than *The TeamNet Factor*, by longtime networkers Jessica Lipnack and Jeffrey Stamps.

## One for the Books

Sometimes these newly emerging organizational forms make one's head spin. To speed innovation, Australia recently created, from whole cloth, a full-blown competitor to Australian Telecoms. The new firm is called Optus Communications. In telecommunications today, information technology is the core competence. So how did Optus, with the benefit of a fresh start, decide to structure its information-systems activities?

Very differently.

At this already big company, the permanent information-systems staff numbers only 23. To perform its information-systems work, Optus created a contracting organization — a stand-alone company called Optus Prime Contract Organization, or OPCO. The OPCO "staff" consists of 220 independent-contractor specialists, who find solutions to customer/company needs, appoint managers to oversee the projects, and pick appropriate external subcontractors to do the work. OPCO even has its own board of directors, including a member from Digital Equipment, Optus's prime subcontractor for information technology. Talk about a wild and woolly — as well as exceptionally flexible and creative — way to execute a/the core-competence task. This one takes the cake. So far.

## Let Your Imagination Soar!

Brenda Brimage, Rick Smolan, the Leap Partnership, Baxter, Draeger's, Optus. Think about "organizing," take the cover off your brain,

**outsourcing—▶outpartnering**

and let your imagination soar. If you can conjure up new ways of working (the InterSolve "talent bank" and its client, First Interstate Bancorp), you can probably make them happen.

Oxford University business school dean Douglas Hague scolds other universities for not delivering education that meets the needs of changing times: i.e., instantly available, instantly tailorable to increasingly divergent student needs. Taking a keynote from Charles Handy's shamrock organizational model, Hague imagines the ideal university staffed mainly with "core academics," well paid, institutional stars who would cadge a ride on the information highway system and offer their lectures and services worldwide. To help them, the university would contract with "media experts" who would aid the stars in packaging and transmitting their material in a variety of ways.

Then there will be "academic impresarios," serving the university "by bringing in leading academics and practitioners — in the flesh, or on a screen — and presenting them to 'students.'" Last but not least are junior teachers, who back up both the stars and academic impresarios and act as "educational consultants." The frontline consultants' role, Hague speculates, "will be to help each student to use personal contact with academics and with visitors from outside the university — as well as the growing stock of books, films, videotapes, and databases — to pursue his or her 'own' education as effectively as possible."

The university, per Hague's *Beyond Universities: A New Republic of the Intellect,* becomes a talent bank and a library, which can be applied across space and time to serve the individual needs of youngsters and seasoned workers bent upon continuous above-the-shoulders improvement. A minority of "students" would be chasing a degree. Even fewer would pursue their needs in a classroom or on a campus. Networked brainfood on demand (anytime, anywhere, for anyone) becomes an (the?) essential element of our national economic infrastructure.

Will such a vision ever become a reality? I don't know. It's the provocative and heretical nature of the operation that lit me up. Sadly, most of our organizational forms, except maybe in places like Silicon Valley or Hollywood, thoroughly lack imagination. And it's my best guess that wild imagination in creating organizational shapes and styles will be at least as important to marketplace victory as imagination in creating products and services per se.

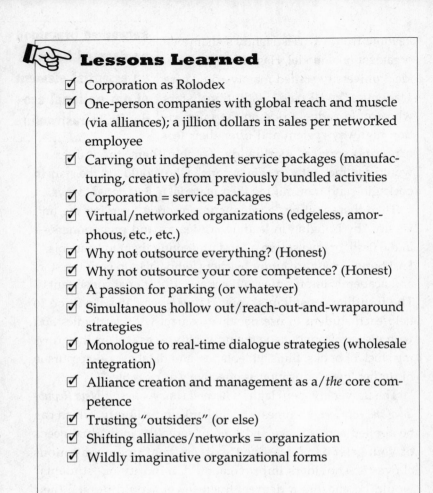

## Lessons Learned

- ☑ Corporation as Rolodex
- ☑ One-person companies with global reach and muscle (via alliances); a jillion dollars in sales per networked employee
- ☑ Carving out independent service packages (manufacturing, creative) from previously bundled activities
- ☑ Corporation = service packages
- ☑ Virtual/networked organizations (edgeless, amorphous, etc., etc.)
- ☑ Why not outsource everything? (Honest)
- ☑ Why not outsource your core competence? (Honest)
- ☑ A passion for parking (or whatever)
- ☑ Simultaneous hollow out/reach-out-and-wraparound strategies
- ☑ Monologue to real-time dialogue strategies (wholesale integration)
- ☑ Alliance creation and management as a/*the* core competence
- ☑ Trusting "outsiders" (or else)
- ☑ Shifting alliances/networks = organization
- ☑ Wildly imaginative organizational forms

### Reprise 1: So Is There a There There?

At one of my seminars, a Federal Express officer exclaimed, "Subcontract everything but your soul!"

I agree. But what is soul? Where do you find it? Will you know it when you see it? And is there any of it left at those outsource-crazy firms I've talked about?

Though there are no short and easy answers, here are a few soul tips:

1. The site of soul is changing. Increasingly, soul does not reside in the ownership of a technology or functional skill. Soul

can be in such skills as alliance management (MCI, Apple), the ability to leverage knowledge (Hague on universities; also see the next chapter), logistics and distribution (Baxter International), information systems (Wal-Mart, FedEx, American Airlines, Citicorp). More and more, soul is "horizontal," a key process skill linked back to suppliers and forward to distributors and ultimate users.

2. Soul *can* be outsourced. Recall the Optus case, where soul is clearly (is it ever really clear?) information-systems activities. To stay flexible and innovative, Optus decided to subcontract most of its soul in order to keep it fresh (more soulful?) in a fast-changing marketplace.

3. Soul today, soup tomorrow. Today's valuable soul is tomorrow's millstone. Soul ages, sours, gets copied, and needs changing, too. If you don't believe me, just ask an IBMer — if you can find one.

4. It is true that, at some point, there's no "there" (critical mass around anything) anymore. On the other hand, critical mass no longer demands ownership of people or assets. How about "virtual soul"? That is, a dormant network that can be awakened overnight as needed. Isn't that the secret to Hollywood productions? And isn't Hollywood a pretty good virtual model for tomorrow's everything? I think so. (And its positive balance of trade suggests that I'm not whistling Dixie.)

### Reprise 2: The Professional Service Firm Model

It turns out that we have superb models — and on a large scale — of "virtual firms." They've been with us for a long time, on the economy's periphery. Now they are center stage.

The winner is . . . professional service firms.

Once, not so long ago, they were considered parasites (accountants, consultants, etc.), head workers

**HOLLYWOOD = VIRTUAL MODEL**

living off the honest sweat of more manly brows. (Pure head work — the money lenders expunged from the temple, "college boys" in heavy industrial companies after World War II — has always been suspect.) Now, head work is the real work and the former "there" (brawn work) is fast becoming parasitical.

So, then, we have these old-but-new exemplars:

■ Pure knowledge ventures (more intellect, less materials; only asset is the human imagination) — nothing is owned; enormous value is created, all above the shoulders

■ Virtual organizations — few professional service-firm workers are "at home" (in the office) on any given day; and when a sizable professional service firm wins a job, it quickly cobbles together a network/project team composed of the best players from around the globe

■ Limitless in size — EDS sports about 80,000 employees, most working on customer sites in 10- to 15-person teams

■ Accountable — organizing around discrete projects provides an automatic focus on results, even though the "assets" are dispersed all over hell and gone

There are good and bad professional service firms, profitable ones and flops, creative ones and duds. (See *Liberation Management*, chapters 10 to 14, for an extensive discussion of project and professional service firms.) In any event, the professional-services/virtual-organizations model is, increasingly, the way the world's work is getting done. It is the model from which all of us can (must) learn.

Here's the deal, like it or not, from Texas Instruments' Steve Truett and EDS's Tom Barrett, writing in *Cyberspace*:

> The traditional equation of "labor + raw materials = economic success" is rapidly changing as American businesses approach the global, highly competitive markets of the twenty-first century. Strategic advantage now lies in the acquisition and control of information. . . . Corporations . . . are becoming bewilderingly diverse and geographically far-flung. The ability to bring dispersed assets effectively to bear on a single project or opportunity is becoming increasingly difficult. . . .

The lumbering bureaucracies of this century will be replaced by fluid, interdependent groups of problem solvers. . . . We believe that cyberspace technology will be a primary drive toward new corporate architectures. The technology will enable multidimensional, professional interaction and natural, intuitive work group formation. The technology will evolve to provide enterprises with what we call Corporate Virtual Workspaces (CVWs) as highly productive replacements for current work environments. . . . Having no need for physical facilities other than the system hosting the CVW, the cyberspace corporation will exist entirely in cyberspace.

With little need for startup capital, cyberspace corporations will form quickly around an individual or group of individuals who have identified an opportunity and formulated a market plan. Additional cyberspace workers will quickly be gathered from previous endeavors or new talent will be recruited. Profits shares will be apportioned across participating members.

The cyberspace corporation may provide a single product or service and then disband, or it may be formed with a longer-term vision and remain to serve the product's market. Other cyberspace firms may specialize in assuming ongoing maintenance of products if the developer decides to pursue other market opportunities.

Cyberspace corporations will be very fast-acting and transient. They will be composed of bright, creative, high-tech nomads who will coalesce into work units for dynamic market opportunities. Personnel turnover will be high as tasks are completed and cyberspace workers decide to migrate to other opportunities. As new corporations form, cyberspace workers may find themselves working periodically with the same people. A very productive informal network will form as cyberspace workers leverage their rich set of experiences and contacts.

That's a mouthful. But it's a brainful, too. And practical. Consider it, alone and with colleagues. If you smirk, you've got a problem. The old model of "own it to control it," "work in one place" is death in today's markets. The new model of "pick and polish your core competence" is probably out of date, too. And, note, this cyberspacial description takes us far beyond today's darling, the neo-Taylorist reengineering approach.

Ah yes, cyberspacial. But, then, it's a cyberspacial world. Remember: crazy times, crazy organizations.

---

### T.T.D. (Things to Do) and Q.T.A. (Questions to Answer)

❶ Does work in your organization mean nine to five? At a desk? In one room? Engaging mostly insiders? If so, why? How many people in your unit are working at home at least one day a week? How about you? Why? Why not?

❷ What are sales per employee at your firm? In your unit? Is the Apple, let alone Kingston Technology or Nintendo, level unthinkable? Are you sure?

❸ Imagine your firm as a collection of "service packages." Make a list of them (it should total 100 percent of what you do). Look for alternative sources for each. Can you find them? No? Try again! Close to home? Far, far away? Keep trying!

❹ Look again at the list of internal-service packages. In the sense of IBM (WFS, manufacturing), Kennametal, and the Lane Group. Can you imagine commercializing, within the next 18 months, each of those services (each, as in every one) and selling them to customers, including competitors? If not, try again! And again!

❺ Per Baxter I.V. (Patient-specific . . .), Andersen CFM, and Draeger's, can you imagine adding significant service "wraparounds" to every product or service, which will intertwine you and your customers? To the point of running significant parts of what are now your customers' businesses?

❻ Per UPS, FedEx, EDS-GM, and Coopers & Lybrand, can you imagine dense information linkages with your customers — that become a core part of your product and service offerings? (Remember, UPS found that doing it was worth billions; not doing it was death.)

❼ Examine the Optus method of introducing innovation and flexibility into a core competence. Does it apply to your organization? Are you outsourcing a significant share of your core-competence areas in order to keep them fresh? If not, why not? On the other side of the same coin, are you willing to sell stand-alone core-competence skills (e.g., manufacturing at Ralston Purina) to archrivals? If not, why not? (Hint: No matter how hard you try, if you don't open them to the market's gusts, they atrophy.)

❽ Do you have an Executive Vice President for Strategic Relationships? Should you?

❾ Is alliance creation and maintenance a core skill in your firm? Should it be? Is there widespread training in "partnering" throughout your firm? Are those who specialize in alliance/relationship/partnering management respected in your organization?

❿ Can you imagine a high-revenue, high-impact company with just a couple of employees? (Rick Smolan, Brenda Brimage.) Try imagining your unit with just two (or one) full-time workers. Is it really out of the question?

⓫ Do you take a shine to the professional service firm as new exemplar? (For everyone.) If not, go back to Chapter 1

## How many people in your unit.........

(yes, "more intellect . . ."). If you do buy the idea, undertake a systematic study of these often dismissed ("not relevant to us") firms.

⑫ Consider Hague's university in the new republic of the intellect, with star academics, media advisors, academic impresarios, educational consultants, etc. Go off to the mountaintop or seaside (literally) and think about "organization." What is your firm really up to? Can you imagine a model for your group/firm/industry that's as wild and woolly as Hague's invention? How much of your thinking time goes into wholesale re-conception of organizational arrangements? Consider creating an outside advisory board of people — from the arts, science-fiction writers, etc. — to help you imagine the unimaginable. Flights of fancy are the most practical work of enterprise these days.

**....work at home at least one day a week?**

Most of the work in advanced economies **(brainwork)** will be done by networks of itinerants, who gather from hither and thither, do their thing, and disband. It's certainly not organization as we've known it. Well, not organization as the Fortune 500 have practiced it; let's put it that way. But it is the path taken by Hollywood, professional-service firms, universities, and other repositories of (among other things) purely intellectual talent. In any event, even if you choke over the more extreme forms of discombobulation, it's certainly clear that do-it-all corporations are dinosaurs. The mad scramble to hollow and expand, to learn how to build (mostly) temporary alliances is on. **Victory will go to the highly imaginative and those least fettered by conventional notions of what an organization has to be.**

## CHAPTER 6

BEYOND REENGINEERING

# CREATING A CORPORATE TALK SHOW

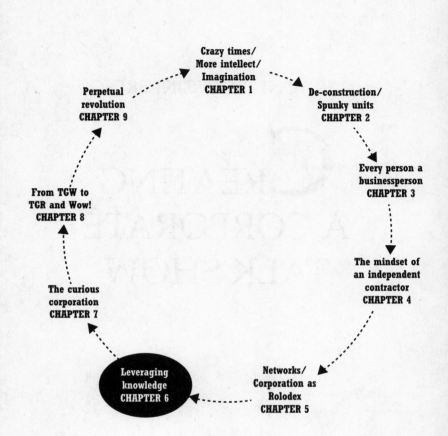

Crazy times/
More intellect/
Imagination
CHAPTER 1

De-construction/
Spunky units
CHAPTER 2

Perpetual
revolution
CHAPTER 9

Every person a
businessperson
CHAPTER 3

From TGW to
TGR and Wow!
CHAPTER 8

The mindset of
an independent
contractor
CHAPTER 4

The curious
corporation
CHAPTER 7

Leveraging
knowledge
CHAPTER 6

Networks/
Corporation as
Rolodex
CHAPTER 5

Disembodied corporations are the new and necessary "it" (Chapter 5). There's no (conventional) there there, or at least it's devilishly elusive. But don't forget, "more intellect, less materials." An economy based on knowledge is, by definition, more disembodied (less materials) and more elusive. But there is a new there there: knowledge per se. Much of the trick of creating value, then, becomes capturing and applying knowledge — on the fly, and from a transient network (corporate virtual workspace, whatever). Capturing and applying knowledge requires a whole new set of organizing skills, and more: a whole new way of conceiving organizations. The Corporation as Rolodex is fine as far as it goes, but we need to go farther: the Corporation as Ongoing Talk Show? **Larry King as prototypical CEO?** Or maybe Oprah (who, after all, does net an estimated $30 million a year)?

**"Nations**

**will**

**wither,**

**knowledge**

**will**

**triumph."**

**Alvin and Heidi Toffler**

**"W**e can no longer compete on the cost of labor with countries like China," Carlo de Benedetti, chief executive of Italy's Olivetti, told the *Wall Street Journal Europe*. "What we have to leverage is our know-how."

Whoops! Not all of de Benedetti's leveraging may have taken place aboveboard. Olivetti is one of many big Italian companies that, along with the politicians they bribed, are caught up in a raging legal and political scandal. But, unintended irony aside, de Benedetti's remarks on the importance of leveraging knowledge strike a powerful note of truth.

He's not the only person to have taken note. "Nations will wither, knowledge will triumph," Alvin and Heidi Toffler write in the *New York Times* (in an article aptly titled "Societies at Hyper-Speed"). "The modern knowledge economy turns on the better use of knowledge," says Xerox's John Seely Brown. Obvious? Yes, but no less powerful for being so. And remember, remember: "more intellect, less materials," "only factory asset is the human imagination."

Knowledge is indisputably the primary basis for value-added in today's companies. But how do we continuously develop, utilize, and leverage knowledge within the company? Especially within "companies" that are more and more ephemeral (see the last chapter)?

Mostly the process has been catch-as-catch-can. Many agree that developing, using, and leveraging knowledge is essential. But we're uncertain and unagreed, to say the least, on how to do a good job at it.

## Small = Big Via Knowledge at ABB

Xerox's Seely Brown seemingly dismisses the virtual organization (though, speaking of irony, he's invented many of the electronic networking tools that enabled its birth) and insists that big corporations may have lurking within them a new basis for advantage in the knowledge-based economy. "The key," he says, "is the ability to learn. The more people you have and the faster you can learn, the more you can capitalize on this."

Seely Brown has a soul mate in Percy Barnevik. Barnevik, you'll recall from Chapter 2, broke ABB into thousands of modest-size units, claiming that doing so was the only way to engender sufficient entrepreneurial zeal to compete in markets that were perpetually clogged by surplus supply. If such zeal was his avowed goal, why didn't he just sell the units off to their managers? He didn't, because Barnevik understands that together the units know more than they could as separate enterprises. It's not that bigger is better; smarter is better, and bigger has the potential (no more) of being smarter.

> **"We are a collection of local businesses with intense global coordination."**
>
> **Sune Karlsson**

Take ABB's Power Transformers business. With revenue of $1 billion, it's four times larger than its closest global competitor. Old-fashioned market muscle through manufacturing scale economics? Hardly. Power Transformers consists of some 25 highly autonomous operations in 17 different countries, and the average local operation is smaller than its local competitor. What, then, makes the ABB Power Transformers units powerful competitors? It's obviously not their size. It's what they potentially know. "We aren't a global business," Power Transformers boss Sune Karlsson told the *Harvard Business Review*. "We are a collection of local businesses with intense global coordination. . . . Our most important strength is that we have 25 factories around the world, each with its own president, design manager, marketing manager, and production manager. These people are working on the same problems and opportunities day after day, year after year, and learning a tremendous amount. We want to create a process of continuous expertise transfer. If we do, that's a source of advantage none of our rivals can match."

Karlsson and Barnevik are betting the future of Power Transformers — and ABB itself — on that enormous "if" above, on the company's potential to learn, develop, and share knowledge among units and across borders.

## The ABB Paradox

Has the paradox at ABB struck you as it struck me? On the one hand, Barnevik radically decentralized the company, torched the fat, and awarded unusual autonomy to several thousand 90 percent entrepreneurs operating profit-and-loss centers close to the front line. For them, it's perform or else. Yet Karlsson and Barnevik are also betting on the company's ability to get these busier-than-the-devil (no central staff support, remember), do-or-die units to cooperate in sharing their knowledge.

To wit: Suppose an Australian unit of Power Transformers has a 96-hour deadline to submit a proposal for a $20 million job. Its German counterpart won just such a bid six months ago, thanks to a clever chief engineer. ABB's corporate strategy (new big = network of small with intense global coordination) will work only if the stressed-out German engineer, in his own do-or-die unit, is willing to drop what he's doing, board a plane, and fly overnight to the aid of his Australian counterpart. And why would he? Developing the right incentives for that kind of cooperative behavior is a — or should I say the — key task Karlsson and Barnevik confront.

Sure, sophisticated electronic networks can help — more later. But the issue, make no mistake, is cultural: how to inculcate a strong norm of sharing among the just-made-independent. Only then can the electronic doodads earn back their hefty price tags.

I'd like to say I'm confident Karlsson's and Barnevik's bet will pay off, but I'd be fibbing. It will pay off only if and when frantic ABB people believe that those who pause today to give to the network will get help in return tomorrow, when they're in need.

That's the way it was at McKinsey & Co., where I worked in the 70s. We were always racing to keep up with the demands of the day; and, moreover, performance on the current project was the make-or-break issue. Yet it was also clearly understood (via "culture" and evaluation schemes) that to get ahead you helped others and developed a reputation for doing so, no matter how much pain was involved.

> **ABB'S PARADOX**
>
> **Perform, as an independent unit, or else**
>
> **and**
>
> **Power stems from constant cooperation among units**

I naively assumed that a similar atmosphere existed in most companies. My mistake. It didn't and doesn't. I've learned that few professional service firms, never mind steel mills, have a knowledge-sharing culture. How to create such a culture, especially with layoffs growing and survivors' workloads exploding, is one of the biggest conundrums that managements, bent on creating value from dispersed knowledge, face today.

### The Greater Paradox

The paradox at ABB is actually a general one. If you flip through the prior chapters, you'll discover I've been talking out of both sides of my mouth.

Out of one side, I've discussed the decimation of central staffs — the elimination of most staff professionals and the transfer of most of the rest to the front lines. Out of the other side, I've asserted that expertise, brainware, and towering competence are more essential than ever to competitive success. I've ripped expertise from its traditional home in the corporate tower; and simultaneously I've proclaimed its primacy. What gives?

The answer is that just because brainware is paramount does not mean it has to be housed in a tall building where the CEO and his top lieutenants hang their hats (and, soon enough — if they don't catch on to the brainware revolution — their heads as well).

John Thompson, former chairman of Computer Sciences Corp. (CSC) Europe, understands. He began his commentary in the firm's 1991 annual report with these surprising words: "We find little added value in a headquarters staff 'coordinating' transnational activities, so we have closed our former headquarters office in Brussels; those functions which provide specialized services are now located in whichever line organization suits them."

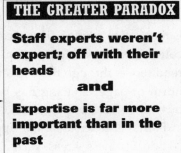

**THE GREATER PARADOX**

**Staff experts weren't expert; off with their heads**

**and**

**Expertise is far more important than in the past**

I ran into Thompson later, during a break at one of my seminars, and remarked that while I loved the part of his commentary that reported the demise of the corporate headquarters, I assumed he had meant it metaphorically. Thompson took my arm and guided me to three empty seats in the room. "Tom," he said, "I brought my two key staffers with me today. We don't have a headquarters, really. Or, rather, our headquarters for the day are these three chairs." He was serious and speaking literally.

Consider Thompson's words carefully. He eliminated the headquarters building, but he hardly said that the skills therein were unimportant. What he said was that the people with necessary skills could work more efficiently and effectively located in the appropriate line organization. "We still need central competence in, say, banking," his annual report message continued, "but we maintain that competence wherever our banking specialists live, and they in turn network with others in each of our country organizations. Rather than gathering all that competence together in some central headquarters, we disperse it across Europe."

"Central" is not a dirty word for Thompson. Central competence is more necessary than ever, central headquarters less so than ever. Expertise is all that he sells, but experts don't have to live cheek-by-jowl in a Brussels spire and devote large chunks

of their days to playing politics and brown-nosing nearby senior management. They should be in the field, where their expertise is most often needed. They "centralize" — that is, leverage their collective knowledge and quickly bring it to bear where it's required — through the network (assuming, once again, that the norm of eager sharing has been firmly established amongst busy, dispersed professionals).

Barnevik takes a similar approach throughout ABB. Each of 60-odd Business Areas, such as Power Transformers, employs a tiny handful of staffer-experts. But these full- or part-time staffers spend most of their time on the road, participating directly in the knowledge-transfer business. Where are their "home" offices? They may change from year to year. But one thing doesn't change: None of the Business Area staffers works at the corporate headquarters in Zurich. Instead, they tend to gather where the action is at the moment. For instance, one Business Area staff relocated itself from Sweden to Germany to the United States in the space of four years as the center of gravity of the global market shifted among regions.

Expertise? It's more important than ever. (That's what the hell this book is all about.) Where does it live? Wherever it's needed for as long as it's needed. How does it move? In person or over the network, whichever works better. If . . .

### Bob Buckman's Scary Observation

If you get those dratted incentives right, as Bob Buckman knows. He runs the $250 million Buckman Labs, a successful, innovative speciality chemical company with headquarters in Memphis, Tennessee. The corporation is privately owned, but Buckman wanted to get a handle on its market value. An estimate provided by a New York investment banking firm stunned him. Though his is a tangibles company, the financiers pegged its market value at about $175 million more than the value of its hard assets. Most companies these days, even manufacturers, are worth more than the value of their hard assets, but this was a lot more.

Buckman imagined that much of that $175 million could be attributed to the firm's "knowledge." Fine. But what's happening to that knowledge? Is it growing? Is it shrinking? Is it becoming obsolete? Where is it? Buckman couldn't answer any of these questions. All he could say was that this golden cache of knowledge was batting around somewhere in the brains of 1,000-odd Buckman folks who were serving various industries in 70 countries. It suddenly seemed imperative to Buckman to get a better handle on something so valuable.

Thus began Bob Buckman's passionate pilgrimage in pursuit of knowledge at Buckman Labs. Knowledge as an asset demands management, and Buckman has assigned all information-services activities at the company to the aptly named Knowledge Transfer Department. The R&D-intense firm now spends more on information systems that support knowledge transfer than on R&D. And that's exactly the way Bob Buckman wants it.

## All Hail the "Director of Knowledge Management"

"As we move toward the chaos of the future," Buckman said in a speech to his company's marketers, "the progress of Buckman Labs relative to other companies will be determined by the growth in the value of knowledge that exists within the company. The acceleration of knowledge transfer is how we will grow this collection of individuals we call Buckman Labs into what it can be. Our strategic advantage lies in the leverage of knowledge."

"The network is the whole thing," Buckman later told me. "It should connect everybody in the organization to everybody outside the organization, and to each other. If you don't let the person on the front line, who is generating the cash flow for the company, have the same connectivity as the CEO, you don't have the connectivity necessary to strategically leverage knowledge."

But, again, people don't instinctively share information. They're used to hoarding it. In our hierarchical organizations, information is power. If I know something you don't, I have an advantage. If I let go too easily, I lose my advantage. How, then, does one "manage" the process of transferring knowledge?

Part of the answer at Buckman Labs has been the creation of electronic "technical forums," usually one for each industry the company serves. Each technical forum, or virtual staff function (to extend the imagery of the last chapter), has a Section Leader, who acts as host. (Get used to that last word.) Where do section leaders live? Buckman's approach is the same as CSC's or ABB's: wherever it makes sense. Section leaders more or less appoint themselves and then do their thing from Australia, South Africa, or Memphis, Tennessee.

Actually, only one part of the network resides at Buckman's Memphis headquarters. That's a seven-person Technical Information Center, which acts as system coordinator, available 24 hours a day, to get anyone in touch with anyone in the cause of helping solve a customer problem as quickly as possible.

Bob Buckman, like ABB's Sune Karlsson, realizes that getting the carrots and sticks right is imperative to igniting a network. "The most powerful individuals in the antibureaucratic future of Buckman Labs," he insists (to anyone and everyone he collars, again and again and again), "will be those who do the best job of transferring knowledge to others." That is, the incentive, evaluation, and promotion system at Buckman Labs, along with the CEO, will recognize and honor those who do the best job of sharing nuggets with others — and ignore or punish those who don't.

Despite what the techno-experts might tell you, then, knowledge management is not primarily a bits-and-bytes issue. Some 17,000 consultants and accountants at Price Waterhouse are using Lotus Development's new workgroup technology system, Notes. Although Notes is state-of-the-art software, *CIO* magazine concludes that so far Price Waterhouse isn't using it in a very interesting way.

Price Waterhouse consultants within a specialty mostly use the software to send messages among themselves. It's a start, but in effect amounts to using Notes as an expensive e-mail system, according to MIT professor Wanda Orlikowski, who's done research at Price Waterhouse. "It isn't the same thing as collaboratively working together on a joint project," she claims. And *CIO* reporter Thomas Kiely adds that "fostering the shared workgroup vision that lies behind Notes has proved elusive" at the giant

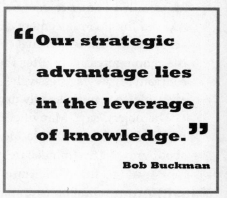

**"Our strategic advantage lies in the leverage of knowledge."**

**Bob Buckman**

accountancy. For the clever software (called groupware) to have value, then, people have to be motivated to fully exploit its latent power.

McKinsey & Co. appears to have moved farther down the right road. The company's avowed intention, says Brook Manville, who until a recent promotion was the Director of Knowledge Management at McKinsey, is to use electronic networks (now including Notes) as one tool supporting a fundamental transformation of the company's professional practice — and culture.

McKinsey has typically thrown very bright, energetic folks at a client project. Manville calls it the "we're-smarter-than-everyone-else-and-that's-enough-to-maintain-our-advantage strategy." But with others catching up, including clients, the logical next step, according to Manville, is to leverage consultant experience. That means moving beyond the traditional catch as catch can approach, and systematically developing and sharing institutional knowledge garnered from the roughly 1,500 projects

McKinsey completes each year.

(Manville's immersion in knowledge management is instructive. He was originally asked to work on a modest-priority project that amounted to spiffing up McKinsey's library activities. It evolved into nothing less than the first strategic repositioning of the company in decades.)

Knowledge development at McKinsey orbits around roughly 30 so-called "practice centers" (in banking, technology, etc.). Akin to the floating centers of expertise at CSC Europe, these are volunteer-staffed, virtual communities of consultant-specialists who aggressively offer their know-how to the rest of the company. I say "aggressively" because they don't just make it available; they unabashedly market it.

The object, says Manville, is to create a "dynamic marketplace of readily available ideas." Each center "should think about growing its 'mindshare' with consultants throughout the firm," McKinsey executive Bill Matassoni adds. To this end, many of the centers measure how much internal customers use the material they offer. Some call queries from fellow consultants "sales leads," and a few centers even publish "bestseller lists" of case summaries and other documents most often requested.

> **Manville wants to turn McKinsey into a dynamic marketplace of readily available ideas.**

The McKinsey practice center that seems to have developed itself most is the Organization Performance Practice. It's one of the biggest, with about 70 volunteer consultant-specialists and a four-person support group (three McKinsey employees, one independent contractor) that runs the practice's Rapid Response Network.

This "central" RRN team (central in function, though it's in fact "headquartered" in three cities, none of which is corporate HQ, and in one member's spare bedroom) promises internal consultant-customers around the world a quick response to any query — usually in the form of pertinent documents retrieved from numerous databases and of referrals to appropriate experts. The human touch counts: Send too many documents, and the already besieged consultant is overwhelmed; send too few and she's disappointed. And each of several thousand staff professionals has a different definition of "how much is enough." Soft-pedaling issues like this one is the Achilles' heel of most knowledge-development programs.

To add more horsepower to the RRN (when will we start saying mindpower?), each McKinsey consultant in the Organization Performance Practice has agreed to act as an "on-call consultant" for a couple of weeks each year. On-call consultants, who still have their own work to do and no time to waste, nonetheless guarantee they'll respond within 24 hours to queries from any of 58 offices in 28 countries. Again, the RRN support staff's touch is decisive: They must not only serve the "customer," but also worry about "suppliers'" distinctive personalities (e.g., varying tolerance for overload among the on-call consultants).

The RRN staff also performs extensive follow-up and religiously tracks customer satisfaction. They even publish a dense, numbers-laden annual report on the practice's progress.

The point of formalizing the network to this extent is to get harried McKinsey consultants to take institutional knowledge development seriously: to use the firm's reservoir of knowledge routinely in their client work (and to make them feel guilty if they don't, Manville admits) and to take the time to replenish the reservoir. Frequent jawboning by management is part of the effort. Managers ceaselessly "talk up knowledge development as a professional responsibility," Manville says.

Beyond that, McKinsey is developing the larger cultural idea that measurable contributions to the knowledge base are a must for consultants' satisfactory performance evaluation. And major contributions to knowledge development also will become significant in promotion decisions, even to the company's top ranks.

Manville has barely begun, he acknowledges, to create a systematic knowledge-development culture at McKinsey, but he is asking the right questions and moving in the right direction.

Knowledge Management Я Us — it's a tough sell, even in a business like McKinsey's, where knowledge is understood to be paramount.

## Roping in Coopers & Lybrand's Couch Potatoes

Andy Zimmerman, at Coopers & Lybrand, is a nut on the topic of "user friendliness" and a soul mate of Manville's. Frustrated by the limits of purely technical solutions to knowledge-transfer problems, he modeled C&L's Knowledge Network, as it's called, on cable television. (Arthur Andersen calls its similar network, based on Notes, the Knowledge Exchange. Are you getting the idea?) The computer-based Knowledge Network features dozens of different "channels," including industry segments (automotive, banking, energy, etc.), C&L specialties (tax law, finance, etc.), and geographic regions. On each channel, users can tune into an assortment of specific "shows," each sponsored by a C&L expert in the field. (Zimmerman calls these in-house knowledge distributors "knowbodies" — more new language.) For example, every Tuesday at noon on the insurance channel, C&L consultants can read (in no more than 200 lines of text) about the latest changes in that industry. Each show stays on the system for a week, then is replaced.

Other selections allow users to read industry reports and order hard copies. But the most powerful and popular offerings are "talk shows." The network's Discuss channel provides more than 80 conferences focusing on professional topics — from mergers and acquisitions by client companies to federal taxes to general calls for help (known, what else? — as "help-wanted ads").

As with TV networks, the Knowledge Network's management follows the weekly "ratings," and tracks overall system usage. The networkers respond by tailoring future content to reflect the users' needs.

## Hooking users into C&L's Knowledge Network:

How helpful is all this? Vicky DeCoster, supervisor of the Reports Department in C&L's 66-person Omaha office, "hosts" (i.e., she created and now oversees) a nationwide discussion group for staffers who prepare client reports and bids. "I started the conference because working in a smaller, midwestern office, I felt isolated," she told my colleague Paul Cohen. "If I was stuck on a software problem, it might take three or four days for someone in another office to return my call — if I even knew whom to call." Now she gets an answer within a day, usually within an hour. "It makes a huge difference for clients," she says, "and if you have the motivation, you can take the network as far as you want."

Zimmerman is trying to spread DeCoster's attitude throughout C&L. "The potential of new technology," he told Cohen, "is to empower individuals and flatten the hierarchy. I've seen a technical-support person in Florida realize she could directly answer a managing partner's question on the network. We have senior managers having conversations with people around the world who, in a classic organization, would probably not get their phone calls returned. We see people creating new roles for themselves as knowledge workers."

What sticks out in any conversation with Zimmerman is his emphasis on the C&L network's anthropological characteristics. Technology enables the network, but practical incentives (the sticks and carrots) and imagination (the friendly cable-TV format and familiar TV language) fuel it. People use the network to exchange knowledge when it's worth their while and easy to do. Period.

### Ensembles of Interconnected Communities of Expertise

Bob Buckman has his electronically based "technical forums," Percy Barnevick his peripatetic Business Area staffers, McKinsey its virtual communities/Practice Centers (and formal facilita-

**"shows"..."knowledge"..."want ads"..."ratings"...**

NORMAN DOW

# It's simple... We either get used to thinking about the subtle processes of learning and sharing knowledge in dispersed, transient networks. Or we perish.

tors, like the RRN), Coopers & Lybrand its friendly, cable-TV look-alike computer network.

The Institute for Research on Learning, a spinoff from Xerox's Palo Alto Research Center, is almost alone in studying the emergence and power of such knowledge-development activities. The center's particularly felicitous term is "communities of practice," as it is used by, for instance, IRL's Susan Stucky. "Learning," she says, "is the process of becoming a member of a community of practice. The motivation to learn is the motivation to become a member."

Becoming a member of a community of practice is literally a requirement of modern-day job success. Nonmembers, IRL researchers insist, can't succeed in an age of knowledge. IRL has examined everything from airline operations centers to insurance companies. In the latter, for example, new insurance claims processors become effective to the extent that they are accepted into (and wish to join) a local community of practice. IRL's Etienne Wenger claims that a knowledge-age organization is nothing but "an ensemble of interconnected communities of practice." Nice.

Nice? Or New Age management-speak? Nice, I say again. It's simple: We either get used to thinking about the subtle processes of learning and sharing knowledge in dispersed, transient networks. Or we perish.

IRL finds that the most exciting communities of practice (which are crucial to innovation and corporate transformation) exist at the borders of organizations, attracting all sorts of characters. Notwithstanding McKinsey et al.'s efforts to formalize them, IRL nonetheless contends that such essential communities of practice can't be created or designed, but can only be discovered and supported.

The issue is critical. McKinsey's programmatic approach is invaluable to the firm's aim to systematically leverage knowledge. Yet it is a fact that quirky and seemingly random bits and pieces of knowledge from unlikely people and places will spark all important leaps of learning. Over time, this emergent knowledge and the informal communities of practice that contain it will stretch and distort the borders that McKinsey (or any organization) tries to maintain around formal practice centers. To overemphasize the formal structure and fail to nurture, as IRL would have it, such oddball connections would be disastrous.

(And more: The subtleties are overwhelming. IRL researchers have frequently discovered that apparently sensible reorganizations have destroyed a company's core competence by breaking up unsung, informal but crucial communities of practice that were essential to, say, the company's key technology. Zounds.)

## Work as Conversation

A laudatory article in *Training & Development* magazine about IRL was titled "The Search for the Poetry." Knowledge output and the poetry of networks are part of a dramatic shift in the way we think about work — work as conversation, business journalist Alan Webber has described it. In the *Harvard Business Review*, Webber wrote:

> Time was, if the boss caught you talking on the
> phone or hanging around the water cooler, he would

have said, "Stop talking and get to work!" Today, if you're *not* on the phone or talking with colleagues and customers, chances are you'll hear, "Start talking and get to work!" In the new economy, conversations are the most important form of work.

Conversations are the way knowledge workers discover what they know, share it with their colleagues, and in the process create new knowledge for the organization. The panoply of modern information and communications technology — for example, computers, faxes, e-mail — can help knowledge workers in this process. But all depends on the quality of the conversations that such technologies support.

Quality of conversation is precisely what most concerns Bob Buckman, Sune Karlsson, Andy Zimmerman, and Brook Manville. In fact, Webber suggests that Manville's erstwhile title, Director of Knowledge Management, is highfalutin. Why not, he asks, Director of Conversations or Internal Talk-Show Host?

Lovely. Why not?

Consider what technology guru Michael Schrage has written: "Real value in the sciences, the arts, [and] commerce . . . comes largely from the process of collaboration. What's more, the quality and quantity of meaningful collaboration often depends upon the tools used to create it. . . . Collaboration is like romance . . . it can't be routine and predictable. People collaborate precisely because they don't know how to — or can't — deal effectively with the challenges that face them as individuals. . . . The issue isn't communication or teamwork — it's the creation of value. Collaboration describes a process of value creation that our traditional structure of communication and teamwork can't achieve."

> **"Collaboration is like romance. It can't be routine and predictable."**
> **Michael Schrage**

Are these characterizations from experts like Webber ("work as conversation" and "internal talk-show host") and Schrage ("collaboration is like romance") just chitchat? I don't think so.

They indicate that technologists and others understand that an increasing number of people are worrying about out how to develop and use knowledge together, in real time, and across space and time; and they are quickly realizing that there's much more to the story than the electronic network's baud rate.

### Cybrarians and Virtual Communities

Tune into the nascent discussion of value through knowledge development, and you'll end up collecting tidbits from the darndest places. In early 1993, for instance, I received "The Cybrarians Manifesto" from Michel Bauwens, an information professional at British Petroleum. He said that characteristically centralist corporate librarians should learn to be democratic — to see themselves "in the middle of a concentric circle of cyberspace levels, consisting not only of external databases, but also of e-mail, bulletin boards, and computer conferencing systems."

These information spider's webs amount to what Bauwens calls an "unlimited, virtual library." The corporation that's serious about leveraging knowledge, he adds, may contemplate having at its disposal a network of cybrarians (librarians able to navigate in cyberspace), who'd perform three key functions: (1) "infomapping," or serving as institutional memory and knowing where the knowledge and expertise lie in the organization; (2) acting as gateways (not gatekeepers, Bauwens insists) to external data sources; and (3) "networking, networking, networking!"

And consider San Francisco Bay Area technology expert Howard Rheingold, who's spent many of his waking hours over the last seven years networking, mostly online with the WELL, the Whole Earth 'Lectronic Link. Rheingold characterizes the WELL as a virtual community. People in such collectives, he writes in *The Virtual Community*, "argue, engage in intellectual discourse . . . make plans, brainstorm, gossip, feud, fall in love, find friends and lose them, play games, flirt, [and] create a little high-art and a lot of idle talk." He often refers to the WELL as a small town where there's "always another mind." It is, he says, "like having a corner bar" nearby — or a cafe, pub, or common room.

But even the WELL, as informal as it might seem to be, engages volunteer (but officially designated) "hosts," who are nominally in charge of topical discussions ("conferences"). Rheingold says the hosts play the same role in cyberspace that they would at a party or salon; they "welcome newcomers, introduce people to one another, clean up after the guests, invoke discussion, and break up fights if necessary."

Bauwens and Rheingold, like Karlsson, Buckman, Manville, Zimmerman, Webber, Schrage, et al., are right. The human, cultural concerns are the really important ones in creating and operating a knowledge-creating, knowledge-sharing network, and these are the issues that are usually absent from most discussions (when there even are discussions) of knowledge development and electronic networks today.

## Michelle Cliffington Gets Religion

Are we making progress toward bringing corporations into the postindustrial, knowledge-sharing, information age?

Absolutely.

We've flattened the organization, and now we're concentrating on the horizontal, value-adding processes. But, essential as this is, it won't be the final step for a company. There is always another, and I'm betting that the next one will be work-as-conversation in "organizations" that consist of people here and there, on and off various payrolls, sharing knowledge and working together to create new value and exploit transient market openings.

How? I got a vivid snapshot of this oddball form from, of all things, a magazine ad for Lotus Notes. It featured Michelle Cliffington, a fictional manager at a made-up bicycle company. Using her spiffy new Notes software and assorted networking

accoutrements, Cliffing-
ton realizes within mo-
ments of the fact that

reorders for her company's most popular model are shaky in
several important markets. She instantly convenes a company-
wide electronic forum to propose a strategic pricing change (a
discount — nothing new there). Her CEO, on the road, taps into
the conversation that night and suggests that it might be time to
add a new product instead of hacking away at margins. The
frenzied conversation continues and an R&D team member
jumps in to suggest dusting off a proposed model that has long
been in the works. Cliffington meanwhile busily scours external
databases for more information. More people jump in. The ad
continues until, in the final frame, Cliffington reports the decision to build the new bike to key customers — Lotus Notes
users, of course — with a promise to deliver within 60 days.

This little commercial parable destroys practically everything
we thought we knew about organizations: (1) the hierarchy is
ignored; (2) functional barriers are routinely bypassed; (3) outsiders participate in the decision-making process in a haphazard
but intense fashion; (4) constant informal chatter goes on without meetings, traditional presentations, or political posturing;
and (5) something of significance happens, quick.

Is this story realistic?

Oh, yes, but it's mostly future realism. Against the standards
of the last several hundred years, and even 1994, it still amounts
to borderline fantasy.

### VeriFone's 24-Hour Workdays

Mostly future realism. But not entirely so. Michelle Cliffington
is a fictional character, but Hatim Tyabji is not, although his true
story is stranger than Cliffington's fictional one. Tyabji is CEO
of fast-growing VeriFone, a Redwood City, California, company
that dominates the U.S. market for credit card authorizations
and is also a player overseas (we were briefly introduced to
VeriFone in Chapter 3).

At VeriFone, all new employees get the laptop computer of their choice "before they get desks," *Forbes ASAP* reports. The company, which prides itself on a "culture of urgency," is wired from top to bottom. VeriFone, as of this writing, may be the most network-dependent sizable company in the world. People "tap in . . . or they die," one manager said, only half in jest.

Virtually all the company's work processes are linked electronically. Take a rush-project proposal for a consortium of German banks that, once started, blazed forward 24 hours a day. When the project team in Redwood City shut down for the day, team members also shut down their egos and passed off their work (electronically) to mates in VeriFone's Taipei office, who, at the end of their day, passed the project, part and parcel, to colleagues in London, who zapped it in another eight hours to Redwood City. Needless to say, VeriFone got the order, shocking the bankers and shaming competitors with its responsiveness.

Internal "p-mail" (paper mail) is outright banned at VeriFone, and the average manager, at home or away (mostly away, close to customers), gets 100 e-mail messages a day. In fact, all VeriFone employees, and many of their families, are linked to one another via the Internet. Three keystrokes will get nearly any employee complete access to information on bookings, shipments, progress with prospects, personnel data, people's travel schedules, and a customized, up-to-the-minute selection of useful articles.

Yikes! It's exhausting just to think about.

## Help Wanted, Circa 1999

Gasping as I contemplated VeriFone's crazy new world, I then came upon a claim that Sun Microsystems' 12,500 employees "do" a million e-mails each day. CEO Scott McNealy himself gets a couple hundred messages every day. It led me to imagine a help wanted ad in, say, *The Economist* in 1999:

> CEO, Lrg. multinat. Must type min. 90wpm. Other rqmts. optional.

Maybe even that's not fantasy.

CHRISTOPHER SPRINGMANN

VeriFone's Hatim Tyabji creates a "culture of urgency."

## New soul = knowledge development

### The Most Exciting Development

"The most exciting developments," writes Douglas Hague in *Beyond Universities*, "will be [when] human brains . . . work out radically new ways of understanding situations and events, solving problems, running organizations and transmitting knowledge. . . . The best [organizations] of the 21st century will bring together brain power *where it is,* not where it can be institutionalized. The aim must be to create a republic of the intellect, open to all, whose natural constituency will be those who keep themselves intellectually aware throughout their lives."

Understand my position (which I'm trying to make yours): In today's developed nations, organizations in which human brains have fulfilled Hague's vision will be the creators of all (or nearly all) of tomorrow's economic value-added.

### Pollocking for Profits

Anyone who has followed my work knows that I'm no fan of organization charts. I think they're a waste of even recycled paper. But maybe I'm mellowing. I recently ran across *Autumn Rhythm*, a Jackson Pollock painting (see below), which to me

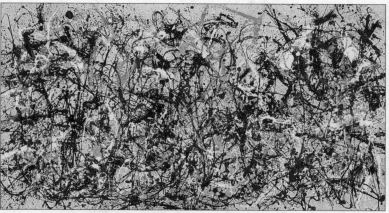

THE METROPOLITAN MUSEUM OF ART, GEORGE A. HEARN FUND, 1957

"Autumn Rhythm" by Jackson Pollock

looks the way a corporate organization chart should look. It's a depiction of Oticon's spaghetti organization, of VeriFone's tap-in-or-die culture, of Hague's new republic of the intellect, a total intertwining of people without regard to rank or function or location.

Autumn Rhythm goes far beyond reengineering (hence the title of this chapter). The "engineering" part of that increasingly popular word worries me, because it smacks of neo-Taylorism. In linking up functions, reengineering substitutes a horizontal bias for Taylor's vertical one. That's great as far as it goes. Yet I worry that reengineering is just the latest "one best way" approach — different, but still engineering. I think we've got to move instead toward work as conversation, corporate talk shows, ensembles of interconnected communities of practice, Pollocking our way to growth and profit.

## Soul-Through-Networked-Knowledge: A (Very) Big Deal Indeed

At the end of Chapter 5, we wrestled briefly with the issue of soul in a disembodied (virtual) organization. This chapter extends that wrestling match into overtime. (Is there overtime in wrestling?)

This entire chapter has been and is a discussion of a new kind of soul for most organizations. Managers of Soul (Corporate/Network Talk-Show Hosts, Directors of Knowledge Management) may be the central keepers of tomorrow's (today's, for some) core competence.

This is, I maintain, a very big deal.

## Learning, Learning Everywhere: An Even Bigger Deal

"In a knowledge age economy," Louis Perelman writes in School's Out, "the learning enterprise is strategically crucial." Far too crucial to leave to the schools, he adds.

> **"Personal learning, on demand, just in time, whenever and however the opportunity is wanted."**
> **Louis Perelman**

> ## "You can't live without an eraser."
> ### Gregory Bateson

Perelman, like Oxford's Hague and then some, imagines all the world turned into a giant learning network (no doubt with sci-fi cult hero and author William Gibson's *Neuromancer* the first entry on the new list of 100 Great Books On Line). The guiding principle is "personal learning 'on demand', 'just in time', whenever and however the opportunity is wanted." Brookings Institute scholar and educator Diane Ravitch likewise touts learning "anything at a time and place of one's choosing." Teachers become, by Ravitch's description, "coaches and guides who help students . . . through the new technology and the vast array of databases and teaching programs that will be available."

Perelman decries the wretched inefficiency of the current school system and the stupidity of the traditional "Yak in the Box" educational model: Detached from reality, teachers in ancient buildings ringed by barbed wire stand at the front of rooms and contextlessly hammer facts into little heads during 50-minute periods regularly interrupted by bells and an endless stream of trivial announcements on the P.A. system. He frets that we are all aglow about learning-as-the-basis-for-economic-value, but spend (as a nation) less per year on learning research than Gillette devoted to research for its latest razor blade, the Sensor.

Besides spending on learning research, Perelman advocates a flexible scheme that includes "microvouchers" (consumer-students are in full charge of their own learning, via educational debit cards), "intellectual food courts" (educational offerings can come from anyone, anywhere, and are not dependent on hierarchical school bureaucracies), and "attendance-free accounting" (outcome measurement, rather than attendance, becomes the basis for the student-provider contract).

- ☑ Leveraging knowledge as sole basis for economic and corporate security
- ☑ New models of knowledge development at ABB, CSC Europe, Buckman Labs, McKinsey, Coopers & Lybrand
- ☑ No headquarters, "the network is the whole thing"
- ☑ Incentives to share, culture of sharing, the anthropology of effective virtual communities; final score:

|  | 1 | 2 | 3 | 4 | 5 | 6 | 7 | 8 | 9 | Total |
|---|---|---|---|---|---|---|---|---|---|---|
| **Electronics** | 1 | 1 | 1 | 1 | 1 | 1 | 1 | 1 | 1 | 0 |
| **Anthropology** | 0 | 0 | 0 | 0 | 0 | 0 | 0 | 0 | 0 | 1 |

- ☑ Paradox: Expertise is prized but homeless
- ☑ Electronic hierarchy-flattening (Coopers & Lybrand)
- ☑ Conversations (work as), talk-show hosts, corporate cybrarians
- ☑ Ensembles of interconnected communities of practice
- ☑ VeriFone: "tap in . . . or they die"
- ☑ Pollocking your way to competitive advantage
- ☑ Student-workers for life

At one point, Perelman admiringly cites Harvard's Professor Shoshana Zuboff, who reports working with a plant manager in an advanced manufacturing operation "who was toying with the idea of calling the plant a college [because] . . . work and learning [there] had become increasingly interconnected." Shakespeare said all the world's a stage and all the men and women merely players. Perelman, Hague, Ravitch, Zuboff, and others now say that all the world must become a university and all of us student-workers within it.

## Rebuttal: The F. Scott Fitzgerald Test —
## To Forget Is Sublime

"The test of a first-rate intelligence," F. Scott Fitzgerald once wrote, "is the ability to hold two opposed ideas in mind at the same time and still retain the ability to function." So, regarding the issue at hand, can you pass the F. Scott Fitzgerald test? Namely: Can you grasp the notion that creating and leveraging knowledge to create value makes sense (the point of this chapter) while simultaneously embracing the idea that there exists an equally important need to forget what you know?

*Business Week* management editor John Byrne spent years examining the impact of the post-World War II "whiz kids" on business practice. Their quantitative bent was a much-needed counterbalance to prewar, seat-of-the-pants management. Eventually, though, the whizzers' helpful techniques were over-

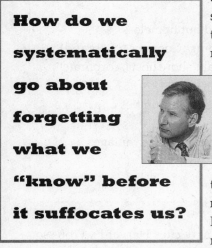

**How do we systematically go about forgetting what we "know" before it suffocates us?**

done. Byrne offers a general lesson: "All useful ideas are taken to the extreme, and the exemplar managers are cloned and cloned again until 'one right way' thinking captures the firm. Enter corporate rigor mortis."

University of Michigan management expert Karl Weick has long championed the application of biological models to organization design and strategy. How collective organizational minds selectively notice "facts" and frame problems is his passion. So is forgetting. Learning how to do some things well and establishing a largely invariant corporate culture is a must for success. Weick pointedly reminds us, however, that "adaption precludes adaptivity." To establish rituals and become effective (and then better and better still) at something, by definition extends the blinds that limit our ability to adjust to the unforeseen.

The way to avoid blindness, per Weick, is to develop an "ambivalent stance toward past wisdom" and "treat memory as a pest." He also nods to Gregory Bateson, who said, "You can't live without an eraser."

But how do you erase a long-dominant and eventually poisonous attachment to numerical analysis at a company like Ford (home to the "whiz kids" studied by Byrne)? IBM's lingering attachment to mainframe computers? Or, at some future date, Wal-Mart's obsession with its discounting formula?

Almost none (none?) of the conventional methods work. Decentralization sounds like a solution, but as Chapter 2 pointed out, decentralized unit chiefs typically came up through the ranks together; they mostly talk and think alike and produce products that look and smell alike.

How about "skunkworks," formed in the corporate boondocks and staffed by renegades? Tragically, even undeniable skunkwork successes are written off, rationalized, or ignored by the company's establishment. The people-first success of NUMMI, GM's skunkworks with Toyota, should have induced similar practices throughout GM. (In accordance with the joint-venture contract, GM rotated numerous managers through NUMMI toward precisely that end.) Instead, throughout most of the 1980s chairman Roger Smith dismissed the emerging saga, because it directly conflicted with his salvation-through-technology strategy (which was consistent with GM's long-term traditions). At IBM and Xerox, skunkworks produced interesting products; but once the mavericks' success became visible, they were absorbed by the dominant culture and lost their quirky edge.

Is there no way out of this dilemma? Near-death experiences and/or the professional deaths of their leaders can partially erase institutional memories. GM and IBM are forgetting a little of their glorious, but now constraining, pasts in the wake of their chairmen's involuntary departures. In fact, boards of directors can play a useful role in questioning tradition, but only if they are genuinely independent, which is a still rare condition.

(To be fair, you're damned if you do and damned if you don't. A board that's too cantankerous may pull the plug on a sound strategy before it's been fairly tested. Many overly touchy venture-capitalist board members have done just that to budding companies, stopping their progress cold. Ah, life!)

Then there's the Silicon Graphics route. CEO Ed McCracken told the *Harvard Business Review* that he scorns normal strategic planning. Instead he insists that the company's best and brightest technologists stay in intimate contact with "lighthouse" (pioneering) customers. When the company, at least partly on the basis of this contact, decides on a product, it virtually drops whatever else it's doing and goes flat out to develop that new offering. If the fresh product knocks off one of the company's current, high-margin winners, even one that's still rising, that's fine. At Silicon Graphics, apparently, forgetting (ignoring the beauty of, and even the cash flow from, today's winner) has itself become part of the culture.

Outsourcing is another ploy for reducing attachment to yesterday's culture and inducing forgetfulness, but outsourcing only works if the company has the guts to outsource a substantial share of its core competencies (R&D, logistics, whatever). As we saw in Chapter 5, only a few firms, such as MCI, play this game well.

Yet, sadly, none of these techniques works completely or for very long. They can help companies forget, but even the firms like Silicon Graphics and MCI are still wedded to notions of "the way we do things around here," and those beliefs (even strategies for outsourcing core competences) eventually will trip them up or, quite possibly, destroy them.

Though I'm not optimistic about inducing forgetfulness, I offer a small piece of practical advice: Consider organizing your 1994 off-site strategy session around the following questions. "What do we know we know for sure?" "How do we systematically go about forgetting what we 'know' before it suffocates us?" Hint: If everyone in the meeting dresses alike (I typically find more uniformity in off-site leisure wear than in office attire), you're off to a shaky start.

## Rebuttal 2: Institutionalizing Forgetfulness at Big Firms

■ Change divisional product portfolios regularly and almost without rhyme or reason (3M does this occasionally).

■ Relocate corporate headquarters to a new region or country every 15 years. (Big one-time moves have worked overnight miracles for groups like GM Europe — so why not keep doing it?)

■ Limit CEO tenure to 10 (five? seven?) years.

■ Manage the share of outsiders in key positions (e.g., a minimum of 25 percent of division chiefs should have arrived within the past five years; 10 percent should have spent most of their career in other industries).

> **Develop a systematic plan to attack your most cherished beliefs.**

■ Sell off one-third of the corporate portfolio every 10 years, regardless of economic logic (and including some of your most successful units).

■ Make sure at least 20 percent of your board members are independently wealthy businesspeople who founded their own firms (e.g., Warren Buffett look-alikes).

■ Every two years, have a team of outsiders and insiders develop a list of 10 statements that summarize "how we do things around here" (based on interviews with insiders, customers, vendors, etc.); then develop a plan for attacking each of the 10 core beliefs.

■ Beware the absence of contention (i.e., fiery disagreement) in meetings you attend; be even more wary of pronounced, public contention that's phony — i.e., that an outsider would say are wars over the number of angels that can dance on the head of a pin (e.g., IBM's famous faceoffs, called "performance shootouts," among potential new products were actually debates about minute variations on traditional approaches).

## Warning: Garbage at the Speed of Light

The emerging information highway system could be a boon to civilization or it could, as one info-industry wag put it, deliver "garbage at the speed of light."

Knowledge-development networks sit on many a knife edge. The new technologies are the essential enablers, yet network anthropology is more important than network software. Likewise, while remembering (learning) is important, forgetting is at least as important; most so-called learning, even in the likes of McKinsey's elaborate new scheme, amounts to no more than embellishing current ideas.

Also, it's imperative to make the distinction between information and knowledge. The poet Donald Hall contends that, "Information is the enemy of intelligence." Even I will admit that, for example, the VeriFone case worries me some. So far so good there, to be fair, but does life at that pace permit the sort of reflection that leads to genuine breakthroughs?

Samuel Johnson once said that "all intellectual improvement arises in leisure." When stuck, Thomas Edison would unfailingly take a nap. U.S. poet laureate Rita Dove, in an address to Phi Beta Kappas at the University of Virginia, worried that we don't pay enough attention to daydreaming, "without which no bridges would soar, no light bulbs burn, and no Greek warships set out upon Homer's 'wine-dark sea.'"

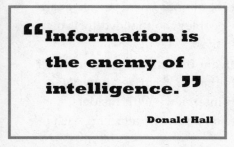

**"Information is the enemy of intelligence."**

**Donald Hall**

Reflecting on the possibility of cyberspace navigators producing garbage at the speed of light and on the absence of naps and daydreaming as a central element of corporate culture leads us not only beyond reengineering, but also beyond "learning networks" and toward the ultimate essential of brain-based competitive advantage: curiosity. Stay tuned.

### T.T.D. (Things to Do) and QTA (Questions to Answer)

❶ Can you pass the Bob Buckman test? That is, do you buy the basic premise of this chapter, that networked knowledge development is the essence of added value for you, your department, your company, your customers, and your vendor-producer-distributor-customer chain? If not, why not? (If not, go back to Chapter 1 and start again: "more intellect, less materials," "only asset imagination.")

❷ Do you know where the knowledge lies in your organization? What the knowledge is? What it's worth? (Bob

## CAN YOU PASS **THE BOB BUCKMAN TEST?**

Buckman couldn't answer those questions at first.) Have you identified the "communities of practice" (informal learning networks, which often include outsiders) in your firm? And nurtured them?

❸ Are you (personally, in your department, across the corporation) experimenting with these network technologies? (Is your home computer hooked up to CompuServe, for example? What? No home computer?) If you're not experimenting, why not?

❹ Reflect on the anthropological issues — a culture of knowledge sharing versus hoarding, user democracy versus authoritarianism (or anarchy). Are such attributes primary issues in your knowledge-development activities? (I.e., do those who share knowledge get clearly and publicly applauded, rewarded, promoted? Are those who don't hissed? How much time do you spend talking up knowledge-sharing per se?) Or is your effort driven by know-it-all techies who are bits-and-bytes freaks and closet (or out-of-the-closet) centralizers?

❺ Reflect on work as conversation, virtual communities, and other such terms. Are they just the latest biz babble? Or do they have meaning for you?

❻ Do you get (and buy) the distinction between reengineering and the organic work-as-conversation?

❼ Revisit the VeriFone story. Use VeriFone as a benchmark. Can you imagine your unit going that far? No? What if a competitor did first?

❽ Are you ready to Pollock?

❾ Reread this chapter. Take a day off and discuss it with colleagues. Isn't it true that adopting my position would force you to reinvent your company and alter every fundamental internal and external relationship? If so, what's holding you back? (If not, what did I do wrong?)

❿ Having bought all of the above (I just know you have), are you now also ready to turn off the computers and daydream or take a nap, to invest in erasers, and take forgetting as seriously as learning? Really. F. Scott Fitzgerald and all that. . . .

"Nations will wither, knowledge will triumph" —
Alvin and Heidi Toffler. Many nations still seem to be acting up, but a glance at the Fortune 500 or the Forbes 400 tells of the triumph of, indeed, "more intellect, less materials." Yet it's barely overstatement to say we haven't a clue about what that means for organizing. This chapter raises, by design, more questions than it offers answers. In fact, **the geniuses of leveraging knowledge are the first to admit that they still have many more questions than answers.** No matter (for now at least). My goal is to agitate your mind, regardless of the rung of the corporate ladder you're on, to get you to at least say, "What if he's even half right?" I'm not sure I'd give myself credit for being that accurate — but I am flatly confident that this is the right issue.

**leveraging knowledge as the first to**
**all that they still have many more**
**questions the answers to seek**

## CHAPTER 7

BEYOND LEARNING

# CREATING THE CURIOUS CORPORATION

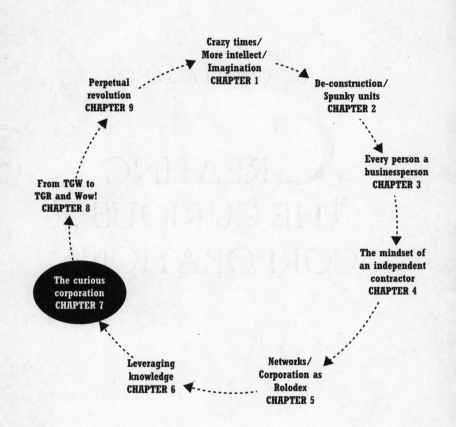

Crazy times/
More intellect/
Imagination
CHAPTER 1

De-construction/
Spunky units
CHAPTER 2

Perpetual
revolution
CHAPTER 9

Every person a
businessperson
CHAPTER 3

From TGW to
TGR and Wow!
CHAPTER 8

The mindset of
an independent
contractor
CHAPTER 4

The curious
corporation
CHAPTER 7

Leveraging
knowledge
CHAPTER 6

Networks/
Corporation as
Rolodex
CHAPTER 5

# Corporations are hurricanes

of activity. "Members" come from hither and thither and are not necessarily on the company payroll. The workplace is as often cyberspace as a corporate tower. It's enough to make your head swim, all right. But it's not enough to keep you in business. The workplace as cyberspace begs the issue raised in Chapter 1, and which will be the centerpiece of the next chapter (Beyond TQM: Toward Wow!): Is it interesting? Remember "garbage at the speed of light," from the end of the last chapter. Fact is, we're still a long way, in this book and in business, from the curious corporation. Now's the time to take the ideas of the first six chapters and raise the ante once again.

"What a distressing

contrast there is

between the radiant

intelligence of the

child and the feeble

mentality of the

average adult."

Sigmund Freud

**"More intellect, less materials."** "Only factory asset is the human imagination." I'm repeatedly drawn back (as you know) to those words and the line from Wal-Mart CEO David Glass about the "absolute dearth" of exciting, fashion-forward products. More products, yes. Developed faster than ever, yes. But most of them aren't exactly scintillating, to put it mildly.

So we've created new corporations, virtual corporations, and corporate virtual workspaces. So we've turned the average person into a businessperson, placed her or him within a moderate-size unit, and networked her or him with everyone from everywhere. So we've worried ourselves to death about leveraging knowledge.

But is *it* (whatever our company is about) interesting?

Is *it* exciting?

### Bored Stiff

Most organizations bore me stiff. I can't imagine working in one of them. I'd be sad if my children chose to. Most organizations, large and even small, are bland as bean curd.

Ugly thoughts? They're terrifying thoughts, when we realize we're relying on these organizations to be and remain commercially viable in a marketplace gone bonkers.

"What a distressing contrast there is between the radiant intelligence of the child and the feeble mentality of the average adult," Sigmund Freud once said. Sorry to say, Freud was right. So is turnaround executive Victor Palmieri: "Strategies are okayed in boardrooms that even a child would say are bound to fail. The problem is, there's never a child in the boardroom."

What do you do about a bland organization? How do you get a child (virtual child?) into the boardroom? It's obvious: Build a curious corporation. But how? Can we get our arms around such a . . . curious term? Are we willing to try? Are we willing even to use the words? In public?

### A List, No More and No Less

What follows is a list, and not all that great a list. Fact is, I hastily sketched it out a while back, then immediately transferred it to 35-mm slides. On the slides it looks great, it looks tidy. But the list wasn't meant to be great, certainly not tidy. Its only purpose is to show that one can make such a list. Okay, how do you create a curious corporation? Try these 14 ideas:

> **The curious kids are the ones, age 6 or 66, who are constantly in trouble.... Right?**

1. <u>Hire curious people</u>. Yes, it's that simple. Except that it flies in the face of conventional wisdom. I sometimes think Rule No. 1 in the corporate recruiting manual is, "Thou shalt not hire anyone who has as much as a nanosecond's gap in her or his résumé between nursery school and now."

Whom do we hire? The person with the perfect grade-point average, who didn't miss a day of class in kindergarten, elementary school, or junior high. Perfect folks. Blemishless. And unspeakably dull. Never a hair out of place, never done a thing wrong. But they haven't done much interesting, either. Curious? I doubt it. After all, the curious kids are the ones, age 6 or 66, who are constantly in trouble. Right?

I'm not alone, if not in a majority, in these observations. Stanley Bing, writing in *Esquire,* offers this marvelous snapshot of an encounter with a job candidate that went nowhere:

> He comes in and seats himself carefully on the edge of my guest chair. He is staring at the toys on

my desk, trying to suppress the realization that I am an infantile nit whose job he could probably do much better. . . . Of course he does not play with the toys. . . He looks out my window instead. "Nice view," he says rather perfunctorily, but he does not say, "Wow!" — which is what my view of the canyons and spires of high-mercantile capitalism deserves. . .

"I'm looking for an entry-level position in public relations. Maybe corporate marketing, if I get lucky," he says.

"Really?" I say. "Like, out of the entire realm of human possibility, that's what you want to be doing?" I'm sorry. He's really starting to tweeze my bumpus. What twenty-four-year-old really and truly wants to be in *corporate marketing*, for God's sake?. . . I look him over as he burbles on about targeting demos or retrofitting corporate superstructures or some frigging thing like that. The guy makes me want to stand up on my desk and yell, "*Booga-booga!*" Instead, I say, "Didn't you ever want to be a rock musician or a forest ranger or anything?" He looks at me like I have a banana peel on the end of my nose. It's quite clear to me that, since he was in high school, he's been preparing to be a . . . communicator. That's actually what he says.

Screw it. There is no poetry in this dude. No soul. No surf or wind or whalebone in his eye. He's . . . desiccated. He makes me sad. I kick him out of my office.

Is Bing on the money? ' Fraid so. Too harsh? I don't think so. Whom do I suggest we hire? A dude with poetry? A gal with soul? Absolutely. I suggest we search for the young woman who went to MIT to study computer science, was doing fine, and then mysteriously dropped out midway in her sophomore year, said the place was the dreariest institution ever created, and took off around the world, maybe to work with Mother Teresa, maybe just to hang out. We really don't know.

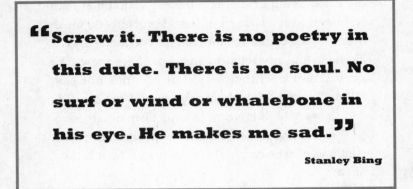

Why would I hire her? I'll tell you. She's demonstrated — at least at one point in her life — the gumption to do something exciting, something extraordinary, something that breaks the mold. Maybe we'll get lucky — and she'll do it again. For us.

VCW, Inc., of Kansas City, Missouri, is in what would hardly be labeled a glamorous, "happening" business. Or so it would seem. Peddling insurance to independent truckers? Yawn. But founder Cheryl Womack, *Fortune* reports, has turned her firm into a high-growth, high-profit gem. Hiring is key. "We look for passion, flexibility, and excitement," Womack asserts. I like that. And I'm dead serious when I suggest we make the first line in the corporate recruitment manual: "Thou shalt not consider for employment anyone who does not have a gap and a couple of glitches in his or her résumé." How about it? Got the nerve? I doubt it. But then I suspect your company is among those routinely offering me-too products and services. (Hey, I'm only saying that because the odds are on my side and long.)

2. <u>Hire a few genuine off-the-wall sorts</u> — collect some weirdos. Curious and the occasional gap in the resume are not enough. We need some real kooks. If we want original products, they're likely to come from original people. What else would you call Ted Turner, George Lucas, Steve Jobs, Anita Roddick? Original they are, oddballs they are. And they've given us breakthrough products and services.

I swiped this idea from Gary Withers, head of the brash

British marketing-services firm, Imagination. Some have called Withers Britain's Walt Disney. He makes his money by creating fabulous events, marketing campaigns, and corporate culture makeovers, for clients wild and not so wild. His personal key, he told me, is looking for flaky sorts who have insatiable "appetites for adventure." It doesn't matter one whit whether there's a job for them or not. He says he comes in contact with a lot of zesty nuts, and if he hits it off with them, he hires them. If they're as good as he thinks they are, they'll make a special niche for themselves in the company, and take Imagination someplace it's never been (praise be, since "topping our last" is the company's strategy). Collecting weirdos sounds to me like one dandy idea.

Civil War historian Shelby Foote reports that General Ulysses S. Grant was once relieved from high command because of his boozing. General William T. Sherman was also once relieved — because of "suspicion of insanity." Yet these two ended up saving the Union, whereas their predecessors, who had boot-licked their way to the top, were disasters when times got tough. What if Lincoln had stuck with the squeaky-clean résumé, had failed to take the plunge for weird?

Words are revealing. How about weird? Withers has no problem with it. Do you? How about maniac? One Nintendo exec says that's what his firm wants — "maniacs." Listen to Guy Kawasaki, the former Apple software executive. He begs us to "turn everyone into raging, inexorable thunder lizard evangelists." Can you imagine that rolling off your tongue while talking with your boss's boss? In a personnel manual? If the times are upside down, the language must be, too. And believe it or not, the choice of words and images is near the center of business strategy.

> **"We look for passion, flexibility, excitement."**
> Cheryl Womack

3. <u>Weed out the dullards, nurture the nuts</u>. Power to the peculiar! Mike Koelker, creative director at Foote, Cone & Belding, says, tongue nowhere near his cheek, that he's "learned

to predict the future. Anyone who comes to see you more than once every two years to discuss their 'career path' probably doesn't have one." On the other hand, he insists that "without exception, the people in the account group and creative department who I find the most brilliant will have the hardest time fitting into . . . the agency structure." It's his job No. 1 to nurture these misfits.

Advertising legend David Ogilvy doubtless would nod in agreement. One listless soul, he said in his official statement of agency philosophy, can infect a cast of hundreds. (Or more.) Out they (should, must) go. Vamooski! — you don't want the wet noodles dragging down the live wires.

You've seen it. I've seen it. We unconsciously learned it at age seven, when we first observed leadership in Sunday School, or with Brownies or Cub Scouts. There's that person (leader) who walks into the room, things are going moderately well, but the whole place clams up and goes stiff. Then there's that other person (leader) who walks in, and even if things are going badly, you feel just a little bit better, there's a little more buzz in the air, just because of his or her presence. We know all this, we know what it means. We even agree on it. But we don't use the dull-is-deadly, cherish-the-live-wires criterion in hiring and especially in promoting. I suggest we do. I suggest we must. Again, the point is strategic, not peripheral.

4. Go for youth. One big reason PepsiCo stays vital at $25 billion in revenues is that it's willing to place big bets on exciting people that others would veto as untested. Time after time, you'll find the company has appointed a 28-, 29-, or 30-year-old to run a big part of the business. (Hey, Thomas Jefferson penned the Declaration of Independence at age 33. It's held up pretty well.)

The 85-year-old *New Republic* magazine, though respected, was in a rut. In 1991, the owner, Martin Peretz, appointed 27-year-old Andrew Sullivan as editor of the venerable publication. He shook things up. "I can't imagine a 45-year-old having the effect he's had," said staffer Jacob Weisberg. Why? "The younger people are much more irresponsible and more willing to do things on the edge," staffer Michael Lewis explains.

I like that: the pursuit of irresponsible greenhorns. How many of your company's leadership cadre are under 35? 30? . . . 25? (You'd be amazed at the number of companies that refer to the appointment of someone 45 years old as part of a youth movement.)

5. <u>Insist that everyone take vacations</u>. When you're blessed with phenomenal growth or extraordinary problems, people, especially in key positions, tend to work 13-hour days, six or seven days a week. They think they're strong, tough, invincible — and as fresh as ever. They may be strong as oxen. But fresh? That's a bunch of baloney. People need to rejuvenate themselves, especially these upside-down days.

I had a good friend at McKinsey, one of the cleverest folks I ever worked with, who each summer took a month's vacation. We were a macho, type-A organization. I couldn't imagine why he did it. At any rate, I knew that I didn't need a month off, I of boundless energy. Then one year I spent August at a cabin on the Northern California coast. When I got back, I was immediately aware of what a burned-out shell I'd been. Let me say it — to toughen up, lighten up.

6. <u>Support generous sabbaticals</u>. For refreshing the overtilled soil. And reinventing ourselves. Vacations, aye. But unless we go farther and occasionally take megabreaks, of several months (or more), to radically ream out and retool, the chances of hitting a second home run (if we've been lucky enough to hit the first one) are very low indeed. Been on the job for five years without a three-month (six-month) break? You're flat. Trust me.

7. <u>Foster new interaction patterns</u>. Create a physical environment that (a) lets people express their personalities, (b) allows project teams to form at a moment's notice, (c) encourages getting together and hanging out, and (d) aggressively snubs traditional functional groupings.

Space reflects (and shapes) corporate culture, spirited or blah, like no other variable. Managers, by a wide margin, don't take it

> **Does your company have a clean-desk policy? If so, the company's nuts and you're nuts to stay there.**

seriously enough. And, in these pages, we don't either (wait until the next book). "We need to change underlying beliefs about how we view and perform white-collar jobs," designer Duncan Sutherland told *Industry Week.* "It's still typical to view offices as information factories or places that produce data. So our traditional response has been to see how much we can produce — how many keystrokes we can coax out of workers, or how many memos. But the purpose of an office is to create knowledge. That is an intellectual process, not a production process." Most offices bore the hell out of me. And if they bore me — I've learned, almost unfailingly — nothing very interesting is going to happen there.

It's the tiny telltale signs, too. Does your company have a clean-desk policy? If so, the company's nuts — and, frankly, you're nuts to stay there. (Yes, based on that criterion alone.) Oh, how many businesses have I visited where you'd never guess at human habitation! Then we wonder why they produce another dozen copycat products (even if they're quick copycats, TQM'd to a fare-thee-well).

8. <u>Establish clubs, bring in outsiders, support offbeat educational programs</u>. Don't invite Tom Peters or Peter Drucker, damn it! Invite Steven Spielberg or Kenneth Branagh or Tim Burton. Or your favorite science-fiction writer — how about William Gibson? Invite somebody who's doing something beyond the pale, clearly contrary to the ordinary corporate usage. P-L-E-A-S-E!

9. <u>Measure curiosity</u>. Yes, I'm serious. Time for semiannual performance reviews? Consider having each employee submit a

one-page essay on (a) the oddest thing I've done this year off the job, (b) the craziest idea I've tried at work, (c) my most original screw-up on the job, and off, or (d) the five stupidest rules we have around here.

Hey, I'm not kidding. (I stole this idea, though not the questions, from Herman Miller's very special boss, Max DePree. He asks execs to answer queries that force them way out of the box.) Why not? We're trying to get people to explode from the traces that hold them back. At the very least, this will make the reading of performance reviews more fun. And it might even do some good.

10. <u>Seek out odd work</u>. Imagination's Withers says he won't take a job, even if it means forgoing megabucks, unless he figures out some way to make it exciting — some way it can force him to push his company's performance to new heights.

11. <u>Look in the mirror</u>. If the chief ain't curious, the troops ain't likely to be. (And that's an understatement.) How many times have I seen the video on "culture change" featuring the CEO? Dressed in black, at least it seems so. The office tidy (i.e., sterile). His animation zilch. And he's telling us (droning on) to get more excited. It doesn't get through. He's a stiff. And then he wonders why his talk doesn't ignite the troops, why they don't race out and do some absolutely madcap stuff. If you're not zany (I don't mean loud, I mean infectiously enthusiastic), then the joint's not going to be zany. By the way, I'm talking to supervisors running eight-person accounting operations as well as CEOs running 100,000-person corporations.

12. <u>Teach curiosity</u>. Brainstorming is not *the* answer to creativity. But it is *an* answer. There are time-tested techniques for milking people's wackier ideas (you'd do no better than to attend one of creativity guru Edward de Bono's seminars); invest heavily in using such techniques to solve all problems — from purchasing and accounting to quality and marketing.

All, as in solving *all* problems. The curiosity mandate does not just apply to marketing or research and development. Curiosity applies to everything, especially if you think of the company, as I suggested in Chapter 5, as "packages of services." Curiosity is at least as important in accounting, purchasing, and logistics as it is in science and design.

13. <u>Make it fun</u>. Not ha-ha fun. (Though there's nothing wrong with that from time to time.) But fun as in enjoyable, or refreshing . . . you know what I mean. A place that makes you smile and makes you want to go to work on Monday morning, even if you had a terrific weekend — that's the ticket. And it is possible.

"We've always said that Silicon Graphics is all about making technology fun and usable," says CEO Ed McCracken, "and that means that working here should be fun. Too many corporations in the United States and Japan have cut the fun out of their businesses. . . . Fun and irreverence also make change less scary." McCracken doesn't have trouble with the three-letter F-word. Can you say the same? (And live it?)

14. <u>Change pace</u>. Go to work next Thursday and declare it miniature-golf day. Showing a training film this afternoon? Order popcorn. Hotter than hell on an August morning? Buy 10 water guns, the good ones, at lunch — and go back and start a water-gun fight in the accounting department. (I stole this one from a software company — yup, the part about the accounting department, too.) Curiosity has a lot to do with perpetually looking at the world through slightly cockeyed glasses.

I'm sure that if you and a few of your colleagues, running a group of six or 60 or 600 people, got together for half an hour, you'd come up with a different — and better — list than mine. The important thing is to understand that you can turn this mushy — and strategic — idea of "creating the curious corporation" into hard, doable suggestions.

And, by the way, while I don't think my list is great, I do earnestly believe that every idea on it makes sense. In these wacky times . . . only asset imagination . . .

## Ken Midura

*Raging Inexorable
Thunder Lizard Evangelist*

LEVI STRAUSS EUROPE
AVENUE LOUISE 489
1050 BRUSSELS BELGIUM
TELEX 65480

MICHAEL ROSSITER
KNOWLEDGE SHARER AND PROMOTER OF ENQUIRING
& CURIOUS MINDS

TEL. (02) 641.60.71

FAX (02) 641.64.96
RECYCLED LEVI'S DENIM

C. Kelly Ange

Pov... ...erations Division
Charlotte ...
Training & Develor..nent
Disorganizer

Westinghouse Electric Corporation
5101 Westinghouse Boulevard
Post Office Box 7002
Charlotte North Carolina 28241
(704) 551-5260
WIN 430-5260

Whoops, I plumb forgot item number 15. While I'm against
adding staff slots in this Age of Lean, I will make an exception:
How about a Vicar of Vitality, Grand Panjandrum of
Pandemonium, Crown Prince of Curiosity, Master of Madness?
And even if you don't add the slot, how about at least changing
your job title on your business card, including the Japanese-lan-
guage version, to one of the above? I'll say it again. I'm serious
about all this. As for you, admit it. When was the last time you
kicked up your heels in the corridor? Danced the length of the
cafeteria? Your place of work bores you silly, too — and it's
costing you. Right?

### Innocence Renewed

"One of the lessons you learn in becoming an adult," John Seabrook wrote in the *New Yorker*, "is that it doesn't always pay to be curious. Some people learn to avoid curiosity altogether. [Microsoft's Bill] Gates appears to have completely failed to absorb this lesson." Gates is not alone. Harvard psychology professor Howard Gardner discovered that geniuses in general lived on the margins of society (perpetually skeptical of conventional wisdom and its purveyors) and maintained, throughout life, "intellectual innocence."

Most of us aren't geniuses, aren't Bill Gates. But at least we can create corporate cultures, and workplaces, that nurture innocence and don't actively stomp out curiosity.

### Snared by the Great Blight of Dullness

We grotesquely underestimate the role of physical space in setting organizational tone. (Remember the Acordia companies in Chapter 2: giving the small units separate physical homes dramatically increased the sense of ownership.) It was urban planner-philosopher Jane Jacobs who taught me that lesson. In fact,

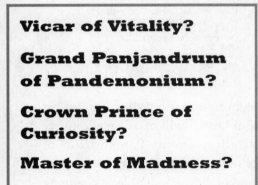

**Vicar of Vitality?**

**Grand Panjandrum of Pandemonium?**

**Crown Prince of Curiosity?**

**Master of Madness?**

few books have influenced me more than her *The Death and Life of Great American Cities*. "Nobody enjoys sitting on a stoop looking out at an empty street," Jacobs writes at one point. She claims that most significant urban problems stem from cities that are engulfed by the Great Blight of Dullness (she's very fond of capital letters), that are perfectly planned (by urban planners), but are boring up close. Her winning formula includes energetic sidewalks, short blocks, lots of old buildings, mixed uses (houses and stores and offices and bars all squeezed together). At its best it adds up,

Microsoft-er (and toys) at work

Jacobs says, to "exuberant variety."

Most of our corporate stoops look out on empty streets, devoid of spirit. And, oh my, I do love that phrase "exuberant variety." How do (a) you, (b) your unit, (c) your company score on the EVI — or Exuberant Variety Index? (A perfect 10 is Microsoft or Planet Hollywood, a stifling 1 is, still, GM.)

Which brings me to the copy of The 39th Annual Design Review edition of *I.D.* (*International Design*) that landed in my mailbox a while back. A frustrated architect, I flipped to the sections on buildings, interiors, and furniture. Without exception, I was repelled by the award winners. They deaden the human spirit.

What are spaces that enliven the spirit? They are comfortable, friendly, awake. I'm for sweatshirts and sweatpants at home and, if I can get away with it, at work. I like to be surrounded by familiar objects, to look up at 100-year-old roughhewn rafters, to gaze at trees and birds or an electric street scene. Like *Esquire*'s Stanley Bing, perhaps, I can no more imagine an office without toys than a computer without software.

At first, as I reacted so strongly to *I.D.*'s winners, I wondered if I was a crank. So I did a smidgen of research.

Architect Christopher Alexander, in his widely acclaimed, Zen-ish *The Timeless Way of Building*, describes "a central quality which is the root criterion of life and spirit in a man, a town, a building, or a wilderness. This quality is objective and precise, but it cannot be named."

Nameable or not, Alexander evokes it: "The first place I think of, when I try to tell someone about this quality, is a corner of an English country garden, where a peach tree grows against a wall. . . . The sun shines on the tree and as it warms the bricks behind the tree, the warm bricks themselves warm the peaches on the tree. It has a slightly dozy quality."

> "I sometimes wonder what sort of quality my work would have if I worked in a harsh, rectangular, smooth-surfaced, evenly lit glossy office."
>
> **Christopher Day**

Mark the words (remember, words!) "alive," "whole," "comfortable," and "eternal." Alexander says they describe places that "let our inner forces loose, and set us free; but when [spaces] are dead, they keep us locked in inner conflict." I believe the same qualities are central to creating value in our companies.

Too much corporate experience is anesthetized by work environments that squash our spirits. I shake my head in wonder — and sometimes am moved to anger or sadness or both — by most facilities I enter. From reception area to research lab, they lack ferment.

Surfaces are smooth and polished. Glass-topped, chrome-legged desks are barren. Light is synthetic. "For proven physiological reasons, people can feel ill if they work all day in artificial light," architect Christopher Day says in *Places of the Soul*. "Yet the light of spring can bring such joy to the heart, it can get the invalid out of bed!"

Gary Withers hires zesty nuts with "appetites for adventure."

Does your workspace suck you out from under the covers in the morning? Does it up the likelihood of clever, collaborative, and energetic problem-solving?

Doubtful. The typical corporate landscape, urban stone or rural lawn, breeds hunkering and hiding, not sharing and openness.

These are, I repeat, critical issues. If value in the new economy is to come from spunk, energy, talk, collaboration, and imagination, then the places where we hang out to do commerce must reflect the principles of that new economy.

Is space everything? Of course not. But you'd be surprised at the role it plays in creating a corporate signature — curious or incurious.

(P.S. In the for-what-it's-worth department, Duncan Sutherland, writing in *Design Management Journal,* reports that Benjamin Franklin did his best work in the nude and Martin Luther on the can. Supercomputer maven Seymour Cray, when stuck, digs tunnels in his backyard. What's around you is inside you.)

## New Realities

A different sort of character (curious) in a different sort of place (spunky) is required to create value in today's, let alone tomorrow's, marketplace. In fact, Peter Drucker wrote in the *Harvard Business Review,* "The relationship between knowledge workers and their organization is a distinctly new phenomenon." Drucker goes on to suggest that we should treat all knowledge workers as "volunteers." We can demand that people show up at work on time, especially in this problematic economic period. But we cannot demand, ever, that people bring passion along, or exuberance, or imagination. We must attract the special worker, then tap into his or her curiosity. But what, specifically, do these new knowledge workers want? In a July 1993 article, *Inc.* magazine presented this fictitious memo, which ought to be framed behind every executive's desk:

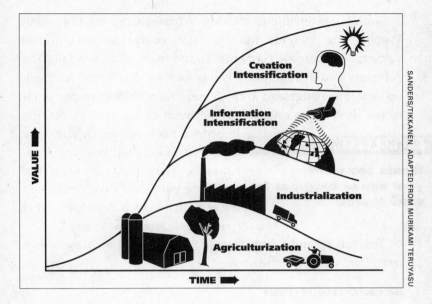

To: *Inc.* magazine
From: Determinedly Seeking the Perfect Job

I don't want to screw around anymore in a place that's badly managed, poorly run, and so stupid I'm just wasting my time. Or a place where you have to be a vice-president to get a window. I want to take my dogs to work, at least on Saturdays, and if I break into a chorus of "Oklahoma" at 4 p.m., I want two people to harmonize with me — not look at me sideways.

I want to work cooperatively in a team. I don't care so much what industry it is, but the more socially conscious, the better. I want an environment that's honest, supportive, fair, inclusive, and playful. I'm really great at what I do, and now I'm going to find a really great place to do it in. I want flex time and exercise space and community service and lots of chances to learn. I want trees and easy parking!

Signed, Determined

Sounds reasonable to me. Mr. Work-as-Conversation, Alan Webber, understands, too. He wrote in the *Harvard Business Review*, "In the new economy, individuals at all levels of the company and in all kinds of companies are challenged to develop new knowledge and to create new value, to take responsibility for their ideas and to pursue them as far as they can go.

People who manage in the new economy [must] tap into the emotional energy that comes from wrestling with their own destiny. In the end, that's a job description that most people would welcome."

Yes, most would, but in early 1994 it's still a chimera — a long, long way from the norm.

### Something Great!

David Sheff's *Game Over* traces the meteoric rise of Japan's controversial, unconventional Nintendo. The spirit of Nintendo is best captured by a simple exchange. A game designer, Gunpei Yokoi, asked his boss, "What should I make?" Nintendo chief executive Hiroshi Yamauchi replied, "Something great."

That brief exchange made my head spin for days. Not long after, I started asking seminar participants, "Has any boss, in your career, ever said to you, 'Do/make something great'? Or, perhaps more to the point, have you ever said that to one of your subordinates?" (No rounding off allowed: not something important, good, or even nifty, but something great, or Something Great, to mimic Jane Jacobs.)

Sad to say, barely a hand has gone up. None for 500 in London. None for 200 in Frankfurt. One out of 5,000 in Sydney and Melbourne. None in Kuala Lumpur. None in large gatherings in Silicon Valley or Chicago either. One out of 1,200 in Atlanta.

What should I make? Something great. Wow! What a turn-

**"What should I make?"**..................

on! What a motivator! What a challenge to the human imagination! What a wake-up call to curiosity! Recall our discussion about Tom Strange and Joe Tilli, the Rapid Deployment Team at Titeflex: Making something great is not just for software developers at Nintendo or Microsoft, chefs at Chez Panisse, or aircraft designers at Boeing. It's for hosemakers. Or a hotel's housekeeping department. "Do something great" — I can imagine a marvelous response coming from a housekeeping department given just such a challenge. "Make something great" is the sort of challenge we must embrace, as bosses at all levels and in all departments and in all firms, if we really do believe that imagination is the only asset, if we really do believe that economic security in developed countries is wholly dependent on leveraging knowledge.

## Yo, Creation Intensification

Drucker gets it. Nintendo's Yamauchi gets it. So does Murikami Teruyasu at Nomura Research Institute. He claims history can be divided into four epochs. First, the Age of Agriculture, which is largely behind us. Then, the Industrial Age, fast fading. Next, the Age of Information Intensification, where most of us would say we are today (in fact, most of us would say we're befuddled by it). But that's not the end of it, says our friend at Nomura. We're quickly moving into the Age of Creation Intensification.

And that's a whole new ball game. Providing and helpfully packaging information is one thing. Getting a handle on that is tough enough (most of us haven't). Ripping out layers is also one (good) thing. Reengineering is another (good) thing. But this is different: This is creation intensification. Creation of the curious corporation. Label it any way you want, it will separate tomorrow's (today's) winners from losers.

## The Practicality of "Correct" Imagery

Words are important. Images are more important. To deal with

..............**"Something great."**

the new era calls for new metaphors. Jazz combos (per researcher Karl Weick). Improvisational theater (per Digital Equipment's Charles Savage). Organization as carnival (me, *Liberation Management*). Shamrock organizations (per Charles Handy). Intellectual holding companies (per Dartmouth's Brian Quinn). Corporate virtual workspaces (courtesy Steve Truett and Tom Barrett). Work as conversation (from Alan Webber). Collaboration as romance (thanks to Michael Schrage). Spider's webs (Quinn again). We must really *see* these new images. "Competition is now a 'war of movement' in which success depends on anticipation of market trends and quick response to changing customer needs," wrote George Stalk, Philip Evans, and Lawrence Schulman in the *Harvard Business Review*. "Successful competitors move quickly in and out of products, markets, and sometimes even entire businesses — a process more akin to an interactive video game than to chess."

Interactive video. I like that.

"Mr. Andy Grove, chairman of Intel . . . compares [Silicon Valley] to the theater business in New York, which has an itiner-ant workforce of actors, directors, writers and technicians, as well as experienced financial backers," wrote Geoffrey Owen and Louise Kehoe in the *Financial Times*. "By tapping into this network you can quickly put a production together. It might be a smash hit . . . or it might be panned by the critics. Inevitably, the number of long-running plays is small, but new creative ideas keep bubbling up." Theater as model. Good. Think about it. Please.

> **Most important suggestion in this book: When you go to work tomorrow, try to look at "your place" as a fearful, first-day employee would.**

## Lessons Learned

- ☑ Traits of the curious corporation (your list or mine)
- ☑ Loving "weird"
- ☑ Hot words
- ☑ Staving off the Great Blight of Dullness
- ☑ Spaces with spunk
- ☑ New relationships with knowledge workers
- ☑ Make something great
- ☑ Creation intensification
- ☑ New metaphors needed
- ☑ Vicar of Vitality

### Reprise: A Place for Your Kids

In *In Search of Excellence,* Bob Waterman and I defined and measured excellence in terms of long-term financial health. Truth is, we could hardly have cared less. But we knew we needed to go through the drill to be taken seriously by the 5,000 conformists we hoped would buy the book.

Nothing wrong with financial measures, mind you. Can't live without them. But they're far from the whole picture. In recent years, for example, we've taken to measuring quality and customer service with a vengeance. (Good for us!)

But I'm thinking in other terms these days. In fact, I've got a new one-dimensional measure of excellence:

Would you want your son or daughter to work there?

What would such a place be, in order to be good enough for your kids? Ethical? Profitable? Growing? Yes. Yes. Yes.

Also, if you ask me, spirited, spunky. And curious. And a place where they're routinely told, "Do something great!" Maybe the list for your kids is different. Somehow I bet it isn't, or not much. That's another vote for going all out to create the curious corporation as we traverse these oh-so-curious times.

### T.T.D. (Things to Do) and Q.T.A. (Questions to Answer)

❶ Most important suggestion in this book: When you go to work tomorrow, try to look at "your place" as a fearful, first-day employee would. (It's very hard to do.) Start with the parking lot, front door, or reception area. Does "arriving" add a little spring to your (first day, remember) step? Or are you shut down a bit? Exuberance or Great Blight? Repeat this exercise with a handful of colleagues. Ask a first-day employee (if you're lucky enough to be hiring).

❷ Score yourself (and colleagues) on my list of 15 ideas for the curious corporation. How do you do? (I bet agreement among you is high.) Now create your own list. S-t-r-e-t-c-h, please. Score yourself again. Then repeat quarterly.

❸ How do you do with words like "weird"? Are you uncomfortable with them? Why? The times are weird, aren't they? (Think about it. "More intellect . . .," remember. "Only factory asset . . ." I didn't make this stuff up, dammit.)

❶ Review the comments on space. Invent a "Vitality of Space" audit, or something like it. Do your spaces turn folks (you) on? Or off?

❺ Have you ever been asked to, or asked someone to, make something great? (Not good, nifty, but . . .) If not, why not? Does it actually apply to hotel housekeeping departments? If not, why not? (And if you run a hotel, is your housekeeping department great — not "TQM good," but zesty, zippy, zany good?)

❻ Ready to sign up to be Vicar of Vitality? If you're a big cheese, why not create such a position? Or assign it to yourself for six months? (P.S. If you're not interested enough, or nervy enough, to change your business card title to Master of Madness, please throw this book away promptly. It's a waste of time to keep reading and sorry to have bothered you to this point.)

**This is the craziest chapter in the book. This is the most sober chapter in the book.** The times: Zany. Our organizations: sandtraps of sobriety. This won't do. The thing is, this chapter, championing lunacy as it unabashedly does, follows logically in the line of the argument I've been developing since, literally, the title page. The steps we've taken in Chapters 2 through 6 markedly loosen up the organization and reconstruct it in a far more flexible fashion (spider's webs, etc.); but they avoid, still, the subject of curiosity per se. Now we've hit it head on. And having done so, it's high time we move to the ultimate "why?" Obviously enough: To meet customers' needs in ways that will stand out in an incredibly crowded and kinetic marketplace.

## CHAPTER 8

BEYOND TQM

# TOWARD WOW!

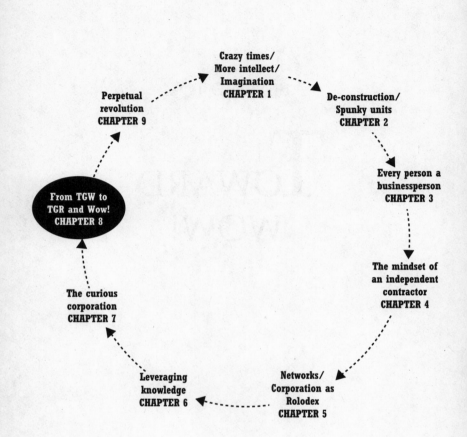

The market is crowded and getting more crowded. Do you stand out? To make his company stand out — to get it obsessed with customers and innovation — is the reason Percy Barnevik dismantled his headquarters and unleashed 5,000 profit-and-loss-center managers on the marketplace. And it's for the same reason our quality obsession of the last decade or so, valuable as it has been and incomplete as it still stands, is not enough. New competitors from around the globe, quality-conscious all, are joining us in flooding the market with flawless products. Flawless, but usually far from dazzling; and therein lies the basis for the next big steps in cozying up to customers: **Be your kinkiest**, and try to wow them. **Be your loving best**, and try to move in with them. In any event, marketing strategies that go far beyond TQM as practiced in the 80s are called for — **now.**

"In today's environ-

ment it's pretty

boring for consumers,

there has to be

some excitement to

get people to come

into the stores."

**Bill Wyman**

# So finally we'll talk about customers? Wrong.

Customers have been the topic of every page of this book. "Crazy times call for crazy organizations." "More intellect, less materials." "Only asset is the human imagination." All three of these rallying cries, raised at the outset and echoing through this book, are plain and simple market-driven imperatives.

Why deintegrate the firm, per ABB's Percy Barnevik and The Associated Group's Ben Lytle? Answer: To get energetic; to get modest-size business units obsessing about their customers.

Why "self-DESTRUCT," per stellar printer Quad/Graphics? To offer persnickety customers, caught in competitive whirlwinds of their own, far better than today's best.

Then I raised several topics in rapid sequence:

■ "Businessing" — turning every job into a business and every worker into a businessperson à la Tom Strange and Joe Tilli

■ Networking — linking directly into the heartland of customer operations per Baxter, UPS, et al.

■ Knowledge development — quickly bringing systemic global knowledge to bear on customer problems at ABB, Buckman Labs, McKinsey, VeriFone

■ Creating the curious corporation — attacking the Great Blight of Dullness that marks most companies and, by obvious extension, their products and services

The point of all of these? To demonstrate that it is possible, not just desirable, to deal imaginatively and speedily with the customer in a market chockablock with good products, good services, and good competitors from here, there, and heaven knows where else.

But, still, we haven't yet spent any time on quality per se. Ah, quality! It was the management and marketing tidal wave of the 1980s.

## TGW vs. TGR

The new American fixation on quality was the most important thing that happened to our economy in the last 15 years. Period. Make no mistake, our historical bent was not toward quality production. There was no Golden Age of Craft in our grandpop's time that we shamefully left behind. We were the build-it, then discard-it bunch from the get go. Later, we became the world's best churn-it-out mass producers. We don't have — and never had — the centuries-long quality tradition of Germany, the millennium-long quality tradition of Japan.

Through brute force and sheer willpower, then, we've executed a phenomenal turnaround recently, and in no place more than in Detroit. Our auto quality, relative to Japanese and German competitors, was a joke 15 years ago. But not today.

For instance, one of the most closely watched Motown measures is "things gone wrong," or TGW — more precisely, TGW per 100 cars produced. In reducing its TGW score, Detroit has all but closed the gap with Japan. But while American manufacturers were fixated on minimizing TGW, the Japanese began to shift their sights to *miryokuteki hinshitsu*, or "things gone right." Call them TGR.

"The Americans are building nice, average cars," industry expert Robert D. Knoll told *Newsweek,* "but few 'gee-whiz-look-at-this' cars." The Japanese are emphasizing "the more subtle sensory side [such as a] turn-signal lever that doesn't wobble [and] the feel of a climate-control knob." That is, we've made fabulous, even stunning, progress. But not enough progress.

"Any manufacturer can produce according to statistics," Mazda chairman Kenichi Yamamoto said dismissively to

**MINIMIZING TGW = necessary but not sufficient**

*Business Week.* Well, it's not that easy. Nonetheless the man from Mazda has a point. These days, getting the quality right by the numbers, according to the statistical measures, amounts to no more than a pass for the player's entrance at the stadium; it doesn't put points on the board. Top-quality products now routinely come from all over Western Europe, from Japan and Taiwan and Korea and Thailand and Malaysia and India and parts of China, from the U.S. and Canada, from Mexico and Argentina and Brazil. Is top quality by the numbers essential? You bet. Is it enough? Get serious.

> **More than half of the products tested rated a grade of D or F on the "new and different" scale.**

Richard Saunders Technologies, in Cincinnati, tests a random sample of the more than 15,000 new products vying for space on U.S. grocery-store shelves each year. In late 1993, according to a report in *Advertising Age,* the firm's researchers gave more than half the products they rated a grade of D or F on the important "new and different" scale. Included among the failed or barely passed: P&G's Mr. Clean Glass and Surface Cleaner, Spic and Span with Bleach, Sterling Winthrop's Aspirin Free Bayer Select, and Fabérgé's Lady Power Clear Roll-on antiperspirant.

When you get to the stores themselves, the story is the same. "In today's environment," says retail consultant Bill Wyman, "where everyone is matching everyone's lowest price, it's pretty boring for consumers. There has to be some excitement to get people to come in the door." You might see that excitement at Barney's new Taj Mahal in midtown Manhattan, but in general it's missing.

And missing even in high tech. Though computer warehouse stores offer block-long arrays of software and hardware, few products stand out. Even Apple seems to have lost its touch. A recent poll in *Computerworld* suggests that Apple's trademark ease-of-use distinction has been eclipsed.

It would be foolish (and condescending) on my part to dismiss as trivial the gargantuan strides that companies have made in quality since 1975. I don't intend to do that. But quality, where quality = low TGW scores, is far from the only measure of a product or service.

## Never the Twain Shall Meet

The problem: As measures, things gone right and things gone wrong are fundamentally apples and oranges. Significantly reducing TGW has a human element, our old friend empowerment; but in the end it is an engineering task, a statistical task, a by-the-numbers task. Increasing things gone right takes unadulterated flair. In fact, the *Business Week* article discussing TGR that attracted my attention was unabashedly peppered with words like "fascinate," "bewitch," "dazzle," and "delight." Sorry to say, lessening your TGW is no way to increase "fascination" or "bewitchment." You can only do that by working directly on TGR.

**"Fascinate," "bewitch," "dazzle," "delight."**

Tommy Boy Records, a standout in a phenomenally competitive industry, gets it. "We don't think we're in the record business," founder Tom Silverman told *Fast Company* magazine. "We *know* we're in the lifestyle business." Ditto Nike, MTV, Body Shop, and, in its heyday, Apple. Also an offbeat company from a country obsessed with precision, Swatch of Switzerland.

In his book *Sur/Petition* (beyond competition), Edward de Bono examined the trials and tribulations of the Swiss watch industry, which, he said,

> invented the quartz movement, but did not use the invention because it felt that this invention would kill [its] existing market. Anyone could use the quartz movement, whereas only the Swiss had the skills to make little cogwheels and balance springs. They were

right in their thinking . . . but wrong in their strategy. Watchmakers in Japan and Hong Kong eagerly grabbed the quartz movement, and in one year the sales of Swiss watches dropped by 25 percent.

What rescued the Swiss watch industry was the very unSwiss concept of the Swatch. The sales of the Swatch at most accounted for only 2 percent of a $4 billion market, but the Swatch . . . signaled that telling time was no longer the most important thing in a watch. A $5 watch tells time every bit as well as a $30,000 watch. The Swatch was not selling time so much as fun and costume jewelry.

The Swiss watch industry recovered as soon as it realized it was not selling watches, but jewelry. Indeed, wearing an expensive watch is sometimes the only legitimate way a man can wear, enjoy, and flaunt jewelry. And that has become the nature of the watch business today.

The equally fastidious Japanese are also getting the idea, and not just in the auto industry. "Until now, Japan has relied on its technological advances and high quality to sell products," said Yoshihara Fukuhara, chief executive of Shiseido, a leading cosmetics company. "But in the next era, that alone will not be enough. We must begin to make products that also have spirit."

There was no better proof of Fukuhara's point than a small, front-page article I came across in the *Press Democrat* of Santa Rosa, California. It was called "Japan Markets Noodles with Classical Bent," and I read it the morning I happened to start writing this chapter.

The billion-dollar noodle market in Japan was saturated. But one leading manufacturer, Takasago Shokuhin, had a strategy for breaking away from the pack. It would sell "music-assisted" products, that is, *udon* (wheat noodles) whose raw materials have been exposed to Beethoven and Vivaldi. "The theory behind these classical music-assisted products," the paper reported, "is that while humans relax by listening to music, enzyme and yeast fungus activity becomes livelier at the sound of classical music." The product has garnered rave reviews in test-market trials, and the manufacturer plans to charge a 50 percent to 70 percent price premium (!) for its music *udon*.

### Go for the Glow!

Paul Sherlock would make a surprising candidate for the music *udon* fan club. He developed and marketed products for Raychem, a high-tech materials company headquartered in Menlo Park, California. Yet in *Rethinking Business to Business Marketing*, engineering-trained Sherlock insisted that the two most important attributes of a sophisticated technical product are "glow" and "tingle." (Okay, Sherlock was trained as a psychologist, too. Engineer and psychologist = weird. Gary Withers' kinda guy.)

You're sitting across the table from a would-be customer, he continued. You lovingly describe your new gee-whiz gizmo. At some point you see the prospect's eyes light up. You've got him.

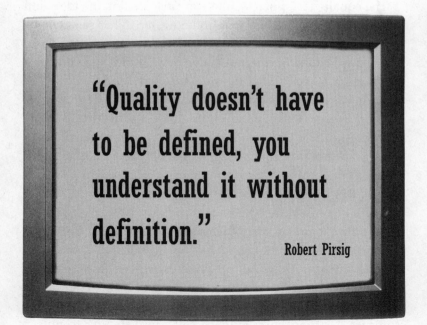

"Quality doesn't have to be defined, you understand it without definition."

Robert Pirsig

Sure, he works for a savvy company, and his corporate controller will demand a detailed justification for the purchase of your product (with its doubtless healthy price premium). Sure, regression analyses must be ginned up and appropriate factor-weighted scoring schemes derived. But any engineer worth her or his salt can churn those out in a flash. In the end, the buyer is determined to get hold of your "glow" and "tingle."

Sherlock's experience mirrors my own — whether the product is bizarrely high-tech material that thinks (from Raychem), a $2,000 personal computer, a $100 million contract for information services, or a jet aircraft engine. Sherlock really got to me with his short list of favorite products. Ziploc bags and Velcro were at the top. Amen! Ziplocs? Can't live without them. Use them for a million things. Grab a half-dozen before I head out on a two- or three-day trip. Love them.

Ziplocs and Velcro are not easy to make, and the quality process associated with their manufacture had better be buttoned down. But, c'mon, we both know I'm buying something more than quality as measured by the producer's SPC charts. I'm buying glow, tingle, and wow.

At the very least, we must understand, appreciate, respect, and accept a far broader concept of quality than the techno-freaks and TQM-maniacs preach. "Quality doesn't have to be defined," writes author Robert Pirsig (best known for *Zen and the Art of Motorcycle Maintenance*) in his recent novel, *Lila.* "You understand it without definition. Quality is a direct experience independent of and prior to intellectual abstractions." Once again, amen!

Did you see a terrific play last night? Why did you like (make that love) it? Because the actors didn't botch any lines? (TQM comes to Broadway: The Method is replaced by zero-defects training.) Hardly. No, the actors didn't botch their lines in the last play I attended. But actors getting their lines right is not the reason I loved the play. I loved it for its emotion, zip, and delight.

# BREAK THE MOLD..............

## Chado-master Rikyu's Lesson

The practice of tea service in Japan, called *chado*, is an art refined over centuries. To this day, devotees put years into learning the details. But *chado*, says one tea-master, also requires a "sincere heart." This saga, about the ancient tea-master Rikyu, has an important message for today's corporate denizens:

> Rikyu was watching his son Sho-an as he swept and watered the garden path. "Not clean enough," said Rikyu, when Sho-an had finished his task, and bade him try again. After a weary hour, the son turned to Rikyu: "Father, there is nothing more to be done. The steps have been washed for the third time, the stone planters and the trees are well sprinkled with water, moss and lichens are shining with a fresh verdure; not a twig, not a leaf have I left on the ground." "Young fool," chided the tea-master, "that is not the way a garden path should be swept." Saying this, Rikyu stepped into the garden, shook a tree and scattered over the garden gold and crimson leaves, scraps of the brocade of autumn! What Rikyu demanded was not cleanliness alone, but the beautiful and the natural also.

The cleanliness comes under the heading of SPC charts, TQM, and the reduction of TGW. The genius of shaking the tree and scattering the leaves is pure TGR.

## Cabbies with Mission Statements

Imagine the first focus group that gathered to review Post-it Notes prototypes. "Folks," the suave marketer began, "what I have here are little squares of yellow paper. They have glue on one side. Not very good glue. I mean, it doesn't stick very well. It sort of sticks, but, you know, then it doesn't. Well, this thing is going to replace paper clips. We think it will be a $1 billion market someday." Would you have bought that act? Don't be silly. Can you live without Post-its today? Maybe, but would you want to?

"When I meet a friend who has just returned from a visit to the hospital, clinic, or doctor's office," wrote the respected health-care futurist Leland Kaiser in *Healthcare Forum Journal*, "I ask, 'Did you have a good time?' This is the same question I might ask a friend if she or he just returned from a trip to Disneyland. A visit to a health-care facility should be a great experience." I love that. (Yes, I love using "love.") I love Kaiser's question because it's beautiful, because it's surprising, breaks the rules, and because it's TGR to the core.

(Actually, I hate Kaiser's question. Why? Because I didn't think to ask it myself. I didn't break out of the box. Yikes, how things like this bug me! D'you suppose it's a residual from my three-decades-old engineering training? Boy, linear thinking dies hard. Or not at all, is more like it.)

Sure I'm foursquare for "reengineering" at hospitals (see our discussion in Chapter 2 of Lakeland Regional Medical Center). And, sure, I'll personally lead the cheers for the quality team that redesigns the admission process to remove annoying, unnecessary, time-consuming steps. Fine. Great, even. But that doesn't go far enough. "Did you have a good time?" That's a challenge, that's a rallying cry I can imagine building a hospital around. I just plain love it.

Transformation. Breaking the mold. Anything — ANYTHING — can be made special. Author Harvey Mackay tells about a cab ride from Manhattan out to La Guardia Airport:

> First, this driver gave me a paper that said, "Hi, my name is Walter. I'm your driver. I'm going to get you there safely, on time, in a courteous fashion." A mission statement from a cab driver!

Then he holds up a *New York Times* and a *USA Today* and asks would I like them? So I took them. We haven't even moved yet. He then offers a nice little fruit basket with snack foods. Next he asks, "Would you prefer hard rock or classical music?" He has four channels.

Mackay goes on, listing more features, such as a cellular phone for his use. Then he concludes, "You know what? This man makes $12,000 to $14,000 extra a year in tips. You should have seen the tip I gave him. Incredible."

How fabulous! Take the most mundane experience imaginable — a cab ride — and transform it into something special. "Did you have a good time?" It's not a bad question to ask about either a cab ride or a trip to the doctor's office, but it implies a standard that most of us don't even think about suggesting, let alone meeting, in our businesses. Make that, more important, don't even think about at all.

### The Valerio's Test

During my first trip to Auckland, New Zealand, my wife Kate and I were looking for an evening meal. We took a taxi to Parnell Street, which was supposed to have a bunch of nice eateries. We picked a block for no particular reason and told the driver to stop, trusting that we'd find someplace decent. About 15 feet away was Valerio's, which displayed the world-standard outside menu board. But there was no menu. Instead, this statement was posted:

> Sometimes menus don't reflect what you might find in a restaurant. So I didn't bother with one.
>
> In our restaurant you will find atmosphere and character. Friendly and witty staff. A half-crazy owner, and real food.
>
> The kitchen is in open view to the customers, and you are welcome to inspect it.
>
> The cockroaches left me a long time ago. The only animals remaining are my cats, Jeffrey and Luigi.

Otherwise I am left with a bunch of paranoid human beings to deal with.

If you are accustomed to all this, then come on in and join us for a pleasant lunch or dinner.

It was more than enough for us. The setting was cozy, and we ended up at a table across from Valerio himself. Greet us? Forget it. He was busy, rummaging through stacks of invoices and receipts. We were promptly handed a menu, though, that was consistent with the warning posted outside. It began with the rules of the house:

"May I remind you that we don't do family counseling. We still love children (ours!). Nothing is for free in this place. We do welcome uncomplicated tourists. If the noise level is too high, adjust your tongue."

It also laid out a culinary philosophy: "Mamma was always right. No fancy sauces, no frills or nouvelle cuisine, but sensible, genuine, tasty, hearty food." Tasty? It was super.

On the way to the gent's at one point, I was drawn to a wall of framed letters. Awards? No way. If you thought so, you've missed the whole point. They were letters of complaint. One, from the sales director of a local TV station, berated Valerio for lousy service and added that the choice of white wines was skimpy. Framed with the letter was a copy of Valerio's insulting response. The customer had "three hours at a so-called 'business lunch' to complain," but hadn't uttered a word. Why now? And, hey, white wine is not a house specialty.

Much amused, I returned to our table. Then a most remarkable discussion ensued. For the next 45 minutes Kate and I talked seriously about dropping both our professional careers and starting a restaurant, restaurant/bookstore, or sidewalk café. Could any other endeavor encourage such individual expression?

What can be learned from Valerio's?

■ Wow. Valerio's had marvelous food, but mostly the place was a kick. Valerio's had spirit, character, quirkiness, and personality.

■ Surprise. The Macintosh, with its mouse and icons, sur-

Valerio reinvented the restaurant experience.

VALERIOS

WELCOME TO VALERIO'S

SOMETIMES MENUES DO NOT REFLECT WHAT YOU
MIGHT FIND IN A RESTAURANT, SO I DIDN'T BOTHER
WITH IT.

IN OUR RESTAURANT YOU WILL FIND ATMOSPHERE
AND CHARACTER, FRIENDLY AND WITTY STAFF, A
HALF-CRAZY OWNER AND REAL FOOD.

THE KITCHEN IS IN OPEN VIEW TO THE CUSTOMERS
AND YOU ARE WELCOME TO INSPECT IT.

THE COCKROACHES LEFT THE LONG TIME AGO.
THE ONLY ANIMALS LEFT ARE MY CATS (JEFFREY AND
LUIGI) OTHERWISE I AM LEFT WITH A BUNCH
OF PARANOID HUMAN BEINGS TO DEAL WITH!

IF YOU ARE ACCUSTOMED TO ALL THIS, THEN
COME DOWN AND JOIN US FOR A PLEASANT
LUNCH OR DINNER. COME IN THROUGH THE
NEW ROOM, PERUSE AROUND, DISCOVER THE
OLD ROOM, ENJOY THE "AL FRESCO" WHERE YOU
CAN FEEL RELAXED AND UNWIND YOURSELF.

Valerio

IF ONE TELLS THE TRUTH, ONE IS SURE, SOONER
OR LATER, TO BE FOUND OUT.

(O. WILDE)

prised most users in 1984 and changed their idea of computing. So, too, did Post-its change our concept of sticky. Valerio's was a complete surprise.

■ Holy Toledo. Beyond wow and surprise, the place was such a happening that we thought (for a couple of hours, anyway) about changing our lives.

■ Subversive. Starting with the anti-menu and extending to the public letters of complaint, Valerio thumbed his nose at conventional wisdom. Likewise, early Apple products were clearly anti-computer computers, symbolized by the fun apple logo and the firm's sandal-clad founders. Such things make the customer a coconspirator in a pirate adventure. I got the same feeling over dinner.

■ Heart. Valerio's made a connection that was refreshingly and joyously human.

■ Lively. Valerio's is energetic. It's not loud (Valerio won't allow it, remember), and it's certainly not glitzy. It's aerobic.

■ Beyond satisfaction. Valerio's does not "satisfy" or even "exceed customer expectations." Such chilly terms! Valerio's redefines expectations. A restaurant? An event? A way of life?

I propose a VT, or Valerio's Test, for each product or service a company offers. Commercial loans. Consumer loans. Travel services. VCRs. Software. Tomato soup. Hot chocolate. Is it a life transformer? Or just another whatever?

Well, you get the point. (So *do* something!)

### Love

Swatch watches. Sophisticated, high-tech material that makes you "glow" and "tingle." A "good time" at the hospital. A cab ride to La Guardia with classical music and a basket of fruit. Noodles nurtured by Beethoven and Vivaldi at a 50 percent price premium. And a restaurant in Auckland that wants you to know that some people had a lousy experience eating there.

What's going on?

"We were convinced that if each of us could add our fantasy and culture to an emotional product, we could beat anybody," Swatch chairman Nicholas Hayek told the *New York Times.* "Emotions are something that nobody can copy."

Likewise, AT&T's recently appointed consumer business chief, Joseph Nacchio, attributes MCI's recent success and market-share surge (Friends & Family, etc.) to having created "emotional ties" to customers; now he'll try to do the same for the slipping market leader. And Marilyn Bruner, president of Ontario's Markham Stouffville Hospital, has taken a page from Leland Kaiser's book (with his help) by reformulating her mission statement to read: "Fundamental to this mission is our commitment that every patient's visit to Markham Stouffville Hospital will be a great experience."

> **Can you learn to use — learn to love, as it were — words like "love"?**

University of Texas marketing professor Robert Peterson gets it. And he can measure it. Peterson has well over 100 technical articles to his credit, and he's studied customer satisfaction for years, but damned if he had been able to find significant correlation between customer satisfaction and repeat business. Whoops!

Then he stumbled over the determining connection. In order for customer experience to lead to repeat business, an emotional link must develop between the consumer and the product or service. "There is a large 'affective' component to service — from the customer's point of view — that we discount and fail to deal with [or] ask about," says Peterson. He reached that conclusion when he started changing the words on customer-approval scales. Instead of using measures that went from, say, "like" to "dislike," he substituted ones that went from "love" to "hate."

But can you learn to use — learn to love, as it were — words like "love"? Can you even include them in strategy documents?

John Peterman can. He's owner of The J. Peterman Company, the upscale cataloger that grew from nothing to $50 million in just six years. Peterman sells fabulous products. At least I think so (and I own several). I'm not sure about the actual product, because I *know* I've been captured by his fantasy. Peterman's whimsical, hand-sketched catalogs associate each product with an adventure. "The great thing about the products we sell is the circumstances of their discovery," he told us. "Every item has a story behind it, making a simple thing very interesting. It puts a lot of pressure on the company to maintain the quality of the products because the story is so wonderful."

Take "The Counterfeit Mailbag," from J. Peterman's summer 1993 catalog:

> The secret thoughts of an entire country were carried in leather bags exactly like this one [sketched below in the catalog]. Except this one, a copy, isn't under lock and key in a museum. It's for sale.
>
> I borrowed an original from a friend, a retired mailman who, like thousands before him, was kind enough to test it out, for years, on the tree-lined streets of small towns everywhere. Before you were born.
>
> The test was successful; even though discontinued, it can't be improved upon. It's simply perfect as a device for carrying important ideas and feelings back and forth.

Sure it's corny, at one level. (So is humanity.) But the idea of "carrying important ideas and feelings back and forth" really got to me. I bought the damn bag. But I've only given you an inkling. Still in the catalog copy, Peterman next tells us in painstaking detail how to take care of our Mailbag:

> The first scratch will kill you, but in fact, it's the first step in the right direction: patina.
>
> So the sooner it gets scratched, nicked, bumped, dug, hit, squeezed, dropped, bent, folded and rained on, the better. Really.

> When you receive your mailbag, it's so fiercely
> new looking I'm almost ashamed of it. But there's no
> choice. It would cost too much to pre-age each mail-
> bag before sending it out to a customer. . . .
>
> Here's my recipe for "accelerating" the aging
> process. First, spend one day (the day you get it) the
> way it is. Brand new. Then, the next day, scratch it *all*
> *over* with your fingernails. Lightly. This will horrify
> you, at first. Then, spray-mist it with plain water,
> lightly. Let it dry. The scratches will lose their raw-
> ness. They will look old. Repeat this treatment as
> often as you can stand to; once a week for five weeks.

What's Peterman up to? He's unabashed about it. He's creating a relationship with customers that he openly compares to a
love affair. "As long as one partner is interesting to the other,
the love affair continues," he says. "If one partner ceases to be
interesting, the affair is terminated."

These ideas are important to catalogers. And to high-tech
materials companies. They're important to 15-person corporate
departments providing accounts-receivable services. To hospitals, to cabdrivers. And to businesses large and small.

## A Passion for Passion

Think about small businesses for a minute. In its array of local
enterprises, your town is probably much like mine: restaurants
and shops come and go. What stuns me is how hard people
work to launch something new only to create a business that is
so, well, ordinary. The new restaurant's food might be tasty, but
there's nothing special about it. It doesn't pass the Valerio's
Test. The passion is missing. So is the soul. The new place does
not make you say "Wow" or "Great," or make you want to
change your life. You don't fall in love.

If you're thinking about starting a new business, restaurant,
or technical consulting service, here's question No. 1: Can you
explain, in 25 words or less, what is absolutely special about it,
what will make people not say "Nice" — but "Zounds!" or

"Holy moly!"

The same question applies to a 35-person hotel-housekeeping department. "What can we do to make us different from any other housekeeping department?" "How can we add our own signature, some things that will elevate the experience that guests have, surprise them, and set our hotel apart?" They're not silly questions, but they mostly go unasked. Or worse, unimagined.

I repeat that I'm not urging hotel housekeeping operations to burn their figure-laden quality-control charts. We ought to know that all the rooms got done on time and that they pass some kind of a test for cleanliness (no hairs in the bathtub, no pretzel crumbs under the bed, etc.). That's essential, for without it we aren't keeping house. Yet it's not enough — not enough to soothe our customers' dreams and stir their imaginations.

Remember: Imagination chief executive Gary Withers says he seeks out the "weird." Guy Kawasaki, software expert turned management guru, wants to change the average employee into a "raging, inexorable, thunder lizard evangelist." And Body Shop's Anita Roddick says she wants the average customer coming into one of her shops to be "thrilled."

"Look, there are two kinds of singers," Luciano Pavarotti told the *New Yorker* magazine. "One who is doing everything very easily. The top note for him is like a — peanut! He just picks it off! And there are the singers who have a little trouble with the top note, but they give you their heart. For me, personally, I like the singer who makes you feel something very important. The first kind comes out of the schools and they have all the pyrotechnics. So? So? I think you need a little effort. A cry. Pain. Something in there to make you think it is true — to the singer and to the audience."

I love Pavarotti's point. Technical excellence is not enough. Heart. Cry. Pain. Give me something special that makes that connection between singer and audience, restaurateur and customer, housekeeper and guest, health-care facility and patient or family member.

# Time to Stop Listening!

The average "new" product on the grocery-store shelf looks like the 47 varieties of the same thing sitting next to it. It's passionless. So, too, the average "new" personal computer. The average "new" automobile. The average "new" catalog that arrives in my mailbox (four per day, typically, in early 1994). The average "new" office supply item I'm considering for my firm. The average professional service rendered, for that matter. So indistinct, so predictable. Part of the problem may be that companies listen too much to their customers. Seriously.

"Talent never asks 'Will they like it?'" talk show host Larry King proclaims. "Talent pleases itself. That's the difference between talent and ordinary." On first reading, I thought that was one of the most arrogant statements I'd ever come across. But then I thought a little more. Almost all the world's progress comes from the people who have it their way.

"It's like a sense for the fashion business. . . . He can read a few years in advance . . . he listens to no one." This is a Nintendo executive on the firm's founder, Hiroshi Yamauchi.

Yamauchi listens to no one. How arrogant!

Sigeru Miyamoto, creator of Nintendo's Super Mario, understands. "I am not creating a game," he says, "I am in the game. The game is not for children, it is for me."

Hmmm?

"A lot of people build products by asking what the market wants and delivering it," says Paul Saffo, director of new media for the Institute for the Future. *Day in the Life of* creator Rick Smolan, he says, "asks 'What's exciting to me?' and delivers that. That's how great products are made."

"I just bought what I liked. I never bought anything that I didn't like. . . . Fortunately," says Chuck Williams, founder of Williams-Sonoma, the high-end cookware retailer and cataloger, "there have been a lot of people out there who like what I like."

Time Warner CEO Steve Ross's "enthusiasm for cable had an emotional source," writes Connie Bruck in the *New Yorker*. "He was a relentless, insatiable consumer."

"He's his own best object of study," said the *New Yorker*'s Terrence Rafferty about Clinton campaign strategist James Carville. "When the body politic itches, he scratches himself."

"Stop worrying about what 'people' think. We believe in our own ideas," insists Imagination's Gary Withers.

"Unless I can design something nourishing to *my* soul — nourishing, not just nice, dramatic, photogenic, novel — I can't expect it to be nourishing to anyone else," proclaims architect-author Christopher Day.

Sure, most companies ought to engage their customers more intimately (see below). On the other hand, job one for the average company these days could be: Get interesting, damn it! And that means, as Joseph Campbell might put it, following your bliss — down blind alleys, all the way to public embarrassment and, occasionally, to the promised land of wild commercial success-via-reinvention in a frenetic retail or high-tech or whatever marketplace.

### Make Way for the 1,000Xers

But how many companies have the nerve to let their Sigeru Miyamotos loose? It's the rare one, run by a rare character like Nintendo's Yamauchi. Or, more likely, it's the Rick Smolan story: a guy who couldn't deal with the normal strictures of the publishing industry, who went out and created his own way of doing things and reinvented a corner of that industry in the process.

We've talked a lot about liberation and democratization — giving people at the front line enough clout to get on with their jobs. Those ideas are phenomenally important. On the other hand, so is the role of the wildly different individual.

"The difference between an average producer and the very best producer can be enormous. A factor of 1,000 sometimes," says Microsoft research head Nathan Myhrvold.

"An ordinary man," says Nintendo's Yamauchi, "cannot develop good games no matter how hard he tries. A handful of people in the world can develop games that everybody wants. Those are the people we want at Nintendo."

Recall, in our discussion of the curious corporation, that I suggested hiring curious people. I also suggested that it was a good idea to lasso the truly weird person and bring him or her into the company, even if the price is wrong and it breaks the bank and disrupts the institution. Getting the special/zany person, the 1,000Xer (1000-times person, per Myhrvold) on board is of growing importance in a crowded marketplace starved for distinct products and services.

Again, the battle cry: Crazy times call for crazy organizations. The time for change is past. The time for revolution is nigh (or post-nigh).

## Beware Improvement-itis

"It is not [price] competition that counts," wrote economist Joseph Schumpeter, "but the competition from . . . the new technology, the new source of supply, the new type of organization . . . competition which . . . strikes not at the margins of the profits and the outputs of existing firms but at their very foundations and their very lives." Consider, then:

Ten years ago, two office-furniture makers (Herman Miller and Steelcase) set the world ablaze with a modular design that revolutionized the way we work. At the same time, a computer manufacturer (Apple) started a revolution of its own by making computing friendly. And for decades, a packaged-goods marketer (P&G) cleverly used consumer information to outwit its competitors and achieve dominance in many crannies of its market.

Now all four companies are at sea. Why? "It's become a discounter's world, a nightmare," says one top exec. In fact, all four companies now sing the same Chicken Little tune: Discounters abound, margins are evaporating, the sky is falling.

The nub of the problem: All four lost their nerve. They allowed themselves to sink into the quicksand of commodity competition.

They didn't snooze. They worked like hell to improve quality, to make their customer service more friendly, and to cut their product-development time smartly. Yes, they even reengineered. But they didn't reinvent. They countenanced change, but not revolution. They cheered the agents of change, but not traitors and anarchists.

I reviewed a catalog from each of the office-furniture makers beset by dastardly discounting competitors and cost-obsessed customers. They put me to sleep. Ten years ago their products wowed me. Now they offered just more of the same. Sure, a dozen (or a dozen dozen) new features were touted, and some were, naturally, labeled revolutionary. And quality was surely top drawer. But, truth is, a broad array of competitors are offering adequate design, and more than adequate quality. What once stood out has been mostly (or more) matched by others. If you want to charge a premium, you'll have to come up with something more.

Apple is in the same pickle, as the *Computerworld* survey I cited demonstrates. Apple is still a pioneer, but it is only a tittle ahead of the pack these days. Tittles don't merit 25 percent (or even 5 percent) price premiums, let alone the 50 percent premiums that the firm was able to command not so many nanoseconds ago.

As for P&G, the *Financial Times* reported on the general malaise in its industry. Private-label and store-brand product quality now rates equal or better with consumers; and the store-brand folks in particular often have more timely and accurate information than their big brothers. So since the big guys' products are a yawn. . . . Well, you get the point.

Rumor in the fall of 1993 had it that owners of leading independent bookstores, reacting to the megastores, such as Barnes & Noble, that had superficially copied their friendliest features (armchairs for leisurely reading, author appearances), were thinking of starting a purchasing and distribution cooperative. Suppose the strategy, aimed at achieving volume discounts from publishers comparable to those given to the biggies, is successful. What will the independents have achieved? Some of them will shave a penny or two (maybe three) from their costs — and come close to imitating the megastores.

How stupid!

Cutting costs any legitimate way you can is fine, mind you. But it's nutty to imagine such a move to be a core strategy that will turn the tables on giant, deep-pocket competitors. Independent bookstores should up the ante by inventing something entirely new. And so, too, should the office-furniture makers, computer creator, and packaged-goods company.

Do it right and the competition will, literally, fold. Take those irritating private-label brands. "[They] thrive on the *status quo*," writes University of California marketing professor David Aaker. "They love to march down the experience curve and exploit economies of scale. They hate innovation. . . . They hate anything that tends to focus competition anywhere but price. . . . A dynamic, innovative environment is not hospitable to store brands."

Look, all your life, if you are imaginative and creative, you will be copied. Copying is what most people, and most companies, do. But the company that wants to stay at the top of its market and command those premium prices can't just copy the copycats by improving its old products, no matter how creative they might once have been.

The history of commerce sadly suggests that market leadership nearly always reduces a company to conservatism — or improvement-itis, as I call it. And even if the company manages to avoid the greater sins of arrogance and complacency, conservatism is more than enough to do it in. If you want to continue to command the heights, you need to keep on creating, and overturning. As Schumpeter understood, it's as simple — and as unlikely and scary — as that. There's no rest.

Combating improvement-itis entails thumbing your nose at yourself and all you stand for. It entails mounting a successful frontal attack on the cherished cash cows that are paying your kids' way through Harvard.

It means questioning the buttoned-down improvement processes you spent most of the 80s putting into place. In an article titled "The Dark Side of Quality," quality researcher Patricia McLagan wrote, "The danger is that an obsession with process will create a myopia that discourages people from testing assumptions and engaging in breakthrough thinking."

Call it breakthrough thinking, call it reinvention, call it cannibalization, call it what you will. The guts to attack themselves mercilessly and ceaselessly is what managements need these days. Without the gumption for self-destruction, any company is vulnerable to the discounter that waits just around the next bend. And that bend is much closer than anybody thinks.

(P.S. It's unfair to single out just four companies, as I did above. In the last year, I've listened to the "commoditization blues" sung by big accountancies, several training companies, a leading engineering firm, a food company, a brace of retailers, and a global insurance company. By firms tallying several billion in revenue, and by independent contractors. But I have no sympathy: zero, zilch, nada. For what it's worth, here's my partial list of once special products that are now distinctly me-too: Procter & Gamble paper towels and toilet paper, American Airlines service, Honda Accords, anything at McDonald's including the once outstanding cleanliness . . . and . . . and . . .)

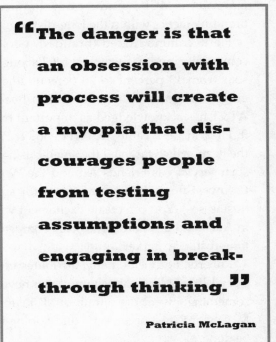

**"The danger is that an obsession with process will create a myopia that discourages people from testing assumptions and engaging in breakthrough thinking."**

**Patricia McLagan**

## Bert Roberts's Prize

I'm mad as hell. As I told several thousand retail executives in January 1994, "My belief No. 1 is this: The refrain that 'Chintzy consumers demand more value these days' is the equivalent of saying, 'We're plumb out of ideas and the only thing we can figure out how to do is match the prices at Sam's.'"

No, dammit, commoditization is not inevitable. Ask Valerio. Or Mackay's Manhattan cabbie. Or Swatch's Hayek. Or the good folks at Rubbermaid, whose passion for innovation and devotion to building brand equity have turned the maker of mundane plastic and rubber doodads into America's most admired corporation, according to *Fortune;* they edged out Merck, no less, in the 1993 poll.

Or ask Bert Roberts.

MCI chairman Roberts bagged *Advertising Age*'s Adman of the Year award for 1993. He helped develop the firm's first TV commercial in 1984, the magazine notes, and "also played a crucial role in MCI's gradual development of personality and branding tactics within the long-distance category."

He decommoditized (branded, personalized) an obvious commodity, and has watched MCI's long-distance market share soar from 13 percent to 20 percent since 1990. He created an emotional consumer bond, which head-to-head competitor AT&T has acknowledged as important by attempting to imitate it. First, in 1991, came MCI's Friends & Family. Then Friends of the Firm, which targeted the small-business sector. And, in 1993, such services as Friends Around the World and Proof Positive (a lowest-possible-rates program for small and medium-size businesses). You can create excitement with a 50-seat restaurant in Auckland or in the ferociously competitive, $65-billion global long-distance market.

Roberts, not incidentally, attributes much of his success to a Gary Withers-like philosophy. "You never assume you can't do something," went the refrain of MCI's former boss, the late Bill McGowan. "Just because no one's doing it doesn't mean it can't be done."

"Every patient's visit to our hospital will be a great experience."

M. Bruner

Amen! The steam rises from my head when I hear, as I often do, a corporate leader respond to a new idea with, "Who else is doing it?" Instead of delighting in originality (if there are other examples, the chief should say "no" in my book), he or she is afraid to plunge in where others have not swum.

Tragic.

## Reinventing: Let All the Line Workers Sell

Reinventing means, from time to time, following your bliss. And tuning in to the wavelength of the frequently disruptive 1,000Xers. But emphasizing TGR also does mean listening to customers. But taking listening a qualitative leap beyond focus groups and customer surveys, which tend to produce "give me what you already sell, but a little bit better" answers, and toward total interconnection. It's what I call the *symbiosis imperative*.

Yes, it's frantic out there. Yes, the market is overcrowded. Yes, quirky passion is imperative. And now I'm going to sound like I'm contradicting myself: If some companies listen too much to their customers, as I suggested above, most companies don't get close enough to customers to hear them.

Close? How close?

Titeflex Rapid Deployment Team members Tom Strange and Joe Tilli are line-workers-turned-supersalesmen, but the idea of getting nonsalespeople into the selling business can be expanded. A lot. Why not let everyone sell? Consider this wacky "sales" approach from the container makers at Ball Corp. The company's development exec, Clifton Reichard, wrote in the *Wall Street Journal*:

> Let's [turn] the process upside down. Don't sell out there; sell in here. Don't let the salesman sell; create conditions where the company can sell itself.
>
> We tell our prospects that if they give us 24 hours, we'll introduce them to our people making the products they will be buying — all the way up to the CEO and his management team. They can judge for themselves if we are the kind of people and company they

would like to buy from.

All of us together can sell better than any one of us can individually. The entire organization from the bottom up — being themselves and demonstrating their capabilities — has a combined credibility that no one salesperson can ever adequately represent. We can convey more in one trip to our plants and offices than one salesperson can convey in a lifetimeof trips calling on prospects.

Of course, if you have plants you don't want customers to see and if you have people you don't want customers to meet, then you are the competition we are looking for. We will fly the prospective customer — at our expense — to see you so we can be absolutely sure the proper comparison and assessment are made.

> **Bringing clients into the process early makes them coconspirators in the creation adventure, which often edges them toward embracing exciting (and risky) ventures that promise a wow-scale payoff.**

Talk about breaking the mold. I wonder how many customers have taken him up on his offer?

### Nothing Short of Symbiosis Will Do

The Ball Corp. approach hints at how far pioneering companies will go to get everyone into the value-creation (and wow) business. The idea of intimately entwining with customers is an idea whose time has come. So just how does one entwine with customers? Ah, imagination.

The Associated Group broke itself into itty-bitty businesses, the Acordia companies, that would have no choice but to schmooze and become intently, intimately, and emotionally involved with microbits of the financial-services marketplace.

Body Shop founder Anita Roddick refuses to spend a dime on conventional advertising. Instead, she works with her shops to create ongoing "conversations" between staff and customers. She wants the Body Shop to be a teaching institution, not just another cosmetics peddler.

The premier German machine-tool maker, Trumpf, plays by similar (self-invented) rules: It is a teaching institution, working hard with customers so that they can clearly understand how to benefit from Trumpf's enormous and unequaled technical skills (which come accompanied by a high sticker price).

Ad agency Chiat/Day has succeeded through its wacky creativity, goes the conventional wisdom. Chiat is creative, all right, but another reason for its success is its unusual (for ad agencies) policy of involving clients intimately in the ad-creation process from the very first rough concept. Conservative agency account execs (perpetually at war with the "creatives" — even to the point of keeping them hidden from the client) rarely share their ideas with the client until they are 90 percent polished. Often as not, a wild approach sprung on the unsuspecting client at this point will lead to quick rejection. By bringing clients into the process early, however, Chiat/Day makes them coconspirators in the creation adventure, which often edges them toward embracing exciting (and risky) campaigns that promise a wow-scale payoff.

### Nypro Snuggles Big Time

As impressive as the Ball Corp., Body Shop, Trumpf, Chiat/Day et al. sagas are, perhaps no one understands the snuggling, symbiotic characteristics of customer relationships better than a $165 million purveyor of mundane injection-molded plastic parts. Nypro, of Clinton, Massachusetts, developed a fabulous quality process, modeled on Motorola's, that sets it miles apart from the

**OPEN CLOSETS=STRATEGIC SHARING**

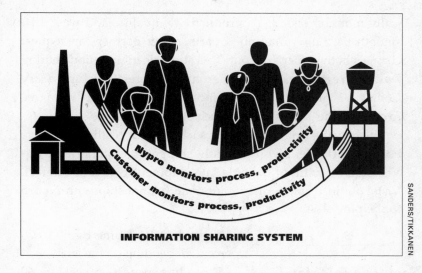

INFORMATION SHARING SYSTEM

SANDERS/TIKKANEN

herd of roughly 2,800 U.S. competitors. With a defect rate edging toward 3.4 per million (the Motorola six sigma gold standard), compared to an industry standard of 10,000 boo-boos per million, Nypro is in a matchless position to single out and pursue only the most persnickety customers, like Johnson & Johnson and Abbott Laboratories.

But Nypro's greatest competitive advantage is the next big step it takes, a virtually unique use of customer teams. Vistakon, the Johnson & Johnson unit that makes Acuvue disposable contact lenses, relies on Nypro for the 120 molds used to produce its lenses. From the start, Vistakon proposed a joint-project team to assess production processes, product quality, and productivity. That team, which meets for two days every six weeks, fosters a partnership that can delve into the most intimate details of both firms' operations.

Vistakon managers in Jacksonville, Florida, are linked by computer to Nypro's shop floor in Clinton and can check Nypro's real-time performance — how many units are being produced, the amount of waste, even the on-line statistical process-control numbers. Still more remarkable, it's a two-way street: Since Nypro must match its production molds to Vistakon's finished lenses, Nypro's team members can electronically monitor Vistakon's productivity, quality, and waste. To smooth the flow of supplied parts, either partner can request changes in the other's output. This strategic information-sharing "will make or break a supplier-customer relationship," Gary Collins, Vistakon quality-assurance manager, told us. "We agree to open all the closets and see each other's skeletons."

The benefits from developing such an open relationship have been remarkable. Nypro recently shipped its billionth part to Vistakon — without a single late shipment or quality defect. Vistakon, in turn, credits its intimate relationship with Nypro for helping slash:

- product lead time by 50 to 70 percent, depending on the lens;
- product inspection costs by 60 to 90 percent;
- inventory by 20 to 80 percent;
- space requirements by 30 to 60 percent; and
- annual costs by 5 to 20 percent.

> **New technologies make it possible for "even the mass marketer to assume the role of small proprietor, doing business again with individuals, one at a time."**
> **Don Peppers and Martha Rogers**

Nypro's latest million-dollar customer, Gillette, awarded it the manufacture and assembly of its Lady Sensor razor — the first time Gillette has relinquished such massive responsibility to an outside source. Nypro and Gillette began planning production of the razor in late 1991, with waves of Gillette engineers and managers visiting Nypro — and reciprocal visits by Nypro staff to Gillette's South Boston plant. Midway through the start-up, Nypro spent $200,000 to further automate the assembly process; the change yielded better quality, 50 percent labor reduction, and 30 percent productivity improvement — savings split 50-50 by Nypro and Gillette. The Nypro-Gillette team then made similar improvements in Gillette's operation.

"We really mean it when we talk about satisfying customers,

because that's all we have. We don't have any 'products,'" says
Nypro CEO Gordon Lankton. (More intellect, less materials, eh?
And this from a plastic-doohickey maker.) "We're like
McDonald's. Like them, we're global . . . but each unit is located
within a few miles — and sometimes a few feet — of the customer." Although most of Nypro's 14 plants were opened at a
customer's request, Lankton sometimes makes the first move.
Nypro agreed to build an $8 million facility outside Chicago to
serve Abbott Labs, even though the relationship was not
assured when construction began.

Talk about snuggling up cozy with the customer!

## Peppers and Rogers:
## The New Electronic Symbiosis

Electronic links are a small but important part of the Nypro
story, but they are near the center of the UPS-Federal Express
battle. (Star Trek redux: Maxiships vs. Powerships, remember?)
But we ain't seen nothin' yet.

In *The One-to-One Future: Building Relationships One Customer
at a Time*, Don Peppers and Martha Rogers suggest that we do
no less than reconsider the fundamental basis for marketing.
New technologies, they claim, make it possible for "even the
mass marketer . . . to assume the role of small proprietor, doing
business again with individuals, one at a time."

The core mechanism is straightforward. Gather as much
information as you can about the customer (Peppers and Rogers
suggest spending 20 percent of the marketing budget on acquiring such info), then recreate the organization to cater to customers' very personalized needs. Customer (rather than product) segmentation already exists — e.g., American Airlines' variety of frequent flier programs, American Express's assortment
of credit cards. Moreover, our mailboxes are increasingly inun-
dated with catalogs tailored, at least loosely, to our individual
needs (as evidenced by past purchases), and with delivery available literally overnight.

But imagination suggests that's only the beginning. In the

near future,
per Peppers
and Rogers, a savvy cataloger could:

■ Allow you to send any number of gifts to friends and relatives, ordered all at once, up to 16 months in advance.

■ Schedule the delivery of each gift on the date you request on the order form; charges would be made two days before the item's scheduled delivery.

■ Send you a "reminder" postcard 10 days before each gift is scheduled for delivery, recapping the item, delivery date, address, and gift message.

■ Subsequently, send you preprinted work forms with each new catalog, including a list of last year's addressees, dates, and gift items.

The goal of such electronically induced intimacy is to dramatically shift the company's (cataloger, whatever) sights from share of market to share of customer. "In the mass-marketing paradigm, which governs the way Kellogg and nearly every other consumer-products company views its business, the brands have managers watching out for them," Peppers and Rogers write, "but the customers don't. The brand manager's assignment is to use advertising to persuade you and 26.7 million other faceless consumers to buy all the boxes of Frosted Flakes that Kellogg hopes to sell this coming quarter. The share-of-customer alternative would be for Kellogg to assign a customer manager the task of figuring out how to increase Kellogg's share of the perhaps 1,800 boxes of dry cereal you will buy in your lifetime."

To get people in existing marketing departments to think this way, the organization must be fundamentally restructured to emphasize "customer management." That is, rather than organizing around products, organize around portfolios of customers arranged, perhaps, according to expected lifetime purchasing value. Even product-development activities would become subsidiary to the customer-management structure.

To be honest, I'm not quite ready to throw in my whole wad with Peppers and Rogers. After all, we've spent the first half of this chapter urging you to get busy adding "wow" to your basic products and services. Putting the product second to customers is hardly a guarantee of success. Nonetheless, there is an exciting message and a stern warning here. To date, most uses of electronics to link up with customers are primitive. The potential *is* enormous. And that potential will probably not be fulfilled unless we do reorganize according to something like predicted lifetime value of various classes of customers. Serious consideration is warranted. And should a competitor get there first (e.g., if Blockbuster Video figures out how to exploit the 48 million membership cards it has issued), well, Katy bar the door.

## Dr. Tattersall Provides a Timeless Lesson

The idea of clever and intense electronic connections, per that only barely futuristic cataloger we examined, is to forge close, lasting, intimate relationships (hey, they know your and all your relatives' birthdays) with customers, even masses of customers, one at a time. Relationships are a process business, dependent on the microscopic details of how a customer is dealt with. Peppers and Rogers say so. Nypro's Lankton says so. And services-marketing guru Len Berry, a professor at Texas A&M, agrees. "The way customers judge a service," he wrote, "may depend as much or even more on the service process than on the service outcome."

Don't tell that to the typical administratively or scientifically trained businessperson. She or he focuses on outcomes. Sure outcomes are important, but Berry's point is that customers are mostly influenced by the way they are handled.

Take the little case of M.H.N. Tattersall, an Australian physician. The *Wall Street Journal* describes an experiment he conducted on office procedures. After the visits of 48 patients, the doctor randomly split them into two categories. Half got follow-up letters, half didn't. Thirteen of the 24 who got letters later said they were "completely satisfied," the highest possible rating. Only four of the 24 nonrecipients made the same assessment. Think about that: A mere letter increased the number of fully satisfied customers by a factor of more than four.

What is a visit to a doctor? It's a complex event. Dr. Tattersall (or Dr. Whoever) brings years of scientific training and experience to bear on a diagnosis. Yet this one tiny twist, a follow-up letter, can completely change the patient's perception of the service rendered. Look at it another way. A doctor's consultation plus a letter is an entirely different service/product from a consultation without a letter.

> **"We always discuss things, then I'll make up our minds."**
>
> A female respondent in a 1993 Australian survey of women's roles in purchasing decisions

Let's go back one more time to TQM. No, I'm hardly suggesting we cut medical school by a year and send the doctor wannabes to charm school instead. I am suggesting that the technical part of the act is far from the whole story and that the worth of the nontechnical elements is often badly underestimated, or not even considered.

In *Verdict Pending*, Fredonia French Jacques examines medical malpractice in the United States. She quotes a hospital administrator: "It is patients who have been slighted or treated abruptly . . . who have been depersonalized, whose feelings have been hurt, who will sue. . . . Patients seldom sue those who have cared for them with kindness." Bottom line: Hospital services are highly sophisticated, but those who get angry enough to call their lawyers tend to do so because of the small, human aspects of the treatment.

### Dazzlements

Yes, Peppers and Rogers have a revolutionary message (and most aren't listening). And yes, UPS's multibillion-dollar tracking system makes an enormous contribution to its customers' perception of the way they're handled (process), and thence the value they receive. But, p-l-e-a-s-e don't underestimate the effect of caring, the Tattersall-ing of a process. Service researcher Ron Zemke even goes so far as to distinguish between the "little touches" and the "spontaneous little touches" that a company offers with its service. The spontaneous little touches he calls "dazzlements," a word I've come to appreciate.

Zemke offers the close-to-home example of Jeff Amland (aka AAgro-Green Corporation), the guy who shovels snow from the Zemkes' Minneapolis driveway during those very, very long Minnesota winters. In one snowstorm, the Zemkes came home from work early. With the snow accumulating quickly, they grabbed their shovels. Then Jeff showed up, and the three worked together. He was performing under a regular contract, with an agreed-upon price. Nonetheless, the next AAgro-Green bill included a 10 percent reduction for the Zemkes' "aiding and abetting removal." That sort of thing makes you chuckle — and keeps you coming back. (To AAgro-Green or to General Electric's aircraft-engine operation.)

Upon reflection, I think Zemke is on the money to make a fuss about the difference between "little" and "spontaneous little." In fact, I think the gap is a gulf. Back to UPS. It's big investment in information systems has brought it close to (or even with) FedEx on that dimension of service. But the paramilitary UPS still lags its archrival badly on the "spontaneous little touches/dazzlements" score. And, interestingly, while a few billion clams can quickly bridge a technology gap, closing a dazzlement gap is much more difficult and much more time consuming, if not so expensive.

"All we need is love," to steal a line from the Beatles.

## Who IS the Customer?

"We always discuss things, then I'll make up our minds." That's the way one female respondent put it in a 1993 Australian survey of women's roles in purchasing decisions. The survey found that women's input tipped the family's choice in: 94 percent of decisions involving major furnishings, 94 percent involving white goods, 92 percent of decisions involving holidays and travel, 91 percent involving the purchase of a family home, 89 percent in choosing a new bank account, 88 percent related to medical insurance, 85 percent for household insurance, 82 percent for car insurance, 79 percent for life insurance, and 71 percent in the purchase of a home computer.

Simple question: Is your staffing in product development and in marketing consistent with these findings? I would be surprised if it was. Very surprised.

---

**Lessons Learned**

- ☑ TGW vs. TGR
- ☑ Glow, tingle, wow (and use those words)
- ☑ Quality doesn't have to be defined
- ☑ Did you have fun at the hospital?
- ☑ The Valerio's Test and Harvey Mackay's cabbie
- ☑ Only love will do (love, love, love, d'ya hear?)
- ☑ Shut your ears ("I just bought what I liked")
- ☑ The deadly commodity trap (beware improvement-itis) and the Rubbermaid-MCI alternative
- ☑ Symbiosis, paying customers to visit your competitors' plants, Nypro and living v-e-r-y close
- ☑ Intimate electronic relationships by the million
- ☑ Process 1, Outcome 0 (Tattersall the scrivener)
- ☑ "Little touches" vs. "spontaneous little touches"
- ☑ Don't men ever make decisions?

---

## Reprise: Symbiosis and Wow — The Twain Do Meet

I said stop listening and tune in to your inner ear ("I just bought what I liked" — Chuck Williams). Then I said listen harder — in fact, go beyond listening to Nypro-style symbiosis. Is there any way to resolve this screaming contradiction between doing what you love and what the customer loves?

Yes, fortunately. Former Apple chief John Sculley, reflecting in the autobiographical *Odyssey* on his years at PepsiCo, said he couldn't recall a single wise marketing decision that had been based on the numbers. Collect them, by all means, but apply them with a big pinch of salt, amended by the intuition developed over a lifetime. (Sculley later admitted, while criticizing some of his deci-

> **Have your 16-year-old daughter review your product catalog.**

sions at Apple, that he figured it had taken him 15 or 16 years to become attuned — good word choice — to the soft drink market.)

Know what the numbers are, but then explode beyond mechanistic TGW-reduction programs to "wow," "glow," and "tingle." Get closer (much, much closer) to the customer, while remembering that tomorrow's triumphant product is much more likely to emerge from the quirky mind of an inspired lunatic than a buttoned-down, Brooks Brothers male, age 46.5 years, who is trying to cope with the statistical revelation that women are making most of the important buying decisions.

Recall that Tommy Boy Records' Tom Silverman said Nike was the first to understand "lifestyle" or "identity" marketing, which moves, he adds, far away from "the dismal science of segmentation" toward the "difficult work of cultural knowledge."

I'm not sure I know what Silverman means, but I sense that he's right, even if prone to jargon. I think Phil Knight of Nike does know what it means. Also Hiroshi Yamauchi at Nintendo, Jay Chiat at Chiat/Day, Chuck Williams at Williams-Sonoma, Clifton Reichard at the Ball Corp, and Gordon Lankton at Nypro.

It blends imagination, intuition, and big-time customer schmoozing. It means being *of* the market ("The game is not for children. It is for me." — Sigeru Miyamoto), not doing something *for* the market. This monumental distinction holds for music recording and industrial plastic-parts making alike. And it underscores the difference — the gap, the chasm — between TGW and TGR.

### T.T.D. (Things to Do) and Q.T.A. (Questions to Answer)

❶ How about it? Is your company's average product offering ho-hum? An imitation? A copy? ("Sure that's true when I go grocery shopping, but not of *our* products/services. . . . You don't get it. Here, bend over, look close, and let me show you this little gizmo we added. . . ." Try again.)

❷ Where's your fixation? TGW? TGR? Do you agree the two are different? Very different? In opposition? So?

❸ How about "glow," "tingle," and "wow"? Are they the basis for your purchases? At home? At work? Low tech? High tech? No? Try being honest. Think again. Talk about three or four recent home and business purchases. Why did you buy from whomever? (Work this through with colleagues. Work it through in the executive suite, and on the front line.)

❹ Does quality have to be defined? (Think back to the last movie you loved, hated.) Is the part you can define decisive in your appreciation of the product or service? Does the very act of defining precisely desiccate the product and obscure the more important elements of quality?

❺ Does "have fun" apply to the experience of customers dealing with your company? Should it? Could it? Does dealing with your (recordings, steel, etc.) company pass the Valerio's Test?

❻ Love. Love. Love. Use that word in business? Do you buy Professor Peterson's research on affection and repeat business (and the insipid nature of mere "satisfaction")? John Peterman's strategy of growth by engaging in "love affairs" with his catalog customers? Are you acting accordingly?

❼ Have recent breakthrough ideas in your business/industry come from systematic listening? Or from someone's inner ear? Is your market segment beset (flooded) by me-too products? Why? And flooded with market research? (Think about the link between the rise of market research and the flood of me-too products, if you dare.)

❽ Curious corporation redux: Do you seek out and retain, difficult as it may be, the 1,000Xers? And, more to the point perhaps, do the 1,000Xers seek out your company?

> **Do you seek out and retain, difficult as it may be, the 1,000Xers? . . . do the 1,000Xers seek out your company?**

❾ Are you hounded by discounters? Have a couple of outsiders (e.g., your 16-year-old daughter and her friends) review your catalog of product and service offerings. Do they see them as genuinely special? Have you reinvented your tiny or large enterprise in the last four years? (If not, why are you surprised by discounters' incursions?)

❿ Who says you can't decommoditize it? Bert Roberts and friends did it with long-distance calling in the face of a bloodthirsty competitor. Why can't (don't) you?

⓫ How's your "entwining quotient" — using Nypro as today's perfect 10? Are you snuggling up — boldly, proactively, lovingly — to your customers? Is everyone a salesperson, per the Ball Corp. model?

⓬ Are you spending 20 percent of your marketing budget on acquiring information about customers, as Peppers and Rogers suggest? Are you obsessed with relationship selling, even if you are a mass marketer (by yesterday's definition)? How about the "customer-management organization" idea? Make sense? If not, why not?

⓭ Are you a process freak, as Len Berry suggests you ought to be? How about the Tattersall experience? Make sense? Do you buy the predominant role of process (vs. outcome)?

⓮ Do you give employees the latitude to perform sponta- neous acts as easily as Jeff Amland was able to give the Zemkes a 10 percent discount? Do you encourage employ- ees to use their imagination as Amland did? (P.S. Check with your frontline people, fresh caught and vets alike, before assigning yourself a high score on these questions.)

We've come so far in the past 15 years, and it's paid off in spades. (Ask a Japanese corporate president about U.S. auto quality these days. And semiconductors. And . . .) **But it's not enough. Not nearly enough,** as revolution chases revolution through the marketplace. Ironically, our very success (and those of others, from everywhere) in going hammer and tongs at quality and speed has leveled the playing field. It's ended up commoditizing quality levels that would have been off-the-charts fantastic 20 years ago. The "What's next?" that is summarized in this chapter (TGR, tingle, symbiosis, electronic links, not listening, listening hard, etc.) has been the subliminal message of this whole book: intimate units furnished with customers, devices to leverage learning, networks of the world's neatest people, curiosity unleashed, innovation and innovators untrammeled. Crazy times . . .

## CHAPTER 9

BEYOND CHANGE (REDUX)

# TOWARD PERPETUAL REVOLUTION

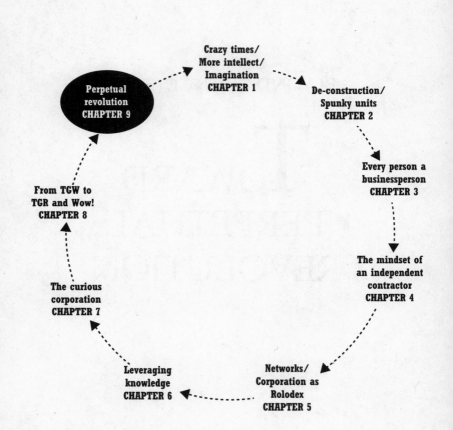

Change and constant improvement (*kaizen*, per the Japanese), the watchwords of the 80s, are no longer enough. Not even close. Only revolution, and perpetual revolution at that, will do. Leaders at all levels must accept what the transformational leaders tell us: that the organization can "take it" (enormous change), that only a bias for constant action and a bold embrace of failure, big as well as small, will move companies forward. The point is to compress 10 years' worth of "change," by yesterday's standard, into one year, if not months. Then draw a deep breath and start again. Forget the calm at the end of the storm. **If you sense calm, it's only because you're in the eye of the hurricane.**

"There is a

revolution in

the company

and we have

to overthrow

the old regime."

David Kearns

"**O**ur feeling is that this rapid, chaotic rate of change will continue forever** and will continue to accelerate," says Silicon Graphics CEO Ed McCracken. "Companies [must] burn themselves down and rebuild every few years," says business consultant Roger Martin.

Most leaders aren't living up to the challenges implicit in McCracken's and Martin's remarks. That's true at the top and true of supervisors, true in big companies and tiny ones. Much of what ails corporations today is traceable to a failure of nerve in every part and at every level of the organization.

### Push the Needle All the Way Over

Nerve. Oticon's chief, Lars Kolind, has got it. He seems to live by the old Chinese proverb, "It's very dangerous to try to leap a chasm in two bounds." Recall that Kolind created a zany "spaghetti organization" overnight. The key to its successful implementation, he insists, was changing everything at once. In his company's case that meant organizational structure, culture, physical setting, and the very nature of work itself.

Former Union Pacific Railroad boss Mike Walsh told his lieutenants to take a "clean-sheet-of-paper" approach to company redesign; a 120-day revolution, which scraped 120 years of rust off the Union Pacific iron horse, followed. "Push the needle all the way over," Walsh counsels others, because, he adds, "Organizations are capable of taking on more than most of their leaders give them credit for."

Silicon Graphics' McCracken says that coping with accelerating chaos (his words) is "simple," a matter of "having the guts to place bold bets. We place bold bets on the strategic portion of our business . . . we place bold bets on the people we hire and then give them their freedom, indeed push them, to make bold bets too."

Sure, most bosses these days know that pat hands will kill and that constant improvement is a must. But even constant improvement will not do. Only revolution will. And, for that matter, perpetual revolution. The *Financial Times* reported a late-1993 speech by Volkswagen's controversial Inaki Lopez to beleaguered European automakers. *Kaizen*, or changes of a few percent, is not enough, he said. The answer, instead, is a quantum leap, "30 to 40 to 50 percent improvement that must be made."

> **"Organizations are capable of taking on more than their leaders give them credit for."**
>
> **Mike Walsh**

Paul O'Neill, CEO of materials giant Alcoa, understands what Lopez means. Continuous improvement is "probably a disastrous idea if you are far behind the world standard," he asserts. Consultant Marion Steeples reports that in 1991 O'Neill set a 24-month goal of closing "at least 80 percent of the gap between Alcoa's practices and world-class benchmarks"; by the end of 1992, "core targets were achieved or surpassed."

Bosses are also championing change agents, which is better than earlier attitudes, but not better enough. As Body Shop founder Anita Roddick puts it, only "anarchists" (her word) can do the trick — i.e., her salvation in the bruising cosmetics marketplace will come, she imagines, from nurturing those in the company with the moxie to thumb their noses at convention, and at her.

Former Xerox CEO David Kearns is one of the few who doesn't choke on the word "revolution." He likes it. "This is a revolution in the company," Kearns said as he launched a quality program that turned his punch-drunk company into a role model, "and we have to overthrow the old regime. The quality transition team is the junta in place to run things on a temporary basis. The standards and measures equate to the laws of the land. The reward and recognition system is the gaining of control of the banks. The training is capturing control of the universities. Communications is the seizing of control of the press, and senior management behavior is putting your own people in place to reflect the revolution. All of these elements are needed to change a culture."

Amen.

## The Action Faction

It's clear, isn't it? Pushing the needle all the way over, unabashedly championing revolution, and getting the company anarchists to the barricades means doing something. Taking action. Once more, Silicon Graphics' McCracken offers a lesson as he guffaws at the very idea of long-range planning. "When we finish one product-development program, we raise our heads and look around to see what to invent next," he told the *Harvard Business Review* in an article aptly titled "Mastering Chaos at the High-Tech Frontier." "We try to get a sense of what customers might want and what is happening with changing technologies. Then we put our heads down, engineer like mad, and get the product into the marketplace. Once we've done that, we do it all over again. That's our planning cycle. If we can do that in nine months or a year rather than three years, we will have a tremendous advantage." Do it he has, and tremendous advantage has been his reward.

A penchant for putting your head down and engineering (a whatever) like mad is the single most important leadership trait in times when market conditions place a premium on doing something. To look more generally at the phenomenon, consider the plight of a corporate staffer who's sweated blood on a 45-minute presentation for her division general manager. Twenty-five years of company watching says the boss responds in one of two ways:

**constant improvement: no**
**revolution: yes**

Response No. 1: "That's a really interesting analysis. The market-research folks, especially Sally Another-Analysis, could give you a hand in fleshing it out. Oh, yeah, the cost thing just seems too low to me. Marty Nitpick, in finance, is a genius with stuff like that. I'll tell him to expect your call. In fact, I'll buzz him while you're here. Why don't you schedule an hour on my calendar for another look in a couple weeks."

Response No. 2 (before the staffer is a third of the way through her presentation): "Smells right. Do what you have to do. Drop by in the next couple of days and tell me how much your next steps are gonna cost. We can scrounge a few bucks from somewhere to cobble together a prototype, then get some quick market feedback. It's risky, but I'm certain you can drum up field support for this — we've got our share of John Waynes out there. This is a terrific opportunity for you."

Boss No. 1, Sam, invariably hits the targets he meticulously sets — not by much, but he hits them. He is as smart as a whip and can ferret out a soft spot in an argument with laser-like precision. Sam is generous to a fault with his time and loves to debate intelligent proposals with bright young staffers. In fact, you could say he provides advanced MBA training.

Boss No. 2, Gwen, has had downs along with ups. But in a six-division organization, she's brought in the lion's share of the parent firm's breakthrough products. Gwen is smart and engaged. But she simply can't sit still (literally) through an entire presentation. She likes committed, well-prepared people ready to go out on a limb to chase their dreams. She'll give them lots of leeway. (Peers such as Sam say it's way too much.) But Gwen expects 15-hour days — and results. She'll put 28-year-olds in charge of big projects quick as a wink if they've produced in the past. If you're on her "out" list, though, be careful. You'll get a second chance if you've busted your gut, but two strikes in a row, no matter what the circumstances, and you better have other plans for the future.

(Incidentally, I'm not slamming Sally Another-Analysis in market research and Marty Nitpick in finance. They're worth their weight in gold. It's just that Gwen-like bosses assume that our fictional staffer is smart enough to seek out such folks on her own, whereas Sam-like honchos inadvertently use Another-Analysis and Nitpick as cops, momentum maulers, and ownership destroyers.)

For my whole adult life I've studied the implementation of corporate strategies and read, it seems, most of the millions of pages that have been written on the topic. The academic buried deep inside me is still put off by simplistic answers to such questions as "What makes for effective strategy implementation?" Yet I keep stumbling across bosses who seem oblivious to hurdles, who assume (for themselves and their associates) that people can do damn near anything they have the will to do so long as they don't wait for one more analysis before starting.

Mind you, action-obsessed chiefs are not prophets, and what they and their hustling underlings accomplish may bear little resemblance to what they first imagined. The action faction nonetheless believes — and I concur — that if you can just get going, you'll learn quickly, and dramatically increase the odds of doing something worthwhile in short order.

Nor are action fanatics necessarily likable or

> **"When we finish one product-development program, we raise our heads and look around to see what to invent next."**
>
> **Ed McCracken**

good company. Sam, the cautious division chief, is the patient professor conducting a tutorial; he loves to chew on ideas, asks good questions, and is a pleasure to talk to. Gwen, in contrast, is often abrupt and, not infrequently, even rude. She doesn't mean to be, but part of her can't figure out why the hell you're there giving the presentation in the first place. If she were you, she already would have recruited some supporters in the field, scraped up some dough, and built something. From the moment she walked through the front door as a 21-year-old junior marketing assistant, Gwen has subscribed to the "It's better to ask forgiveness than permission" school of subordinate behavior.

### The Relentless Pursuit of Failure

Pushing action (a must) has an awkward relative. Namely, tolerating screw-ups galore. It's that simple. And logical. Unfortunately, the typical boss cringes at the very idea of failure. The smart boss, though no fan of half-hearted tries, knows that perpetually pushing the limits means hitting the wall from time to time. "The whole secret of his success," says publisher

> **If we don't make utter fools of ourselves from time to time, we grow smug — that is, we do not grow at all.**

John Brown, speaking of Virgin Group founder Richard Branson, "is his failures. . . . He keeps opening things, and a good many of them fail — but he doesn't give a f---. He keeps on going!" Likewise, Wal-Mart CEO David Glass told me the No. 1 thing that stood out about Sam Walton was his ability to leave yesterday's cockup behind and get on with today's work. "He simply wasn't afraid to fail," Glass flatly asserts.

Fear of failure, on the part of the newly hired receptionist as well as the newly appointed chief executive officer, is the principal cause of paralysis. But even if you can somehow engender, in yourself and among your employees, a taste for small failures,

# Champion Revolution !

it's nowhere near enough in these dizzying times. From time to time, and more often than you think, the failure must be big, bold, embarrassing, face-losing, and public. If we (you and me, our unit, our company) don't make utter fools of ourselves from time to time, we grow smug — that is, we do not grow at all.

The irony, and conundrum, is that the concern over the next round of layoffs that haunts most professionals these days leads to conservatism at precisely the times that we need audacity. "Maybe if I hide behind the desk, they'll miss me when the pink slips are handed out on Friday," goes the implicit refrain.

Mistake. Recall our discussion of achieving the mindset of an independent contractor (Chapter 4): Only those who restlessly and boldly pursue risky projects and career moves, and who laugh off the pratfalls that attend such a strategy, stand much of a chance of making it to the winner's circle, let alone staying there.

## Never Accept a Tepid Response

Division chief Gwen never asked permission. And she doesn't expect her subordinates to. Change the gender, and Gwen could be Mike Walsh (Union Pacific, now Tenneco) or Percy Barnevik (ABB). I'm reminded of the first commandment for teachers from the venerated Notre Dame English professor Frank O'Malley: "Accept anything but a tepid response."

Walsh and the other transformation artists among leaders have this one down cold: They are determined to leap that chasm in one bound. And they're determined that you'll do the same. Sadly, tepid is still the temperature in many corporate corridors. Tepid questions are asked and tepid responses are accepted. "Make something great," said Nintendo's Yamauchi. That's no tepid request. And if you're one of those 892 Nintendoids who generated over $5 billion in revenues in 1992, you'd better be ready to respond in kind.

## Spending Time (Amid the Mess)

Pushing the needle all the way over means action. Action calls for the bold embrace of failure. Replace tepid with hot. Then add one more to the list of leadership imperatives: focus. It's not easy, though. In a classic 1973 study of how managers actually spend their time, Canadian researcher Henry Mintzberg discovered that their days were amazingly fragmented, with the average duration of an activity running only nine minutes.

Fragmented, yes. But the trick for successful managers was turning those microbursts of activity into a consistent tune.

All bosses have hundreds of distractions a day. Hey, it's what they get paid for handling. However, the best bosses use every distraction, no matter how minor and no matter what the apparent issue is, to hammer home their dominant theme. Milliken & Co. CEO Roger Milliken got the quality religion in 1980. He preached the gospel at every occasion. "[Roger] Milliken is obsessed with quality," one company exec told journalist Jeremy Main, "from the way we write memos to [how we maintain] the guest quarters. Once I picked him up at the airport and he asked me how long it would take to drive to the guest house. I said twelve minutes. He said, 'OK, you've got twelve minutes to tell me what you have done this week to improve quality.'"

What an exception to the rule! Many CEOs may loudly sing the quality hymn, chant the reengineering mantra, or dance the speed jig. But look at their calendars, and you'll see that after the entertainment, they're quickly cloistered with 73rd-floor staffers, poring over the quarterly numbers. By all means, make the numbers these days, especially with impatient boards and activist institutional shareholders looking over your shoulder. But just remember that the numbers will only sustain you if the company is transformed — e.g., becomes a quality exemplar like Milliken under Milliken or Xerox under Kearns. And that takes CEO time. Five minutes here. Twelve minutes there. Hour after hour. Day after day. Year after year.

It goes without saying (or it should) that what holds for the CEO who has held his job for 47 years (Milliken) applies to the

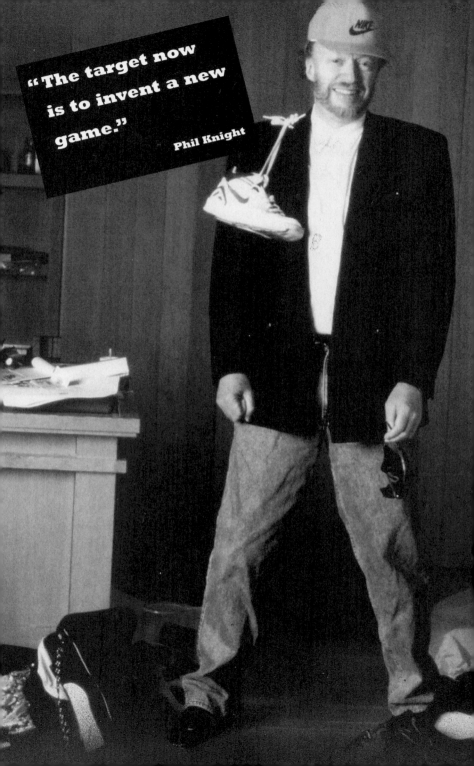

"The target now is to invent a new game."

Phil Knight

| THE FIVE VIRTUES |
| --- |
| **Pedal to the metal** |
| **Action** |
| **Embrace failure** |
| **No tepid responses** |
| **Focus amidst mayhem** |

young woman appointed to her first managerial post yesterday morning. At the end of her 18-month tour of duty, the department will be different. Or not. If it is different — known, say, for phenomenal responsiveness to internal customers — it will only be because she found a way, leveraging those daily distractions, to stay v-e-r-y focused.

Put the pedal all the way to the metal ("organizations are capable of taking on more . . ." — Mike Walsh). Action ("put our heads down [and] engineer like mad" — Ed McCracken). Embrace failure ("he doesn't give a f---" — John Brown on Richard Branson). No tepid responses ("make something great" — Yamauchi). Focus amidst the mayhem ("you've got twelve minutes" — Roger Milliken). These are the five cardinal virtues of the most effective leader-revolutionaries, at all levels, including the front line, that I've met. Tack, jibe, keep your eye on the finish line, and don't look back. Except . . .

### Thriving Amidst Constant Disequilibrium

Except the damned finish line keeps changing. Sun Microsystems "has become a vortex in which you really have a constant state of disequilibrium," said Sun vice president Bill Raduchel. A constant state of disequilibrium is something all of us must get used to. Learning to love change (uh, revolution), thrive on change (uh, revolution), cherish change (uh, revolution) — that's the ticket.

Anita Roddick puts it in slightly different terms. Her corporate philosophy is clear: "First, you have to have fun. Second, you have to put love where your labor is. Third, you have to go in the opposite direction to everyone else." Roddick is almost, but not quite, alone on that last point. Sony cofounder Masaru Ibuka adds: "The key to success for Sony, and to everything in business, science, and technology . . . is never to follow the others."

Ah, how sad it is, in these turbulent times, to watch the average company, small or large, trying to succeed in the herd by moving maybe "a little bit faster than yesterday" or "delivering a little better quality or service than yesterday." Forget it. It'll be trampled.

Furthermore, from inside the herd it won't even see the real competition: the company off to the side and heading in the opposite direction that just reinvented their industry. As one consultant said of a client obsessed with process improvement, "While they're calmly shampooing the carpet for the umpteenth time, the competition is busy pulling it out from under them."

Hearken back to self-DESTRUCTION (and don't forget those capital letters, please), the term Quad/Graphics boss Harry Quadracci favors. Or recall Nike's Phil Knight: "The target now is to invent a new game."

"If your business has anything to do with information, you're in deep trouble." That's the word from His Eminence, Microsoft founder Bill Gates. But all our businesses have lots to do with information, and almost all of them are in trouble. I agree with Gates. (And he'd better watch out, too.)

"There's no way to be careful in this business," says Novell founder Ray Noorda. "All you can do is be aggressive, strong, and give the customer choices." I like that: "No way to be careful." Most firms are far too careful, careful protecting a franchise that's disintegrating before their eyes.

"The most probable assumption is that no currently working 'business theory' will be valid 10 years hence," says management grandee Peter Drucker. But a tough Irishman, MCI's late boss Bill McGowan, put it more bluntly: "The chump-to-champ-to-chump cycle used to be three generations. Now it's about five years."

On your mark! Get set! Reinvent!

## The Last Word

Reinvention must have a particular flavor, one hinted at by Ben Cohen and Jerry Greenfield, cofounders of the quirky and successful Ben & Jerry's Homemade, the high-end of high-end ice cream companies. New products and polices at their firm must pass a test: "Is it weird enough?"

Maybe *Is It Weird Enough?* should have been the title of this book.

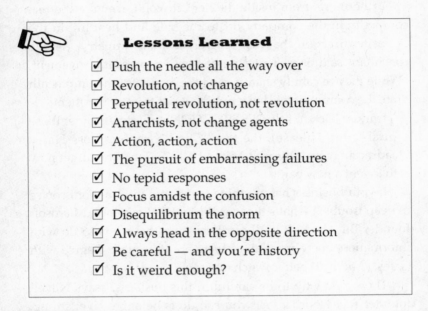

## Lessons Learned

- ☑ Push the needle all the way over
- ☑ Revolution, not change
- ☑ Perpetual revolution, not revolution
- ☑ Anarchists, not change agents
- ☑ Action, action, action
- ☑ The pursuit of embarrassing failures
- ☑ No tepid responses
- ☑ Focus amidst the confusion
- ☑ Disequilibrium the norm
- ☑ Always head in the opposite direction
- ☑ Be careful — and you're history
- ☑ Is it weird enough?

### Reprise: The (Truly) Last Word

At the outset, I recalled having heard futurist Alvin Toffler say that we need to "reinvent civilization." I agree. And I take Toffler's words very seriously. Reinventing civilization begins with reinventing thee and me, and that means we both need:

- ■ A passion for failure
- ■ A thirst for learning and homework
- ■ A bias for action
- ■ A taste for ambiguity
- ■ An abhorrence of pompous and inflexible obfuscators
- ■ A willingness to shoot straight
- ■ A belief in the curiosity of all folks
- ■ A hankering to be weird

- An affection for "hot" words
- A penchant for revolution
- A love of laughter
- An aversion for the tepid responses, and
- A determination not to tolerate the Great Blight of Dullness, whenever or wherever it appears

Got that?

### T.T.D. (Things to Do) and Q.T.A. (Questions to Answer)

❶ Do you discuss "change" and "change agents"? Or do you discuss revolution and reinvention and revolutionaries (and perpetual revolution)? Do you think the distinctions are overblown? If so, why? What do your colleagues say? Is what we are experiencing a once-every-couple-hundred-years change? Or not? Nots, explain yourselves. (Hint: You're wrong.)

❷ Can you imagine changing everything at once, per Oticon's Kolind et al.? If not, why not? What's your experience with the efficacy of two-jump leaps across chasms?

❸ Is there a bias for action (Ready. Fire. Aim.—Harry Quadracci) in your outfit? Or a common plea for "one more analysis," and a tendency to "write it up" and ask permission? How about you? If you're an action fanatic, prove it (i.e., ask frontline folks and customers anonymously).

❹ Have you ever observed any progress without (many) accompanying failures? And leaps forward unaccompanied by major boners? How, then, is failure viewed in your organization? How do you view failure? Big, bold botches? (P.S. If the front line is hesitant, and terrified of failure, despite your pleas for risk taking, I'll give you one guess as to why. . . . Because you and your colleagues in management are terrified yourself. Right?)

❺ Are you helping your colleagues learn to live with (and even get a kick out of) constant disequilibrium? Do you discuss it? With new hires? Old hands? Openly? Constantly?

❻ Can you imagine formally adding "Is it weird enough?" to your product-development handbook? Can your actions, as a leader, in the last day, week, month, or year, pass the I.I.W.E. ("Is It Weird Enough") test? Do you think so? Do your peers think so? Do your subordinates think so? How about group and individual G.W.P.s (Get Weird Plans) for yourself and all your peers and subordinates — with one-week, one-month, three-month, six-month, and one-year goals?

Is it **weird** enough?

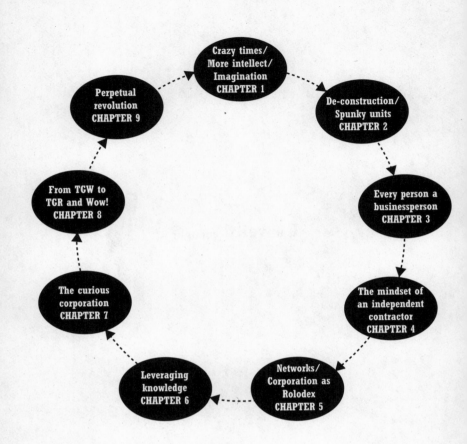

# IT MAY BE CRAZY
# BUT IT ALL MAKES SENSE

So what have we done? We've built a model. A rational model of tomorrow's (today's) business organization.

Its cornerstone is coldly logical, the market-driven case for craziness: Crazy times call for crazy organizations. The design concept for the model, the idea that would influence its eventual shape, was the inexorable fact that most/all value in a business, regardless of its size or industry, is generated by the energy from two sources — the intellect and the imagination.

Next, we deconstructed the old corporation and turned, as the new engine of progress, to the immoderately independent, modest-size sub-unit. Why? Simple. How else, say the likes of ABB's Percy Barnevik , are you going to bring that intellect and imagination to bear whenever an unexpected opportunity (or new competition) pops up.

Flattening the bejesus out of the organization chart (19 out of 20 middle managers and central staffers evaporate) brought us literally face to face with the front line . . . where we discovered workers who were slot-fillers.

That won't do. So we transformed them; we made them businesspeople, 90 percent entrepreneurs, and put them in charge of complex jobs.

Endangered workers? Endangered everyone is more like it. Act like an independent contractor, hit the books with zest, and lifetime commitment (receptionist or biologist). That's the ticket. That, and, of course, Pollocking for profits, in the . . .

. . . in the networked, virtual organization, the new-fangled enterprise-as-Rolodex concocted in order to bring people and little bits of organizations together from hither and thither, for a day, a week, a year, to take advantage of today's opening in the marketplace — that may well be closed tomorrow.

The virtual organization gave us a new form of sorts, but we were still light on substance. Is there a there there? No small question. Well, since tomorrow's (today's) chief substance is going to be (already is) knowledge, we'd better figure out how to find it, corral it, and leverage it. We jumped with both feet into knowledge development schemes, where there are a few pioneers but no experts yet — and where the payoff is the world.

Then we paused. Visions of "corporation-as-Rolodex" and "Pollocking for profits" notwithstanding, the organizations we were cobbling together were still too dull by half for these decidedly un-dull times. What if . . .?

What if we factored into our design the concept of curiosity itself? What if we did no less than create a curious corporation, an enterprise that really is as crazy, zany, sparkling, and innovative as the times demand? So we hired curious people, including a few, disruptive 1,000Xers; and we gave them spunky settings where they could readily bring their dog to work and break into a chorus of Oklahoma at 4 p.m., where their valuable imaginations would be nourished rather than suppressed.

And what did we expect this organization to produce? Quality? Of course. But not just the quality you can capture on charts, expressed as an absence of TGW. This curious, flattened, atomized, networked, Pollocking organization that employs zany, 90 percent entrepreneurs would measure its quality in terms of TGR, expressed in units of Wow!

It would seek customers' affection, not just satisfaction. It would surprise, not just please. And it would intertwine, not just listen to.

And now what, now that we've fleshed out our model? Dotted the i's, crossed the t's? Zounds! We do it all over again. And then again ...

The one mistake I'm not making with this book that I've made in some (all) of the others is to think that I've arrived at THE ANSWER FOR ALL TIME. There isn't just one answer. Not just one strategy. Not just one model. If you're gutsy enough to build one of the strange creatures we've just discussed, work like hell at running it, and start seeing good results, do you now have it made? You do not. Whatever you've built, the best thing you can do, as consultant Roger Martin says, is to burn it down every few years. Ah, yes, words. Don't change it, but b-u-r-n i-t d-o-w-n. In a world where the outrageous has become the norm — in a crazy world — stable, sensible organizations make no sense.

## Acknowledgments

Ian Thomson, my business partner, had the idea for this series. Esther Newberg, my agent, thought it was a good idea. Sonny Mehta, my publisher, agreed with Esther. Donna Carpenter, Tom Richman, and Charles Simmons, my editors and de facto coauthors, labored long, hard, and well to create and polish and polish the "product." Ken Silvia, our designer, taught us that design is as important as words. Kathy Dalle-Molle, independent contractor, meticulously checked the facts and provided a wealth of other support. Kate Abbe, pal (and spouse), was outrageously supportive (as usual). Evelyn Peters, Mom (and dedicatee of this book), made me what I am.

Thank you all.

Donna Carpenter, Tom Richman, and Charles Simmons (and thence I) were ably supported by Cindy Sammons, Mike Mattil, Sebastian Stuart, and Maurice Coyle.

Ken Silvia (and thence I) was assisted by Jessica Robison.

At The Tom Peters Group, Chris Gage was, as always, of enormous assistance from the first to the last. Paul Cohen, Liz Mitchell, and Randy Patnode, of our newsletter team, are coauthors of several of the stories that appear in these pages. Pat Reardon, my boss (scheduler, contract negotiator, etc.), kept the wobbly train on the track.

At Knopf-Vintage, I am enthusiastically assisted by Jane Friedman, Carol Devine Carson, Linda Rosenberg, Katy Barrett, Laurie Brown, and many others.

Needless to say, since this is a book derived from a seminar, thanks are due to the small army of people who have asked questions, written letters, and in general pushed me to sharpen and enlarge my arguments. Then, there's the meat and potatoes: Bob Buckman (of Buckman Labs), Lars Kolind (Oticon), Gary Withers (Imagination), and so many others who have performed the feats that I have tried to recapture in these pages.

Again, thank you all.

—T. P.

# NOTES

## INTRODUCTION

PAGE

xiii     "On October...basketball at the time": "Warriors' Webber Inks $74.4M Deal," *USA Today*, October 18, 1993, p. 1C.

xiii     "On the same...auto parts workers": Kevin Done, "Threat to 400,000 Jobs in EC Auto Sector," *Financial Times*, October 18, 1993, p. 1.

xiii     "Three months later...lay off more employees": "Cautious Optimism in the Corner Office," *Business Week*, January 10, 1994, p. 67.

xiv     "If Hewlett-Packard...staff of four people": Gifford and Elizabeth Pinchot, *The End of Bureaucracy and the Rise of the Intelligent Organization* (San Francisco: Berrett-Koehler Publishers, 1993), p. 9.

xiv     "When we confront...electronic microcontrollers each": Robert E. Calem, "In Far More Gadgets, A Hidden Chip," *The New York Times*, January 2, 1994, p. 9F.

xiv     "Nintendo, with only...all of Japan": "Game Maker Nintendo Reports Super Year," *Asahi Evening News*, May 22, 1993, p. 6.

xiv     *Online Access: The Magazine that Makes Modems Work* (Chicago Fine Print, Inc., 920 N. Franklin, Suite 203, Chicago, IL 60610, 312/573-1700).

xiv     *Going Bonkers?* (Harold Publications, Inc., 322 Royal Poinciana Plaza, Palm Beach, FL 33480-4020).

## CHAPTER 1

5     "The nineties will be...and the dead": David Vice, quoted on the book jacket of Linda McQuaig, *The Quick and the Dead: Brian Mulroney, Big Business and the Seduction of Canada* (New York: Viking, 1991).

6     "Recently...moving these days": Paul Volcker and Toyoo Gyohten, *Changing Fortunes: The World's Money and the Threat to American Leadership* (New York: Times Books, 1992), p. 161.

6     "Since 1979...every three weeks": Steven Brull, "As the Profit Machine Slows Down, Japan Rethinks the Product Cycle," *International Herald Tribune*, March 26, 1992, p. F-1.

6     "spaghetti sauce...1991 alone": Data from *New Product News* in Chicago, IL .

6-7     "A recent Harper's Index...just 34 days": "Harper's Index," *Harper's*, August 1993, p. 9.

7     "In the last three...1,100 to 423 people": "The Wonders of Workflow," *The Economist*, December 11, 1993, p. 72.

# Notes

7-8     "Australia's Kalgoorlie Consolidated...from 1,500 to 720": Steve Bunk, "Super Pit Digs Into the Future," *Australian Business Monthly*, June 1992, p. 94.

8       "Most records no longer...in the Berkshires": Lewis J. Perelman, *School's Out: Hyperlearning, the New Technology, and the End of Education* (New York: William Morrow, 1992), p. 85.

8-9     "...an electronic undergraduate...Lionel Baldwin ": Perelman, *School's Out*, p. 56.

10      "We are trying...less materials": "60,000 and Counting," *The Economist*, November 30, 1991, p. 71.

10      "Nike, a shoe...Industrial 500 one": "Fortune's Service 500," *Fortune*, May 31, 1993, p. 206.

11      "Tom Silverman... the lifestyle business": Bruce Tucker, "Tommy Box Can CD Future," *Fast Company*, November 1993, p. 60.

11      "shoemaker shelling out...just do it": "Juiced-up Ball? Statistics Say No." *USA Today*, April 15, 1993, p. 3C.

11      "Microsoft's only factory...human imagination": Fred Moody, "Mr. Software," *The New York Times Magazine,* August 25, 1991, p. 56.

14, 16  "Research by Isabel...whopping 48 percent": Fredrick W. Gluck, "Recreating the American Dream," *The McKinsey Quarterly*, Fall 1992, p. 58.

16      "Every organization has...everything it does": Peter Drucker, "The New Society of Organizations," *Harvard Business Review*, September-October 1992, p. 98.

18      "In 1981, 2,689...soared to 16,143": Data from *New Product News*, Chicago, IL.

18      "You can have...new and exciting": Scott Donaton, "Bumps Lie Ahead on Interactive Lane," *Advertising Age*, November 1, 1993, p. S-16.

18      "Or as former...Godfather V": Rich Karlgaard, "ASAP Interview: John Sculley," *Forbes ASAP*, December 7, 1992, p. 95.

19      "The obsession with...dreadful wage depression": Roger Swardson, "Downsizing Hits Home: An Inside Look at the Shrinking American Workplace," *San Francisco Chronicle*, August 8, 1993, p. TW8.

21      "In a speech...had been given": Susan Yoachum, "Clinton Promises $5 Billion for U.S. Cities that Lose Bases," *San Francisco Chronicle*, July 3, 1993, p. A3.

## CHAPTER 2

30      "Management consultants...to 'decentralized'": Charles Handy, *The Age of Unreason* (London: Business Books, 1989); and, James O'Toole

**PAGE**

and Warren Bennis, "Our Federalist Future: The Leadership Imperative," *California Management Review*, Summer 1992, pp. 73-90.

33-34    "Lexmark, made the...away from Mom": "The Typing on the Wall: Lexmark," *The Economist*, October 3, 1992, pp. 74-5.

34-35    "New technology...to mean 'failing'": "The Fall of Big Business," *The Economist*, April 17, 1993, p. 13.

35       "As essayist Lance...the individual boss'": Lance Morrow, "The Temping of America," *Time*, March 29, 1993, p. 41.

35       "The job creation...million new jobs": Data from Cognetics, Boston, MA.

35       "*Inc.* magazine's...less than $100,000": Martha E. Mangelsdorf, "Behind the Scenes," *Inc.*, October 1992, p. 72.

36       "the humbling...just begun": "The Fall of Big Business," *The Economist*, April 17, 1993, p. 13.

36       "In his often-quoted...big-company body": "Letter to the Shareholders," 1992 General Electric Annual Report, p. 4.

37       "The Finnish arm...it's 25": Aziz Panni, "Reaping the Harvest," *EuroBusiness*, October 1993, p. 75.

38       "Once people start...corridors of power": Echo Montgomery, "Branson the Bold," *Success*, November 1992, p. 23.

39-41    "In the typical...with the patient": David O. Weber, "Six Models of Patient-Focused Care," *Healthcare Forum Journal*, July-August 1991, pp. 18-25; J. Philip Lathrop, "The Patient-Focused Hospital," *Healthcare Forum Journal*, July-August 1991, p. 26-30; and, "Operational Restructuring: 19 Pioneering Models," *Healthcare Forum Journal*, July-August 1992, p. 5.

40       "We have to...patient's room": J. Philip Lathrop, *Restructuring Health Care: The Patient-Focused Paradigm* (San Francisco: Jossey-Bass, 1993), pp. 192-3.

41       "She especially notices...her efforts": Lathrop, *Restructuring Health Care*, pp. 192-3.

45       "Zurich Insurance...a global scale'": "Taking on the World," *The Economist*, June 5, 1993, p. 75.

46       "Huge CSR...small-business activities": Philip Rennie, "Australia: New CSR Chief Wastes No Time," *Business Review Weekly*, April 23, 1993, p. 32.

48       "all good...of management": "60 Things Every Man Should Know," *Esquire*, October 1993, p. 121.

49       "Xerox reorganized...the nine operations": Martin Dickson, "Settling Down to Small Talk," *Financial Times*, March 24, 1993, p. 12.

# Notes

PAGE

50     "For most companies...the competition": James F. Moore, "Predators and Prey: A New Ecology of Competition," *Harvard Business Review*, May-June 1993, p. 75.

50-51     "Active mutators... also selected against": Carl Sagan and Ann Druyan, *Shadows of Forgotten Ancestors: A Search for Who We Are* (New York: Random House, 1992), p. 87.

51     Donald J. Wheeler, *Understanding Variation: The Key to Managing Chaos* (Knoxville, TN: SPC Press, 1993).

52     "In an era...self-cannibalization": George Gilder, "George Gilder's Telecosm: The New Rule of Wireless," *Forbes ASAP*, March 29, 1993, p. 110.

52     "Quad/Graphics...risk being destroyed": Claire Ho, "Ultimate Think Smalls Help Overcome Barriers," *Quad/Community News*, April 23, 1993, p. 1.

52     "The target now...a new games": Frank DeFord, "Running Man," *Vanity Fair*, August 1993, p. 52.

54     "The creation of...socialist countries": Dwight R. Lee and Richard B. McKenzie, *Failure and Progress: The Bright Side of the Dismal Science* (Washington, DC: CATO Institute, 1993), pp. 61, 153.

54-55     "Outsiders think of...resumes of entrepreneurs": Michael S. Malone, "Silicon Valley Primer," *San Jose Mercury News*, June 27, 1993, p. 4C.

55     "To Washington, I say...and disobedient": George F. Will, "Silicon Valley Doesn't Need This Kind of Help," *San Jose Mercury News*, June 9, 1993, p. 7B.

55     "In 1993, PepsiCo...by outraged citizens": "Pepsi Staged Attacks," *AP Online*, December 17, 1993.

56     "The Nobel laureate...discovery process": Chiaki Nishiyama and Kurt R. Leube, eds., *The Essence of Hayek* (Stanford, CA: Hoover Institution Press, 1984), pp. 254-65.

57     "If people have...emotional involvement":"Rich and titled," *The Economist*, March 30, 1991, p. 64.

59     "We all have...communications technologies": "The Coming Clash of Logic," *The Economist*, July 3, 1993, p. 25.

59     "Successful change...organization over time": Andres K. Sandoval-Strausz, "Reinventing America: The 1993 Business Week Symposium of Chief Executive Officers," *Business Week*, December 13, 1993, Special Advertising Section, p. 121.

59-60     "It's as if...by those revolutionaries": Sagan and Druyan, *Shadows of Forgotten Ancestors*, p. 104.

62     "All success...Wanniski": "Other Comments," *Forbes*, January 3, 1994, p. 28.

# Notes

PAGE

86     "McDonald's founder...hamburger bun": Ray Kroc, *Grinding It Out;
       The Making of McDonald's* (New York: Berkley, 1977), p. 98.

CHAPTER 4

95     "If you can't...you're out": Brian Dumaine, "The New Non-Manager,"
       *Fortune*, February 22, 1993, p. 80.

97     "People do realize...not the organization": Homa Bahrami, "The
       Emerging Flexible Organization," *California Management Review*,
       Summer 1992, pp. 42-3 .

97     "Educator and consultant...in the marketplace": Perelman, *School's
       Out*, p. 77.

98     "For example, Alive Culinary...restaurant owners": Florence
       Fabricant, "Trying to Turn Chefs Into Celebrities," *The New York
       Times*, March 17, 1993, p. B1.

98     "Writing in...until you retire": Oren Harari, "Stop Empowering Your
       People," *Management Review*, November 1993, pp. 28-9.

98-99  "Career-development expert...in organizations": William A. Charland
       Jr., "Career Shifting: Shifting Gears in a Changing Workplace," *Points
       West Review*, September 1993, p. 4.

99     "In the new...take a job": Tom Schmitz, "Teen Girls Get Lesson In
       Entrepreneurship," *San Jose Mercury News*, October 1, 1993, p. F-1.

100    "Support for this...bug yourself": Robert Kelley and Janet Caplan,
       "How Bell Labs Creates Star Performers," *Harvard Business Review*,
       July/August 1993, p. 133.

101    "Doing it...you'll get promoted": Hank Whittmore, *CNN: The Inside
       Story*, (Boston: Little, Brown, 1990), p. 33.

101    "Veronique Vienne has...that present themselves": Paul Cohen,
       "Living on the Edge: Story of a Master Networker," *On Achieving
       Excellence*, February 1992, pp. 2-4.

102    "I've made my...grow everyday": Richard Corliss, "Hot Damn, He's
       Good," *Time*, September 6, 1993, p. 65.

105    "Andersen Consulting...hours a year": Ronald Henkoff, "Inside
       Andersen's Army of Advice," *Fortune*, October 4, 1993, p. 82.

105-106 "Consider David Maister's...be famous for?": David H. Maister,
       *"How's Your Asset?"* (Boston: Maister Associates, Inc., 1991), pp. 1-3, 9.

106-107 "My first music...of a raga": Gita Mehta, *A River Sutra* (New York:
       Doubleday, 1993), pp. 203, 208, 210, 212.

110    "The question always...you are doing": Richard N. Haass, *The Power to
       Persuade: How to Be Effective in Government and Other Unruly*

**PAGE**

*Organizations* (New York: Houghton Mifflin, 1994), uncorrected manuscript, p. 50.

111    "Life may be...taking its place": Mary Ann Sieghart, "I-Know-Best Generation Claims the Soul of the Nanny State," *The Times* (London), December 3, 1993, p. 18.

112    "In his autobiography...time with us": John Sculley with John A. Byrne, *Odyssey: Pepsi to Apple...A Journey of Adventure, Ideas, and the Future* (New York: Harper & Row, 1987), pp. 125-6.

113    Ben Hamper, *Rivethead: Tales from the Assembly Line* (New York: Warner Books, 1991).

114    "Psychologist Kenneth Gergen...and more fulfilled": Walter Truett Anderson, "Multicultural Mix-ups: Postmodern Cowboys and New Age Indians," *Utne Reader*, March-April 1993, p. 127.


**CHAPTER 5**

123    "shamrock organization...Handy in 1989": Charles Handy, *The Age of Unreason*, pp. 70-92.

126    "Take Brenda Brimage...going to be": Mark Henricks, "The Virtual Entrepreneur," *Success*, June 1993, p. 41.

126    "Then there's Rick...he told us": Paul Cohen, "Against All Odds, Entrepreneur Taps Passion and Personal Networks to Shatter Industry Sales Records," *On Achieving Excellence*, June 1993, pp. 2-3.

126-127  "Or consider lawyers...wherever we are": William Charland, "Support System Network Helps Isolated Lawyers," *Rocky Mountain News*, October 3, 1993, p. 3C.

127    "Or how about Edward...networks pay off": Randall Patnode, "The 'Just-in-Time Talent' Network," *On Achieving Excellence*, February 1994, p. 2.

128    "Today, with technologically...value-added providers": Brook Manville, "Tradition and Innovation in the Management of Professional Knowledge: A Case Study of a 'Virtual Library'," (New York: McKinsey & Co., 1993), p. 4.

128    "Several creative stars...all day long": Beth Heitzman, "Leap of Faith: DDB Needham Creatives Jump Ship to Pursue Own Agency," *Adweek*, September 20, 1993, pp. 1, 9.

128    "In 1992...$128,000": "IBM's 'Big Blue' Days Are Over," *San Jose Mercury News*, December 16, 1992, p. 24A.

130    "*Design News* reports...the service firms": Paul E. Teague, "Engineering Services: Where Creativity Thrives," *Design News*, July 5, 1993, p. 106.

## Notes

PAGE

130-131    "Kingston Technology...just-in-time manufacturing": Michael Meyer, "Here's a 'Virtual' Model for America's Industrial Giants," *Newsweek,* August 23, 1993, p. 40.

131    "Andy Grove, Intel's...organized horizontally": John A. Byrne with Richard Brandt and Otis Port, "The Virtual Corporation: The Company of the Future Will Be the Ultimate in Adaptability," *Business Week,* February 8, 1993, p. 98; and, Stratford Sherman, "Andy Grove: How Intel Makes Spending Pay Off," *Fortune,* February 22, 1993, p. 58.

131-132    "What will a...according to need": Davidow and Malone, *The Virtual Corporation,* pp. 5-6.

132    "Professor James Brian...marketing, etc.": James Brian Quinn and Penny C. Paquette, "Technology in Services: Creating Organizational Revolutions," *Sloan Management Review,* Winter 1990, pp. 67-78; and, James Brian Quinn, Penny C. Paquette and Thomas Doorley, "Technology in Services: Rethinking Strategic Focus," *Sloan Management Review,* Winter 1990, pp. 79-87.

133    "Texas Instruments...revenue in 1993": Peter Burrows, "Farming Out Work—to IBM, DEC, NCR..." *Business Week,* May 17, 1993, p. 92.

133    "Ralston Purina...competing with itself": Emily DeNitto, "No End to March of Private Label," *Advertising Age,* November 1, 1993, p. S-6.

134    "Kennametal installed...tool rooms": Barnaby J. Feder, "Kennametal Finds the Right Tools," *The New York Times,* May 6, 1992, p. D1.

135-136    "Draeger's Supermarket...Biscotti and Pesto": *Draeger's Culinary Center Schedule: April, May and June,* p. 1.

136-137    "Then there's Lane...customer's site": For additional information, see *"Management Revolution and Corporate Reinvention,"* (London: BBC Training Videos, 1993).

137    "Services form an...pushing the envelope": Joseph B. Fuller, James O'Conor and Richard Rawlinson, "Tailored Logistics: The Next Advantage," *Harvard Business Review,* May-June 1993, p. 88.

139    "The division managers...the [headquarters] job": Shawn Tully, "A Boom Ahead in Company Profits," *Fortune,* April 6, 1992, p. 77.

139-140    "Take IBM's creation...IBM or elsewhere": Tim Smart, "IBM Has a New Product: Employee Benefits," *Business Week,* May 10, 1993, p. 58.

142    "Introducing Total Track...of your package": *USA Today,* March 4, 1993, Advertisement, p. 6A.

142    "In fact, the speedy...inventory-management services": Laurie M. Grossman, "Federal Express, UPS Face Off on Computers," *The Wall Street Journal,* September 17, 1993, p. B1.

144    "Darrell Miller's...Strategic Relationships": Karen Southwick, "Novell: An Enterprising Company," *Upside,* May 1993, p. 10.

**PAGE**

145     "The thing that...web of trust": Eric Nee, "John Seely Brown," *Upside*, December 1993, p. 30.

145     Jessica Lipnack and Jeffrey Stamps, *The Team Net Factor: Bringing the Power of Boundary-Crossing Into the Heart of Your Business* (Essex Junction, VT: Oliver Wight, 1993).

146     "Australia recently created...information technology": Helene Zampetakis, "Optus Getting Results by Using External Specialists," *Financial Review*, May 31, 1993, p. 49.

146-147  "Oxford University's Hague...on a campus": Hague, *Beyond Universities*, pp. 58-9.

150-152  "The traditional equation...experiences and contacts": Michael Bendikt, ed., *Cyberspace: First Steps* (Boston: The MIT Press, 1991), pp. 383, 403-4.

**CHAPTER 6**

161     "We can no longer...know-how": Philip Revzin, "De Benedetti Envisions Electronic Links," *The Wall Street Journal Europe*, July 2-3, 1993, p. 4.

161     "The modern knowledge...Seely Brown": *Upside*, December 1993, p. 34.

162     "The key...capitalize on this": *Upside*, December 1993, p. 33.

162-163  "We aren't...rivals can match": William Taylor, "Power Transformers—The Dynamics of Global Coordination," *Harvard Business Review*, March-April 1991, pp. 96-7.

165     "We find little...suits them": "Chairman's Letter," *CSC Europe 1991 Annual Review*, p. 4.

165     "We still need...it across Europe": *CSC Europe 1991 Annual Review*, p. 4.

167     "As we move toward...leverage of knowledge": Robert H. Buckman, opening remarks at Buckman Laboratories Canadian Marketing Conference, May 1992.

168-169  "Some 17,000 consultants...practice — and culture": Thomas Kiely, "Learning to Share," *CIO*, July 1993, pp. 38-44.

172-173  "Andy Zimmerman...and easy to do": Paul Cohen, "Accounting Firm Electronically Links Its Experts and Clients, Reaps Strategic Advantage," *On Achieving Excellence*, November 1993, pp. 2-4.

174     "The Institure for Research...become a member": "The Search for the Poetry of Work," *Training and Development*, October 1993, p. 35.

174     "IRL's Etienne...communities of practice": Etienne Wenger, "Communities of Practice: Where Learning Happens," *Benchmark*, Fall 1991, p. 8.

175-176  "Time was...technologies support": Alan M. Webber, "What's So New About the New Economy," *Harvard Business Review*, January-February 1993, p. 28.

**PAGE**

176 "Consider what technology...teamwork can't achieve": Michael Schrage, *Shared Minds: The New Technologies of Collaboration* (New York: Random House, 1990), p. 127.

177 "These information...networking, networking!": Michel Bauwens, "Corporate Bybrary Networks: An Idea Whose Time Has Come," *The Internet Business Journal* 1(1), p. 25.

177-178 "Howard Rheingold...if necessary": Howard Rheingold, *The Virtual Community: Finding Connection in a Computerized World* (Reading, MA: Addison-Wesley, 1993), pp. ix-xi.

178-179 "I got a vivid...within 60 days": Lotus Notes advertisement, *Computerworld*, March 1, 1993, p. 42-3.

179-180 "Hatim Tyabji...of useful articles": David H. Freedman, "Culture of Urgency," *Forbes ASAP*, September 13, 1993, pp. 25-8.

180 "Sun Microsystems...messages every day": Scott McNealy, "To Asia With Hope: Opportunity Lures a U.S. Executive," *The New York Times*, November 28, 1993, p. 5F.

182 "The most exciting...throughout their lives": Hague, *Beyond Universities*, pp. 12, 14.

183-184 "In a knowledge age...opportunity is wanted": Perelman, *School's Out*, p. 100.

184 "Brookings Institute...will be available": Diane Ravitch, "When School Comes to You," *The Economist*, September 11, 1993, p. 44.

184-185 "Perelman decries the...increasingly interconnected": Perelman, *School's Out*, pp. 48, 70, 205, 106; and, the quote from Shoshana Zuboff originally appeared in "Smart Machines and Learning People," *Harvard Magazine*, November-December 1988.

186 "The test of...ability to function": F. Scott Fitzgerald, "The Crack-up," in Charles R. Anderson, ed., *American Literacy Masters*, vol. 2 (New York: Holt, Rinehart and Winston, 1965), p. 1007.

186-187 "University of Michigan...without an eraser": Karl E. Weick, *The Social Psychology of Organizing* (Reading, MA: Addison-Wesley, 1979), pp. 7, 205, 221.

188 "CEO Ed McCracken...of the culture": Steven E. Prokesch, "Mastering Chaos at the High-Tech Frontier," *Harvard Business Review*, November-December 1993, p. 137.

190 "Information is...of intelligence": Donald Hall, "Mo' Info'mation," *PEN American Center Newsletter*, October 1993, p. 5.

190 "Samuel Johnson...arises in leisure": Adrian Furnham, "Decisions Makers Ride a Harder Hobby Horse," *Financial Times*, November 19, 1993, p. R-1.

190 "U.S. poet laureate...'wine-dark sea'": Rita Dove, "To Make a Praire,"

PAGE

*The Key Reporter*, Autumn 1993, p. 1.

**CHAPTER 7**

199     "What a distressing...the average adult": Robert Bly, *Iron John: A Book About Men* (Reading, MA: Addison-Wesley, 1990), p. 7.

199-200  "Strategies are okayed...child in the boardroom": Victor Palmieri, "Now Hear This," *Fortune*, February 24, 1992, p. 18.

200-201  "Stanley Bing...of my office": Stanley Bing, "Dudes! Get a Life!" *Esquire*, May 1993, pp. 76-7.

202     "VCW, Inc....Womack asserts": Charles Burck, "Succeeding with Tough Love," *Fortune*, November 29, 1993, p. 188.

203     "General William...of insanity'": Shelby Foote, *Shiloh* (New York: Dial Press, 1952), p. 39.

203     "Guy Kawasaki...thunder lizard evangelists": Michelle Moreno, "Product Evangelists Make Customers Into Believers," *On Achieving Excellence*, January 1993, p. 5.

203-204  "Mike Koelker...the agency structure": Mike Moreno, "A Creative Man Shares (Some of) What He's Learned," *Advertising Age*, December 13, 1993, p. F-8.

204     "David Ogilvy...cast of hundreds": David Ogilvy, *Principles of Management* (New York: Ogilvy & Mather, 1968).

204-205  "The 85-year old...Lewis explains": Walter Kirn, "The Editor as Gap Model," *The New York Times Magazine*, March 7, 1993, p. 56.

206     "We need to...production process": Charles R. Day Jr., "First Factories, Now Offices," *Industry Week*, September 7, 1992, p. 7.

208     "We've always said...change less scary": Prokesch, *Harvard Business Review*, November-December 1993, p. 142.

210     "One of the...absorb this lesson": John Seabrook, "E-Mail from Bill," *The New Yorker*, January 10, 1994, p. 56.

210     "Harvard psychology professor...intellectual innocence": Howard Gardner, *Creating Minds* (New York: Basic Books, 1993).

210-211  "Nobody enjoys...exuberant variety": Jane Jacobs, *The Death and Life of Great American Cities* (New York: Random House, 1961), p. 161.

212     "Architect Christopher Alexander...in inner conflict": Christopher Alexander, *The Timeless Way of Building* (New York: Oxford University Press, 1979), pp. ix-x, 25.

212     "For proven physiological...out of bed": Christopher Day, *Places of the Soul: Architecture and Environmental Design as a Healing Art* (London: HarperCollins, 1990), p. 50.

# Notes

PAGE

214    "Duncan Sutherland...in his backyard": Duncan B. Sutherland Jr.,
       "Technology and the Contemporary Design Firm: Reflections on
       Time, Space, Tools, and the Mind's Work," *Design Management
       Journal,* Spring 1993, pp. 38-9.

214    "The relationship between...new phenomenon": Peter Drucker, "The
       New Society of Organizations," *Harvard Business Review,* September-
       October 1992, p. 101.

215    "To: *Inc.* ...Signed, Determined": John Kerr, "The Best Small Companies
       to Work For in America," *Inc.,* July 1993, p. 51.

216    "In the new...people would welcome": Webber, *Harvard Business
       Review,* January-February 1993, p. 42.

216    "A game designer...something great": David Sheff, *Game Over: How
       Nintendo Zapped An American Industry, Captured Your Dollars, and
       Enslaved Your Children* (New York: Random House, 1993), p. 21.

218    "Competition is now...than to chess": George Stalk, Philip Evans, and
       Lawrence E. Shulman, "Competing on Capabilities: The New Rules of
       Corporate Strategy," *Harvard Business Review,* March-April 1992, p. 62.

218    "Mr. Andy Grove...keep bubbling up": Geoffrey Owen and Louise
       Kehoe, "A Hotbed of High-Tech," *Financial Times,* June 28, 1992, p. 20.

**CHAPTER 8**

228    "But while American...things gone right": David Woodruff et al., "A
       New Era for Auto Quality: Just as Detroit is Catching Up, the Very
       Concept is Changing," *Business Week,* October 22, 1990, p. 84.

228    "The Americans are...climate-control knob": Larry Reibstein, "The
       Hardest Sell," *Newsweek,* March 30, 1992, p. 45.

228-229 "Any manufacturer...to Business Week": Woodruff et al., *Business
       Week,* October 22, 1990, p. 84.

229    "Richard Saunders...Clear Roll-on antiperspirant": Adrienne Ward
       Fawcett, "In Glut of New Products, `Different' Becomes Key,"
       *Advertising Age,* December 13, 1993, p. 28.

229    "In today's environment...in the door": Kate Fitzgerald, "In Retailing,
       Price Stanglehold Lessons," *Advertising Age,* November 1, 1993, p. S-6.

229    "A recent poll...has been eclipsed": James Daly, "Mac User Loyalties
       Under Stress," *Computerworld,* October 25, 1993, p. 1.

230    "We don't think...the lifestyle business": Bruce Tucker, "Tommy Boy
       Can CD Future," *Fast Company,* November 1993, p. 60.

230-231 "In his book...watch business today": Edward de Bono, *Sur/Petition:
       Creating Value Monopolies When Everyone Else is Merely Competing* (New
       York: HarperBusiness, 1992), p. 111.

**PAGE**

231     "Until now...have spirit": Emily Thornton, "Japan's Struggle to Be Creative," *Fortune*, April 19, p. 134.

231-232   "The billion-dollar...its music udon": Asahi News Service, "Japan Markets Noodles with Classical Bent," *The Press Democrat*, August 3, 1993, p. A1.

232-233   "Paul Sherlock developed...glow, tingle, and wow": Paul Sherlock, *Rethinking Business to Business Marketing* (New York: The Free Press, 1991), p. 65.

233     "Quality doesn't have...to intellectual abstractions": Robert M. Pirsig, *Lila: An Inquiry Into Morals* (New York: Bantam, 1991), p. 64.

234     "The practice of...the natural also": Kakuzo Okakura, *The Book of Tea* (New York: Kodansha, 1991), pp. 36-7.

235     "When I meet...a great experience": Leland R. Kaiser, "The Hospital as a Healing Place," *Healthcare Forum Journal*, September/October 1992, p. 39.

240     "Likewise, AT&T's...slipping market leader": John J. Keller, "AT&T to End Sales of `i Plan' Phone Program," *The Wall Street Journal*, November 10, 1993, p. A5.

240     "University of Texas...love to hate": Letter from Robert A. Peterson to Tom Peters, June 15, 1991.

241     "John Peterman...is so wonderful": Liz Mitchell, "To Deliver Genuine Quality, Create A Customer Experience," *On Achieving Excellence*, December 1992, p. 2.

241-242   "The secret thoughts...for five weeks": *J. Peterman's Unexpected Summer Sale*, 1993, p. 14.

243     "Look, there are...to the audience": David Remnick, "The Last Italian Tenor," *The New Yorker*, June 21, 1993, p. 43.

244     "Talent never asks...and ordinary": "So-o-o Sharp," *Going Bonkers* 1(1), p. 7.

244     "It's like a...Hiroshi Yamauchi": Sheff, *Game Over*, p. 39.

244     "Sigeru Miyamoto...is for me": Sheff, *Game Over*, p. 51.

244     "A lot of people...products are made": Paul Cohen, *On Achieving Excellence*, June 1993, p. 4.

244     "I just bought...what I like": Caroling E. Mayer, "William-Sonoma, Just a Shop That Sells What Its Owner Likes," *Washington Post*, August 8, 1993, p. C1.

244     "Time Warner...insatiable customer": Connie Bruck, "A Mogul's Farewell," *The New Yorker*, October 18, 1993, p. 87.

245     "He's his own...he scratches himself": Terrence Rafferty, "The Battle of Little Rock," *The New Yorker*, November 8, 1993, p. 126.

# Notes

PAGE

245     "Unless I can...author Christopher Day": Day, *Places of the Soul*, p. 18.

245     "The difference between...Nathan Myhrvold": Laurence Hooper, "The Creative Edge," *The Asian Week Wall Street Journal*, May 24, 1993, p. 10.

245-246  "An ordinary man...want at Nintendo": Sheff, *Game Over*, p. 38.

246     "It is not...their very lives": Joseph Schumpeter, *Capitalism, Socialism, and Democracy* (New York: Harper & Row, 1962), p. 84.

247     "As for P&G...their big brothers": Guy de Jonquieres, "A Rose by Any Other Name," *Financial Times*, October 6, 1993, p. 15.

248     "[They] thrive on...to store brands": David A. Aaker, "So How Do the Nationals Beat Back the Store Brand Surge," *CalBusiness*, Fall 1993, p. 21.

249     "In an article...in breakthrough thinking": Patricia McLagan, "The Dark Side of Quality," *Training*, November 1991, p. 33.

250     "MCI chairman Roberts...businesses": Kate Fitzgerald, "Roberts Brings Real Branding to Long-Distance Phones," *Advertising Age*, December 20, 1993, p. 8.

250     "You never assume...it can't be done": Fitzgerald, *Advertising Age*, December 20, 1993, p. 8.

252-253  "Let's [turn] the...assessment are made": Clifton Reichard, "Salesmen Shouldn't Sell; Buyers Shouldn't Buy," *The Wall Street Journal*, September 13, 1993, p. A16.

254     "Body Shop founder...cosmetics peddler": Anita Roddick with Russell Miller, *Body and Soul* (London: Ebury Press, 1991), p. 62.

254-257  "a 165 million purveyor...when construction began": Liz Mitchell, "Manufacturer Rewrites the Formula: Forget Bidding on Jobs, Choose Customers for Value-added, Quality Partnerships," *On Achieving Excellence*, May 1993, pp. 2-3.

257-258  "In *The One-to-One Future* ...customer-management structure": Don Peppers and Martha Rogers, Ph.D., *The One-to-One Future: Building Relationships One Customer at a Time* (New York: Doubleday, 1993), pp. 22, 39, 140, 157, 165, 172, 176.

259-260  "Take the case...more than four": Jerry E. Bishop, "Technology and Medicine: Doctors Get Results by Sending Letters After Treatments," *The Wall Street Journal*, October 11, 1991, p. B4.

260     "In *Verdict Pending* ...them with kindness": Fredonia French Jacques, *Verdict Pending: A Patient Representative's Intervention* (Garden Grove, CA: Capistrano Press, 1983), p. 188.

261     "Jeff Amland...abetting removal": "Ten Service-Obsessed Stars Reveal Secrets to Customer Bliss," *On Achieving Excellence*, April 1992, p. 2.

261-262  "We always discuss...a home computer": Robin Hill, "Vengeance is Hers," *The Bulletin*, May 11, 1993, p. 46.

**PAGE**

263     "Former Apple chief...over a lifetime": Sculley with Byrne, *Odyssey*, p. 37.

263     "Sculley later...drink market": Alan Deutschman, "Odd Man Out," *Fortune*, July 26, 1993, p. 44.

263     "Tommy Boy Records...of cultural knowledge": Tucker, *Fast Company*, November 1993, p. 60.

**CHAPTER 9**

273     "Our feeling is...CEO Ed McCracken": Prokesch, *Harvard Business Review*, November-December 1993, p. 137.

273     "Companies [must]...every few years:" Roger Martin, "Changing the Mind of the Corporation," *Harvard Business Review*, November-December 1993, p. 92.

273-274  "Silicon Graphics'...bold bets too": Prokesch, *Harvard Business Review*, November-December 1993, p. 140.

274     "The Financial Times...must be made": Kevin Done, "Lopez Preaches Gospel of Third Industrial Revolution," *Financial Times*, September 9, 1993, p. 4.

274     "Paul O'Neill...or surpasses": Marion M. Steeples, "The Spirit of Americans," *Industry Week*, December 6, 1993, p. 37.

274-275  "Former Xerox CEO...change a culture": David Kearns, *Prophets in the Dark: How Xerox Reinvented Itself and Beat Back the Japanese* (New York: HarperBusiness, 1992).

275     "When we finish...a tremendous advantage": Prokesch, *Harvard Business Review*, November-December 1993, p. 137.

278     "The whole secret...keeps on going!": "That's Rich," *Esquire* (British edition), May 1994, p. 52.

280     "In a classic...only nine minutes": Henry Mintzberg, *The Nature of Managerial Work* (New York: Harper & Row, 1973), pp. 31-5.

280     "Milliken is obsessed...to improve quality": Jeremy Main, *Quality Wars: The Triumphs and Defeats of American Business* (New York: The Free Press, 1994), uncorrected manuscript, p. 46.

282     "First you have...everyone else": Roddick and Miller, *Body and Soul*, p. 79.

282     "The key to...follow the others": Brenton R. Schlender, "How Sony Keeps the Magic Going," *Fortune*, February 24, 1992, p. 77.

283     "If your business...deep trouble": Sherman Stratford, "The New Computer Revolution," *Fortune*, June 14, 1993, p. 61.

283     "There's no...this business": Karen Southwick, "Novell: An Enterprising Company," *Upside*, May 1993, p. 12.

# Notes

PAGE

283     "The most probable...10 years hence": Peter F. Drucker, "A Turnaround Primer," *The Wall Street Journal*, February 2, 1993, p. A14.

283     "The chump to...about five years": "*Thriving on Chaos*," (Schaumburg, IL: Video Publishing House, 1989).

# INDEX

# INDEX

# INDEX

towering competence, 106–8, 124
training, 105–6. *See also* learning
Training Force, 136
travel budget, businessing and, 73–74
travel services industry, 7
Truett, Steve, 122
Trumpf, 254
trust, 87
 employees as businesspersons and, 79
 survey on, 85
 virtual corporations and, 145
Turner, Ted, 144
turnkey services, 134, 137, 141
Tyabji, Hatim, 179

Union Pacific Railroad, reorganization of,
 30–33
universities, 155
 future of, 146–47
UPS, 142, 153
 tracking system of, 142

vacations, 205
Valentine, Don, 55
Valerio's restaurant (Auckland, New
 Zealand), 236–39
Valerio's Test, 239, 242
value adds, chain of, 137, 138
variation, chaos and, 51
VCW, Inc., 202
Velcro, 233
venture capitalists, 55
VeriFone, 76, 179–80, 190, 192
vertical thinking, 138
Vice, David, 5
Vienne, Veronique, 101
virtual communities, 177–78
virtual corporations, 125–31. *See also*
 corporation(s), as collections of
 services
 professional service firms as model of,
 149–52
 trust and, 145
virtual soul, 148–49
Vistakon, 255–56
Vitale, Alberto, 48
Volcker, Paul, 6

Wal-Mart, 17, 18
Walkman, 6
Walsh, Mike, 31, 32, 273, 282
Walton, Sam, 278
Waterman, Bob, 219
Watson, Hayden, 127
Webber, Alan, 175-76, 218
Weick, Karl, 186
Weisberg, Jacob, 204
Welch, Jack, 36, 107
Wellington, Arthur Wellesley, 1st Duke of,
 82
Wenger, Etienne, 174
Whirlpool, 133
Wilkof, Marcia, 31
Williams, Chuck, 244
Withers, Gary, 202-3, 207, 243, 245
Womack, Cheryl, 202
Woodward, Bob, 48
work environments. *See* physical
 environment
Workforce Solutions, 139
wow test, 18
Wriston, Walter, 20
Wyman, Bill, 229

Xerox, 49, 187

Yamamoto, Kenichi, 228–29
Yamauchi, Hiroshi, 216, 244, 245-46, 279
Yokoi, Gunpei, 216
youth, 204-5

Zemke, Ron, 261
zest, 5
Zimmerman, Andy, 172, 173
Ziploc bags, 233
Zschau, Ed, 48
Zuboff, Shoshana, 74, 185
Zurich insurance, 45

# Permission Acknowledgments

Grateful acknowledgment is made to the following for permission to reprint previously published material:

Stanley Bing: Excerpts from "Dudes! Get a Life!" by Stanley Bing, from *Esquire*, May 1993. Copyright © 1993 by Stanley Bing. Reprinted with permission of the author.

Draeger's: Excerpts from *Draegar's Culinary Center Schedule: April, May and June.* Copyright © 1993 by Draeger's. Reprinted with permission.

Doubleday, a Division of Bantam Doubleday Dell Publishing Group, Inc: Excerpts from *A River Sutra* by Gita Mehta. Copyright © 1993 by Gita Mehta. Reprinted with permission.

Jossey-Bass: Excerpts from *Restructuring Health Care: The Patient-Focused Paradigm* by J. Philip Lathrop. Copyright © 1993 by Jossey-Bass, Inc., Publishers. Reprinted with permission.

The MIT Press: Excerpts from *Cyberspace: First Steps*, Michael Bendikt, editor. Copyright © 1991 by the Massachusetts Institute of Technology. Reprinted with permission of The MIT Press.

William Morrow and Company: Excerpts from *School's Out: Hyperlearning, the New Technology, and the End of Education* by Lewis J. Perelman. Copyright © 1992 by Lewis J. Perelman. Reprinted with permission.

*Newsweek*: Excerpts from "Here's a 'Virtual' Model for America's Industrial Giants," by Michael Meyer, from *Newsweek*. August 23, 1993. Copyright © 1993 by Newsweek, Inc. All rights reserved. Reprinted with permission.

Pollock-Krasner Foundation: Reproduction of "Autumn Rhythm," by Jackson Pollock, 1950. Copyright © by 1994 Pollock-Krasner Foundation/Artists Rights Society (ARS), New York. Reproduced with permission.

Clifton J. Reichard: Excerpts from "Salesmen Shouldn't Sell; Buyers Shouldn't Buy," from *Wall Street Journal*, September 13, 1993. Copyright © 1993 Clifton J. Reichard. Reprinted with permission of the author.

## A Note About the Author

Tom Peters is the co-author of *In Search of Excellence* (with Robert H. Waterman, Jr.) and *A Passion for Excellence* (with Nancy Austin) and the author of *Thriving on Chaos* and *Liberation Management*. Though he is founder and chief of The Tom Peters Group in Palo Alto, California, he and his family spend much of their time on a farm in Vermont, thanks to the information technology revolution.